Strategic Risk Management

Strategic Risk Management

Designing Portfolios and Managing Risk

CAMPBELL R. HARVEY
SANDY RATTRAY
OTTO VAN HEMERT

WILEY

Published by John Wiley & Sons, Inc., Hoboken, New Jersey.
Published simultaneously in Canada.

For general information on our other products and services or for technical support, please contact our Customer Care Department within the United States at (800) 762-2974, outside the United States at (317) 572-3993 or fax (317) 572-4002.

Wiley publishes in a variety of print and electronic formats and by print-on-demand. Some material included with standard print versions of this book may not be included in e-books or in print-on-demand. If this book refers to media such as a CD or DVD that is not included in the version you purchased, you may download this material at http://booksupport.wiley.com. For more information about Wiley products, visit www.wiley.com.

Library of Congress Cataloging-in-Publication Data:

Names: Harvey, Campbell R., author. | Rattray, Sandy, author. | Van Hemert, Otto, author.
Title: Strategic risk management : designing portfolios and managing risk / Campbell R. Harvey, Sandy Rattray, and Otto Van Hemert.
Description: First edition. | Hoboken : Wiley, 2021. | Series: Wiley finance | Includes index.
Identifiers: LCCN 2021005741 (print) | LCCN 2021005742 (ebook) | ISBN 9781119773917 (hardback) | ISBN 9781119773948 (adobe pdf) | ISBN 9781119773924 (epub)
Subjects: LCSH: Portfolio management. | Risk management.
Classification: LCC HG4529.5 .H378 2021 (print) | LCC HG4529.5 (ebook) | DDC 332.6—dc23
LC record available at https://lccn.loc.gov/2021005741
LC ebook record available at https://lccn.loc.gov/2021005742

Cover Design: Wiley
Cover Image: © Mike Robinson
Printed and bound by CPI Group (UK) Ltd, Croydon, CR0 4YY

C9781119773917_170822

Contents

Proceeds from this book will be donated to The Access Project, which supports students from disadvantaged backgrounds to access top universities through tuition and in-school mentoring. Please visit https://www.theaccessproject.org.uk/ for more information.

Foreword

Active funds devote considerable effort to the search for excess returns, but risk considerations often fail to get anywhere near the same level of attention. The authors of this book, Campbell Harvey, Sandy Rattray, and Otto Van Hemert, take risk seriously and give it the consideration it deserves.

Risk considerations can get short shrift in many ways. For example, historical returns typically are reported without reference to the risk taken to achieve them. Unfortunately, without a better understanding of the risk involved, it is difficult to estimate the likelihood that such (possibly fortuitous) returns can be repeated.

In the standard risk management approach, the focus is on setting volatility constraints associated with various targets and benchmarks. Such constraints often are based on the probability of a significant downdraft that could adversely impact the current investment strategy. In actuality, the commonality of such constraints across a wide range of funds suggests that some peer group pressure might also be at play.

Once risk limits have been established, managers generally are permitted to roam relatively freely in the search for higher returns. Risk considerations are then relegated to ensuring that returns stay within the pre-established bounds. In effect, this approach tends to put risk assessment in a box that is removed from day-to-day fund management.

In the asset allocation context, this fence-posting behavior is built on the belief that the maximum expected return is equivalent to the optimal return. However, that may not be the case when the fund's "true" objectives are considered.

This book's authors make the case that the position of a fund relative to its risk boundaries should be integrated into any consideration of investment shifts. The challenge is garnering sufficient incremental return from new investments to justify all incremental risks.

In theory, each incremental investment initiative or allocation shift should be based on a holistic risk/return valuation. This valuation should include an understanding of the interaction between marginal investment changes and the probability of success relative to various absolute and/or market-sensitive performance goals. An absolute goal might be to achieve a specific return or some given level of spending. Market-sensitive goals might include a desired probability that the fund's performance will exceed that of a peer group, market benchmark, or customized reference portfolio.

When such market-sensitive targets are considered, correlations between investment and target returns become important. The incremental return advantage versus a moving target will be improved if the portfolio and the target are closely aligned along the primary dimension of risk.

Significant risk events are likely to spawn a need for portfolio rebalancing. Most funds do rebalance at both prescribed time intervals and following sufficiently sizeable market moves. However, the rebalancing process can easily devolve into a mechanical regimen that simply moves the fund back to its preordained policy portfolio.

This auto-rebalancing protocol is based on the presumption that significant market events do not seriously impact going-forward prospects. This presumption is based on the belief that, over time, the market presents the same face to investors—both before and after major market moves. This equilibrium-mandated framework is comforting because it relieves fund managers of the need to peer into the clouded world of uncertainty and tease out revised policy portfolios. While it is true that a return to a prior equilibrium often occurs, it is also true that significant risk events can change the market's going-forward return characteristics as well as the fundamental risk tolerance of the fund itself!

In this book, Harvey, Rattray, and Van Hemert take a broader view of the rebalancing problem. They make the case that, rather than being based on a fixed periodic timetable, rebalancing should be more closely attuned to market conditions. For example, discernible changes in a market's prospective risk should play an important role in shaping the rebalancing process. It serves little purpose to speedily rebalance against a strongly trending market.

Harvey, Rattray, and Van Hemert provide concrete illustrations and techniques for more fully integrating risk considerations into both the rebalancing process and the day-to-day management of the fund. For example, they show how volatility scaling provides a risk management function by reducing allocations when risks are increasing. They also study a range of investment strategies and assess how each strategy performed historically in times of crisis.

Although the research in this book was conducted prior to the COVID-19 outbreak, a postscript has been added to show how their approach fared during the first two quarters of 2020. It appears that both volatility scaling and strategic rebalancing did serve to improve portfolio performance.

The authors' focus on these asset management issues is grounded in their fund management experience, their deep understanding of the latest financial theory, and their own published work. (In this regard, it should be noted that Professor Harvey was recently named the "2020 Quant of the Year" by the *Journal of Portfolio Management* for outstanding academic contributions to the field of quantitative finance.)

In this book, the authors—each with their exceptional credentials in this area—have been most generous in sharing their hard-won insights with the investment field at large.

President, Advanced Portfolio Studies LLC,
and Senior Advisor to Morgan Stanley

Preface

By Sandy Rattray

One of our core beliefs at Man Group is that risk management of portfolios is just as important as alpha generation. Based on a number of articles we've published over the past five years, this book is derived from some of the key areas of risk management where we have had something to add and the practical experience we have as fund managers. The motivation for writing this book often came from questions asked by our clients that we thought would be interesting to others, and sometimes from specific problems that we were thinking about ourselves.

In *Seeking Crisis Alpha* (Chapter 1), we write about a theme that is close to our hearts: the ability of time series momentum to produce strong returns in weak market environments. We challenge the consensus view that this feature is limited to generating alpha in weak equity markets by finding very similar results in bond markets. We also show that time series momentum has some similar features to a long (put and call) options strategy. Aside from our momentum funds, we have directly used the protective feature of momentum in our long-only multi-asset programs. The chapter was written to respond to the many comments we received: that futures momentum could only protect against equity market drawdowns. Even with a 25-year history for our flagship trend fund, we needed to generate additional historical returns going back to the 1960s to test for protection against bond market selloffs.

We develop this theme further in *Can Portfolios Be Crisis Proofed?* (Chapter 2) by exploring a range of crisis alpha strategies. These include: long S&P 500 put options, long U.S. Treasury bonds, long gold and long protection on credit spreads, as well as futures momentum and long high-quality, short low-quality equities. We argued that put options are the most reliable, but most expensive, strategy, and that U.S. Treasury bonds have historically been unreliable. Credit protection and long gold fit somewhere between options and Treasuries, on both reliability and cost. Time series momentum and quality combine the attractive features of positive returns in both good and bad periods (at some reliability cost).

We have, over the years, built solutions for clients utilizing equity options, credit protection, times series momentum, and equity quality to fit specific investor preferences. Our motivation was to try to create a single framework for these strategies.

Risk Management via Volatility Targeting (Chapter 3) takes a different approach to risk management by focusing on methods to keep asset and portfolio volatility stable over time. This is in contrast to most investment strategies, which try to keep exposure stable over time. Many systematic hedge fund strategies use some form of volatility targeting, while risk parity is one of the few long-only approaches to use this technique. We show that scaling positions by an expected volatility (using recent historical returns) produces more stable risk outcomes in all the asset classes that we study (i.e., reduced tail losses and more stable experienced volatility). In equities and credit, volatility scaling somewhat increases historical Sharpe ratios, perhaps because these assets show a leverage effect themselves (becoming naturally more volatile with lower prices). Volatility targeting has been a mainstay of our Man AHL hedge fund and long-only strategies for many years, and we continue to believe that it has helped us limit portfolio drawdowns historically.

In *Strategic Rebalancing* (Chapter 4), we summarize several years' worth of research on the impact of rebalancing on portfolio returns. For us, rebalancing is core to almost all portfolio management, and yet its risk characteristics are woefully underexplored. Rebalancing has many benign features, including the obvious risk balancing and less obvious return improvement. However, we show that rebalanced portfolios generally underperform buy-and-hold portfolios in extreme market environments where assets show strong momentum (because the rebalancing keeps buying the underperforming asset and selling the outperforming asset). It is possible to rebalance better by taking account of this momentum effect (i.e., delay rebalancing when momentum is against you). This has maintained the advantages of rebalanced portfolios by retaining the asset class balance, but reduces the underperformance that rebalancing introduces in stress periods. The chapter was prompted by a client remarking that rebalancing is a "short volatility" strategy, which caused us to start exploring the topic in much more depth and realizing the importance of active choices in rebalancing strategy.

In *Drawdown Control* (Chapter 5), we explore the impact of cutting risk when drawdowns occur. This is an approach very commonly used by investors and yet barely mentioned in academic literature. We show that drawdown rules can be effectively used to weed out strategies (or managers) who lose the ability to generate alpha, and that this improves portfolio risk-and-return characteristics.

All of the tools we advocate are quantitative. In *Man vs. Machine* (Chapter 6), we look at both the risk and performance of systematic versus discretionary hedge fund strategies. This started as a performance comparison project in response to a client query. It ended up focusing on risk-adjusted returns. We found that discretionary and systematic macro managers are united in their long exposure to volatility, which can help in crises. For equity funds, discretionary managers have shown higher performance than systematic ones, but this difference is entirely explained by discretionary managers having larger factor exposures, especially to the market and size factors.

How have our suggestions held up in 2020? Well, at the time of writing, it's too early to tell. But in *Out-of-Sample Evidence from the COVID-19 Equity Selloff* (Chapter 7), we take a look. The results show that these risk management techniques remained effective and we continue to rely on them in our own fund management strategies. We have added this analysis as a final chapter to the book.

Many of the chapters of this book are based on work that was published in the *Journal of Portfolio Management* with a number of our colleagues at Man Group. We are grateful for their support over the past few years and their comments on our manuscript.

The book provides, we hope, a practical insight into how to manage risk well. There has been no better test than the recent market events of the first half of 2020. While we are clearly not out of this period of turbulence, we believe that our approach to strategic risk management provides some guidance on how to better manage risk through difficult periods. That's half the challenge of being a portfolio manager, and often the more-overlooked half.

Acknowledgments

The authors have greatly benefited from the insights of their coauthors on much of the foundational research for this book: Mark Ganz, Nick Granger, Carl Hamill, Edward Hoyle, Russell Korgaonkar, Eva Sanchez Martin, Matthew Sargaison, Andrew Sinclair, Daniel Taylor, and Darrel Yawitch.

The authors also appreciate both detailed comments and discussion with many of their colleagues at Man Group, including Giuliana Bordigoni, Richard Bounds, Tom Bowles, Paul Chambers, Michael Cook, Yoav Git, Keith Haydon, Chris Kennedy, Lawrence Kissko, Anthony Ledford, Charles Liu, Andrea Mondelci, Shanta Puchtler, Jayendran Rajamony, Mark Refermat, Graham Robertson, and Drake Siard.

The authors would like to thank their colleague, Darshini Shah, for her great help in this production of the book, her unceasing good humour and her encouragement in bringing this to the finish line.

CHAPTER 1

Seeking Crisis Alpha

INTRODUCTION

The idea of risk management is to provide some protection during adverse events. However, the cost of that protection must be balanced against the benefit. For example, in a strategy that uses costly long put options to eliminate the downside, the portfolio's return should not be greater than the risk-free rate. By contrast, we focus on the idea of crisis alpha, which uses dynamic methods that lower risk and also preserve excess returns. In this sense, they provide alpha when it is most needed—during crisis periods.[1]

Trend following is one technique that works especially well with a crisis-alpha strategy. Theoretically, trend-following strategies sell in market drawdowns (mimicking a dynamic replication of a long put option) and buy in rising markets (mimicking a dynamic replication of a long call option). This resembles a long straddle position and induces positive convexity. While it is possible to purchase the long straddle directly, that is expensive. Implementing a trend-following strategy is not expensive, but it is not as reliable as taking option-based insurance.

Much of our book focuses on these costs and benefits. We assess the after-cost performance of different strategies (including option-based strategies) in various risk-on events.

Our starting point is a deep dive into time-series momentum (trend-following) strategies in bonds, commodities, currencies, and equity indices between 1960 and 2015. Over the last few years, institutional investors have turned to futures trend-following strategies to provide "crisis alpha."[2] Our analysis shows that these momentum strategies performed consistently both before and after 1985, periods which were marked by strong bear and bull markets in bonds, respectively.

We document a number of important risk properties. First, returns are positively skewed, which is consistent with the theoretical link between momentum strategies and a long option straddle strategy. Second, performance was particularly strong in the worst equity and bond market environments, giving credence to the claim that trend following can provide equity *and* bond crisis alpha. Putting restrictions on the strategy to prevent it being long equities or long bonds has the potential to further enhance the crisis alpha, but reduces the average return. Finally, we examine how performance has varied across momentum strategies based on returns with different lags and applied to different asset classes.

Backdrop

Government bonds have experienced an extended bull market since 1985. This is illustrated in the left panel of Figure 1.1, where we plot the cumulative excess return of U.S. 10-year Treasuries and the S&P 500 index, relative to the U.S. T-bill rate. This shows a steady increase in cumulative bond returns since 1985. The right panel of Figure 1.1 plots the drawdown level, which rarely exceeded 10 percent for bonds in the post-1985 period. A trend-following strategy holding a (predominantly) long bonds position would have benefited from the consistent upward direction after 1985.

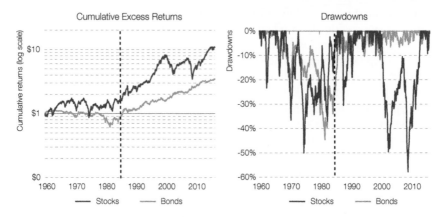

FIGURE 1.1 Cumulative excess returns and drawdowns in the stock and bond markets (1960–2015). The left panel shows the cumulative return of stocks (S&P 500 index) and bonds (U.S. 10-year Treasury), in excess of the U.S. T-Bill rate. The right panel shows the drawdown relative to the highest cumulative return achieved to date for both stocks and bonds. The data period is January 1960 to December 2015 and the dashed, vertical line separates the pre- and post-1985 period.

The strong bond performance was driven by significant interest-rate compression. U.S. yields fell from almost 16 percent in the early 1980s, to below 2 percent in March 2016. While in some countries yields have turned slightly negative, most economists believe yields cannot become very negative, and as such we are unlikely to see a similarly large yield compression in future decades. In light of this, it is natural to ask whether, in the absence of a bond market tailwind, trend-following strategies can maintain performance and protect against bond-market stress similar to that seen in the 1960s, 1970s, and early 1980s.

Outline

In this chapter we seek to shed light on three questions by studying trend-following strategies from 1960 onwards:

1. Should we expect futures trend following to be profitable in an environment where government bond yields rise?
2. Are the protective characteristics of trend following confined to equities, or do they work for government bonds as well?
3. Is it possible to improve the protection characteristics of a futures momentum strategy by removing the ability to be long equities?

Importantly, there is a stark difference between the pre-1985 period and the post-1985 period. Between 1960 and 1985, bonds experienced negative excess returns on average while stock markets provided modest positive average excess returns and quite frequent drawdowns (Figure 1.1).

In the first section, we discuss the available data to ground our understanding of the markets between 1960 and 1985. The second section defines a straightforward momentum strategy. Extending our analysis back to 1960 requires us to use monthly data and augment the available history of futures and forward returns with proxies based on cash returns, financed at the local short-term rate.

In the next section, we show that strategies based on the past four months' returns (lag 1 to 4) experience consistently strong performance, as do strategies based on returns of almost a full year ago (lags 9 to 11). However, strategies based on returns at the intermediate horizon (lags 5 to 8) underperform consistently over time and across asset classes. Next, we form a momentum strategy that places weights on historical lagged returns, such that it best matches the representative BTOP50 managed futures index (we label our strategy *momCTA*) and find that this replicating strategy allocates almost all weight on lags 1 to 4, thus largely ignoring the predictability of lags 9 to 11.

In the two sections that follow, we show that *momCTA* inherits two important risk characteristics that are particularly associated with momentum strategies based on recent returns. In the section about skewness, we show that *momCTA* has positively skewed returns, in particular when returns are evaluated over multiple months. (We specifically consider 3- and 12-month evaluation windows.) We argue this result is intuitive and related to the strategy's property of adding to winners and cutting losers, which is similar to the dynamic replication of a long option straddle position.

Then, in the section on crisis alpha, we show that *momCTA* performed particularly well in the worst equity and bond market environments, giving empirical support to a claim that trend-following can provide crisis alpha for both equities *and* bonds. Performance was strong in not only the worst but also the best equity and bond market environments, revealing a well-known equity market smile and a lesser-known, but even more pronounced bond market smile.

We find that the equity and bond crisis alpha was further enhanced when we restricted the equity and bond position to be non-positive. However, this comes at the cost of lower general performance and unfavorable cross-market effects. Indeed we find that a non-positive equity (bond) restriction worsened the performance during bond (equity) market declines.

DATA

Many other papers that have looked at trend-following strategies start their analysis well after 1960. Moskowitz, Ooi, and Pedersen (2012), for example, evaluate trend-following strategies from 1985 onwards "to ensure that a comprehensive set of instruments have data." We believe that starting in 1960 strikes the right balance for our research question; however, using a sample period that starts in 1960 presents certain challenges. Starting earlier than 1960 is problematic for commodities because one either has to omit the asset class before 1960; rely on imperfect and only intermittently available data; or rely on spot returns, thus ignoring the roll yield component of return.[3] Starting in 1960 provides an opportunity to study the worst bond market drawdown the United States experienced since at least 1900, as the 10-year yield rose from below 5 percent in 1960 to a peak of almost 16 percent in the early 1980s.

In Table 1.1, we provide an overview of the securities used in our analysis, and report the start date and some summary statistics. While we start the evaluation of momentum strategies in 1960, our data start as early as 1950 to allow for a so-called warm-up period for obtaining the volatility and correlation risk estimates needed in the strategy construction. For securities with data starting after 1960 only, we maintain a warm-up period of one year so that they are included in the momentum strategy return one year after the reported data start date.

TABLE 1.1   Data. This table provides the start date for the securities used in this chapter, as well as some descriptive statistic for monthly security returns. The euro (EUR/USD) is augmented with the deutsche mark prior to the January 1999 introduction of the euro.

	Cash start date	Futures/ forwards start date	Mean (annual)	Standard deviation (annual)	Skewness	Kurtosis
BONDS						
Australian 10yr Bond	Jan-77	Dec-84	0.21%	3.60%	−0.45	23.48
Canadian 10yr Bond	Jan-50	Feb-90	1.68%	6.31%	0.25	6.12
French 10yr Bond (OAT)	Jan-50	Jun-12	2.17%	5.68%	−0.29	5.50
German 10yr Bond (Bund)	Jan-50	Jun-83	3.08%	5.10%	−0.33	1.95
Italian 10yr Bond (BTP)	Jan-50	Sep-11	2.72%	10.14%	0.40	2.26
Japanese 10yr Bond (JGB)	Jan-72	Mar-83	3.16%	5.86%	0.13	6.39
UK 10yr Bond (Gilts)	Jan-50	Nov-82	1.85%	6.32%	0.25	3.00
US 2yr Note	Jan-50	Jul-05	0.83%	2.70%	0.71	12.16
US 5yr Note	Jan-50	Oct-91	1.52%	5.06%	0.24	6.12
US 10yr Note	Jan-50	May-82	1.87%	6.80%	0.43	3.86
US 30yr Bond	Jan-50	Sep-77	1.84%	9.80%	0.27	3.40
COMMODITIES - AGRICULTURALS						
Cocoa (CSCE)	N/A	Sep-59	3.76%	30.68%	0.65	1.40
Coffee (CSCE)	N/A	Aug-73	4.73%	37.20%	1.22	4.24
Corn	N/A	Jul-59	−2.06%	23.66%	1.20	6.57
Cotton	N/A	Jul-59	2.58%	23.29%	0.68	3.49
Lean Hogs	N/A	Sep-69	3.45%	26.00%	0.24	1.23

(*Continued*)

TABLE 1.1 (*Continued*)

	Cash start date	Futures/ forwards start date	Mean (annual)	Standard deviation (annual)	Skewness	Kurtosis
Live Cattle	N/A	Nov-64	4.76%	16.95%	−0.29	2.11
Soyabeans	N/A	Jul-59	5.58%	25.66%	1.56	10.81
Soyameal	N/A	Jul-59	9.79%	30.29%	1.94	13.86
Soyaoil	N/A	Mar-68	7.57%	31.38%	1.42	6.64
Sugar (CSCE)	N/A	Jan-61	0.55%	42.53%	1.10	2.99
Wheat	N/A	Jul-59	−1.59%	24.89%	0.72	3.29
COMMODITIES - ENERGIES						
Brent Crude Oil	N/A	Jun-88	13.05%	34.42%	0.47	3.13
Gas Oil	N/A	Apr-81	8.41%	31.73%	0.49	2.03
Heating Oil	N/A	Mar-79	7.97%	32.88%	0.70	3.22
Natural Gas	N/A	Apr-90	−5.70%	54.36%	1.82	10.71
RBOB Gasoline	N/A	Dec-84	16.42%	36.43%	0.43	2.52
WTI Crude Oil	N/A	Oct-83	7.29%	33.35%	0.25	2.04
COMMODITIES - METALS						
Aluminium (LME)	N/A	Jan-80	−2.10%	22.21%	1.00	4.23
Copper (COMEX)	N/A	Jul-59	10.06%	27.32%	0.36	3.41
Gold	N/A	Dec-74	1.43%	19.30%	0.39	3.27
Nickel	N/A	Jul-79	7.04%	34.74%	1.44	9.15
Palladium	N/A	Nov-05	11.62%	32.63%	−0.15	3.92
Platinum	N/A	Mar-68	4.31%	27.77%	0.36	4.46
Silver	N/A	Jan-72	4.58%	32.39%	0.65	4.85
Zinc	N/A	Jan-75	1.97%	24.65%	−0.02	1.33

TABLE 1.1 (*Continued*)

	Cash start date	Futures/ forwards start date	Mean (annual)	Standard deviation (annual)	Skewness	Kurtosis
CURRENCIES						
AUD/USD	Jan-73	Jan-75	2.02%	10.83%	−0.76	3.77
CAD/USD	Jan-73	Jan-77	0.48%	6.64%	−0.88	7.83
EUR/USD	Jan-73	Jan-75	1.25%	12.14%	0.37	2.51
JPY/USD	Jan-73	Nov-76	0.82%	14.69%	2.41	25.44
NZD/USD	Jan-73	Dec-88	2.63%	9.18%	−0.34	3.68
NOK/USD	Jan-73	Dec-88	1.08%	9.38%	−0.24	1.96
SEK/USD	Jan-73	Dec-88	0.71%	10.07%	−0.40	2.64
CHF/USD	Jan-73	Feb-75	2.78%	14.91%	1.57	12.22
GBP/USD	Jan-73	Feb-75	1.07%	10.18%	0.06	2.19
EQUITIES						
Australia SPI200	Jan-50	Mar-83	7.08%	16.61%	−1.15	11.34
France CAC 40	Jan-50	Nov-88	6.68%	18.87%	−0.10	1.17
Germany DAX	Sep-59	Nov-90	3.75%	19.53%	−0.17	1.61
Dutch All	Dec-50	Oct-88	7.72%	17.82%	−0.42	2.10
U.K. FTSE	Jan-50	May-84	6.67%	18.22%	0.84	14.14
Spain IBEX 35	Jan-50	Jan-92	6.19%	18.79%	−0.09	2.06
Italy All	Jan-50	Dec-94	5.16%	23.10%	0.40	2.08
U.S. S&P 500	Jan-50	Apr-82	6.99%	14.41%	−0.37	1.35
Canada S&P 60	Jan-50	May-87	5.74%	15.22%	−0.67	2.39
Japan TSE	Jan-50	Jul-92	8.23%	18.89%	0.02	1.31

For commodities, we have data on various agricultural futures contracts and some metals going back to the 1960s. The first oil futures contract, however, was only introduced in the early 1980s. For currencies, we have data from 1973 onwards only. Before that, from 1944 to 1971, the rules of Bretton Woods provided a system of fixed exchange rates that led to limited exchange-rate moves and an unsuitable investment environment. For the initial years, we use spot exchange rates, corrected for the short-rate differential to make it comparable to futures returns. For equities and bonds, we have monthly cash data going back well before 1960 from Global Financial Data for a number of countries. We deduct the local short rate from the return to make it comparable to the return of an unfunded instrument like a future. The equity and bond market data requires us to do our analysis based on monthly data.[4]

As a general rule, we use cash, and then futures or forwards data as soon as it is available. However, we make an exception for securities that are subject to market regulation that is so severe that the price hardly fluctuates, making those securities unsuitable for investment. Specifically, we filtered for securities for which the rolling 12-month volatility estimate at some point dropped to a level of 0.05 times the average 12-month volatility. Three securities were identified by this filter. The first is silver, which we include only from 1972 onwards. Before that, silver prices did not fluctuate freely because they were tied to the U.S. monetary system until 1968; in the years immediately following 1968, they were subject to government intervention. The other two are the Japanese and Australian 10-year bonds, which will be included only from 1972 and 1977, respectively, because before that price fluctuations were severely subdued due to a combination of capital controls, currency intervention, and other monetary policies.

STRATEGY

After analyzing the data, we explore a basic momentum strategy. As discussed in the previous section, extending the equity and bond data back to 1960 means we have to work with monthly rather than daily data. We consider the following general formula for the momentum signal of security k, observed at time $t-1$:

$$mom_{t-1}^k = \frac{w_1 R_{t-1}^k + w_2 R_{t-2}^k + \ldots}{\sigma_{t-1}^k \sqrt{w_1^2 + w_2^2 + \ldots}} \tag{1.1}$$

where:

- R^k_{t-i} is the monthly return of security k at lag i
- w_i is the weight given to lag i, which is assumed to be the same for all securities k
- σ^k_{t-1} is the standard deviation of monthly returns for security k, observed at time t-1[5]
- $\sqrt{w_1^2 + w_2^2 + \ldots}$ is to achieve a unit standard deviation (approximately) for the signal[6]

In the next section, we will consider different weights, w. The weights will typically be positive to capture momentum (rather than reversal behavior) and are required to sum to one.

The signal value indicates how many risk units one would want to hold in a security. To turn this into a dollar position, we need to divide by the volatility estimate a second time (so that all assets are trading the same amount of risk for a given strength signal).[7] The strategy performance is found by summing over the performance for each traded market, which in turn is found by multiplying the signal–volatility ratio, the next period return, and a leverage or gearing factor to scale to a given risk target:

$$Performance_t = \sum_k Gearing^k_{t-1} \frac{mom^k_{t-1}}{\sigma^k_{t-1}} R^k_t \qquad (1.2)$$

The gearing factor is such that, on average, the resulting portfolio has an ex-ante annualized volatility estimate of 10 percent, and risk is spread equally over the four asset classes: bonds, commodities, currencies, and equities. Within equities, bonds, and currencies, we allocate equal risk weights to the different constituent securities. Choosing equal weights is quite common in academic studies (albeit usually for dollar allocations), as it's in a way a model-free choice. Any other weighting scheme would require justification for exactly how and why you deviate from equal weighting. Within commodities, we give equal weight to the agriculture, metals, and energies subsectors, and within these subsectors we give equal weight to the different constituent securities. For securities that have data available only at a later date, we redistribute the risk in the preceding period equally to the other securities in the same asset class.[8]

We use unfunded instruments for our security returns in this analysis (i.e., futures, forwards, or cash instruments financed at the local short rate).

This means that the performance in Equation 1.2 should be interpreted as an excess return. If you wanted to know the total performance, you would add up the short rate, possibly with a haircut to reflect the fact that some margin needs to be posted and that the interest rate on the margin account may be below the short rate. Between 1960 and 2015, the U.S. T-bill return and inflation rate averaged 4.8 percent and 3.9 percent, respectively, and, unsurprisingly, they moved mostly in line with one another, revealing a correlation of 0.72. An 18 percent haircut in the short rate, which we think is reasonable, would equate with the average interest income rate and inflation rate. Thus, the reported excess returns can alternatively be considered as a reasonable proxy for the inflation-adjusted (real) returns.

Finally, we ignore transaction costs and fees, which would impact the general profitability of momentum strategies, but less so the dynamics of momentum returns, which is the main focus of this chapter. Assuming a two-basis-point transaction cost for outright trades leads to a reduction in the annualized return of 0.42 percentage points for the main strategy, which we will call the *momCTA* strategy. This estimate is broadly in line with experience over current trading conditions for a medium-term trend strategy, whereas it is harder to make statements about earlier periods.

PERFORMANCE

In Figure 1.2 we present the annualized excess return for trend strategies based on a single month's return, where we vary the lag from 1 (past month) to 24 (the return 24 months ago). Using the notation of Equation 1.1, the leftmost bar is based on $w_1 = 1$ (other lags zero), the next bar is for $w_2 = 1$ (other lags zero), and so on, all the way up to $w_{24} = 1$ (other lags zero) for the rightmost bar.

It is noteworthy that returns for lags up to 11 months ago are strongly predictive with a positive sign for the following month's return, as evidenced by the solidly positive performance.[9] In contrast, the one-month return 12 months ago is much less predictive, with only a modestly positive performance. At first sight this may seem odd. In fact, other papers on futures trend-following have claimed predictability up to 12-months out and proposed a trading strategy based on 12-month momentum. In unreported results, we find that the main reason that the return 12 months ago is not as predictive is due to using monthly rather than daily data, which effectively adds a half-month lag on average.[10] Also worth observing from Figure 1.3 is that the annualized returns for lags 1 through 11 display a U-shape, where the curved line represents the quadratic fit.

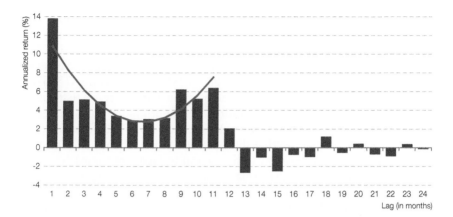

FIGURE 1.2 Performance of single-month momentum strategies. The bars show the annualized return for momentum strategies based on the first 24 lags. The curved line represents the quadratic fit on the first 11 lags. Returns do not include interest income, so they can be considered excess returns and are gross of transaction costs and fees. The measurement period is January 1960 to December 2015.

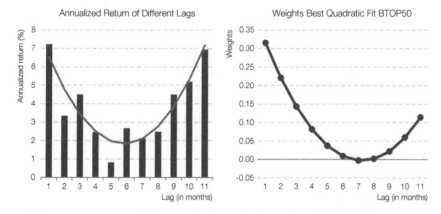

FIGURE 1.3 Single-month momentum performance and weights BTOP50 replication (post-1987). The bar graph in the left panel shows the annualized return of momentum strategies based on the first 11 monthly lags. The quadratic fit is given by the curved line. Returns do not include interest income, so they can be considered excess returns, and are gross of transaction costs and fees. In the right panel, we show the weights to the first 11 monthly lagged returns of the momentum strategy that has the highest correlation with the excess returns of the BTOP50 index, while imposing a quadratic functional form on the weights as a function of the lag. The measurement period is 1987–2015, which corresponds to the time period for which we have performance data for the BTOP50 index.

Next we explore which weights in Equation 1.1 correspond best to the returns of the representative BTOP50 managed futures index, for which we have return data from January 1987.[11] Our goal is to develop a close proxy for the BTOP50 so that we can examine performance in the period the BTOP50 was not available from 1960–1986. We deduct the U.S. T-bill rate from the index returns to give an excess return. In Figure 1.3 (left panel), we first plot the annualized return for single-month momentum strategies, as we did in Figure 1.2, but now we use the data from 1987 onwards, and up to lag 11. Again, we see that the quadratic fit is U-shaped and this time nearly symmetric. To prevent overfitting and to facilitate comparison with the U-shape found for the performance of different lags, we impose that the weights are a quadratic function of the lag and set weights at lag 12 and beyond to zero. Subject to these restrictions, the weights that lead to the highest correlation with the BTOP50 index return are plotted in Figure 1.3 (right panel). We will refer to the strategy based on these weights as the *momCTA* strategy.

The monthly returns to *momCTA* and the excess returns of the BTOP50 index have a correlation coefficient of 0.62 over the 29-year history. We consider this to be reasonably high given that the *momCTA* strategy is defined on monthly data, while BTOP50 managers most likely use daily data for computing signal values and risk measures. What is noteworthy is that the optimal quadratic weights (right panel) are not nearly as symmetrically U-shaped as the quadratic fit of single-month momentum performance (left panel). In fact, 76 percent of the optimal quadratic weights come from the first four lags. This indicates that trend followers seem to have mostly focused on the predictability of recent lags and largely ignored the historically strong predictability of lags 9 to 11.

In Figure 1.4, we plot the cumulative returns for the following momentum strategies, which are all defined by Equation 1.1 and differ only in terms of the weights given to different lagged returns:

- *mom(1,4)* based on the past four months' returns ($w_1 = w_2 = w_3 = w_4 = 1/4$, other lags zero)
- *mom(5,8)* based on returns from 5 to 8 months ago ($w_5 = w_6 = w_7 = w_8 = 1/4$, other lags zero)
- *mom(9,11)* based on returns from 9 to 11 months ago ($w_9 = w_{10} = w_{11} = 1/3$ ther lags zero)
- *momCTA*, based on the past 11 months' returns, weights given in Figure 1.3 (right panel)

We chose *mom(1,4)*, *mom(5,8)*, and *mom(9,11)* such that they capture the different parts of the U-shape in performance illustrated in Figures 1.2 and 1.3 (right panel). To be clear, our goal here is to deliberately examine non-overlapping historical returns to see how far back they are predictive. We use a log-scale, so a constant performance over time would correspond to a straight line. The monthly returns of *momCTA* and *mom(1,4)* have a correlation of 0.92, while the correlations between the other pairs are much lower, ranging between 0.20 and 0.40. The performance of *momCTA* and *mom(1,4)* around 1974 stands out as particularly strong. This can be largely attributed to bonds and commodities whose returns displayed very strong one-month momentum. Besides that, the *momCTA* and *mom(1,4)* perform stronger quite consistently over the 56-year period considered. Comparing the slope of the cumulative return curves of the *mom(9,11)* and *mom(1,4)*, it's clear that the *mom(9,11)* strategy also performs consistently and, since the mid-1970s, has performed about as well as *mom(1,4)*. In contrast, the *mom(5,8)* strategy has consistently underperformed the other strategies.

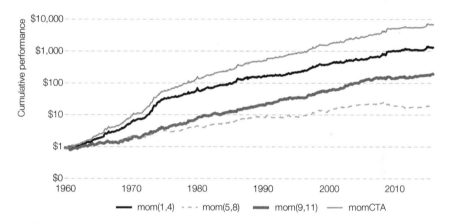

FIGURE 1.4 Cumulative performance for different momentum strategies. All strategies are run at 10 percent ex-ante volatility. Returns are compounded and plotted against a log-scale, so that a straight line corresponds to constant performance over time. This is also reflected on the y-axis, which follows a log scale. Returns do not include interest income, so they can be considered excess returns and are gross of transaction costs and fees. The measurement period is January 1960 to December 2015.

All strategies target an ex-ante annual volatility of 10 percent on average. For *momCTA* and *mom(1,4)* the realized value is slightly above target at 10.5 percent (in both cases), while for *mom(5,8)* and *mom(9,11)* it is slightly below target at 9.2 percent and 8.9 percent respectively. While the cumulative performance plotted in Figure 1.4 is affected by the realized volatility, the annualized Sharpe ratio reported in Table 1.2 is not. We report the Sharpe ratio both for the case where all securities are included and for the individual asset classes. In all cases, *mom(5,8)* clearly underperforms *momCTA*, *mom(1,4)* and *mom(9,11)*.

TABLE 1.2 Sharpe ratio for different momentum strategies. This table reports the annualized Sharpe ratio, determined as the annualized (excess) return divided by the annualized volatility of returns, for different momentum strategies. Returns do not include interest income (i.e., can be considered excess returns) and are gross of transaction costs and fees. Different columns correspond to different sets of securities to which the strategy is applied. The measurement period is January 1960 to December 2015.

Strategy	Securities included in analysis				
	All	Bonds	Commodities	Currencies	Equities
momCTA	1.56	1.18	1.07	0.57	0.64
mom(1,4)	1.30	0.99	0.87	0.48	0.55
mom(5,8)	0.64	0.32	0.56	0.19	0.34
mom(9,11)	1.12	0.54	0.91	0.52	0.51

The strong performance for lags 1 to 4, which then tapers off from lags 5 to 8, seems consistent with the wisdom that price trends often arise from an initial underreaction to news followed by a gradual response in the month immediately after the story breaks. The uptick in performance for lags 9 to 11 is harder to explain with a pure underreaction to a news story; news released nine or more months in the past is likely to have been digested by the market, even if there is an initial underreaction. It is likely partially related to an annual seasonality effect and partially to a footprint left by the prevalence of 12-month windows in reporting and evaluating financial data. The news-based economic interpretation is more difficult to apply to *mom(9,11)*, which may be one reason that *momCTA*, our proxy for the momentum strategy employed in live trading by trend followers, is much closer to *mom(1,4)*. However, another possible explanation is that the risk characteristics of *mom(1,4)* are more favorable than those for *mom(9,11)*, as we show in the subsequent sections.

SKEWNESS

The two most basic parameters of the return distribution are average return and standard deviation of returns, but investors do not necessarily limit their interest to these. Rather they may also care about the asymmetry of the return distribution and may be particularly averse to occasional large negative returns. In other words, investors may dislike negatively skewed return distributions and be drawn to positively skewed return distributions.

We find that the monthly returns of *mom(1,4)* and the highly correlated *momCTA* strategy display considerable positive skewness. The positive skewness is further enhanced when using a three-month evaluation window, which arguably is a more relevant horizon for an institutional investor. Using a 12-month evaluation window also yields similar results. Table 1.3 shows the outcome, both where all securities are included and for individual asset classes. The *momCTA* and *mom(1,4)* strategies have considerably positively skewed returns for all asset classes while the *mom(5,8)* and *mom(9,11)* strategies have much lower (and often negative) skewness statistics. This suggests that much of the positive convexity is being driven by faster momentum speeds. That is, the segments from lags 5 through 11 are not substantially contributing to positive skewness.

TABLE 1.3 Skewness for different momentum strategies. The annualized skewness of three-month overlapping returns for different momentum strategies are reported. Returns do not include interest income, so they can be considered excess returns, and are gross of transaction costs and fees. Different columns correspond to different sets of securities to which the strategy is applied. The measurement period is January 1960 to December 2015.

Skewness three-month overlapping returns

Strategy	Securities included in analysis				
	All	Bonds	Commodities	Currencies	Equities
momCTA	1.04	0.71	1.21	1.40	0.96
mom(1,4)	1.13	0.53	1.08	1.59	0.81
mom(5,8)	−0.06	−0.41	0.01	0.51	−0.24
mom(9,11)	0.16	0.38	0.41	0.17	0.11

Skewness 12-month overlapping returns

Strategy	Securities included in analysis				
	All	Bonds	Commodities	Currencies	Equities
momCTA	1.48	0.08	0.97	1.86	0.89
mom(1,4)	1.80	0.24	0.95	2.38	0.88
mom(5,8)	−0.07	−0.70	−0.13	0.86	0.26
mom(9,11)	−0.07	0.23	−0.16	0.24	−0.05

We have confirmed the robustness of these findings in a number of ways. First, we have looked at the pre- and post-1985 time periods separately. Second, we have rerun the models omitting 2008, which is when most extreme positive returns occurred, giving that year a disproportionate impact on a higher-order moment like skewness. Finally, we have recalculated the statistics using the alternative Bowley and Pearson measures of skewness.[12] All three of these tests give a similar conclusion to the original experiment: that *momCTA* and *mom(1,4)* display considerable positive skewness for 3- and 12-month evaluation periods.

The positive skewness at a multi-month evaluation window for *momCTA* and *mom(1,4)* seems intuitive given the close parallel between a momentum strategy and a long straddle strategy.[13] With a long straddle strategy, one frequently loses a limited amount of money when the underlying asset price stays bound within a limited range, but sometimes one makes big gains when the underlying asset makes big moves up or down.[14] In fact, the trading profile of a trend follower involves adding to winning positions (called *riding winners*) and reducing losing positions (called *cutting losers*), much like the dynamic replication of an option straddle strategy. This involves holding an amount in the underlying equal to the delta of a straddle.[15] In Figure 1.5, we illustrate this point by plotting the delta of a straddle as a function of the distance to the strike price, expressed as a number of standard deviations.[16] On the same graph, we plot the position

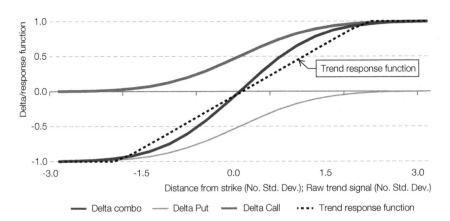

FIGURE 1.5 **Delta of straddle versus momentum response function.** Figure 1.5 shows the delta of a call, put, and the straddle (i.e., call plus put) as a function of the distance from the strike price, expressed as a number of standard deviations. Plotted alongside this is the response function of a trend follower as a function of past returns and also expressed as a number of standard deviations.

of a trend follower, as a function of his or her past returns, also expressed as a number of standard deviations, and scaled and capped such that the most extreme positioning is achieved for +/−2 standard deviation moves.[17]

CRISIS ALPHA

After determining skewness, we evaluate the performance of the *momCTA* strategy during different equity and bond market environments. To this end, we form quintiles based on rolling three-month equity (S&P 500) and bond (10-year U.S. Treasury) returns and report the average return of the *mom-CTA* strategy for each of the quintiles. As noted before, we argue that using three months for the evaluation window may be more appropriate because it may take an institutional investor at least a couple of months to reposition when faced with a changing market environment.

Figure 1.6 shows the result for different equity (left panel) and bond (right panel) performance quintiles; the rightmost bar corresponds to the unconditional average return. We note that *momCTA* performs particularly

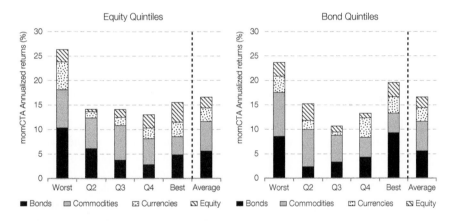

FIGURE 1.6 *momCTA* performance, equity and bond quintiles, rolling three-month window. The figure shows the annualized average *momCTA* return for rolling three-month windows, attributed to the four asset classes covered, under different general equity and bond market conditions. In the left panel, the results are reported for equity market quintiles, with quintile 1 corresponding to the worst three-month S&P 500 returns and quintile 5 to the best. The rightmost bar corresponds to the average return across all periods. Similarly, the right panel shows results for different bond market (U.S. Treasury) quintiles. Returns do not include interest income (i.e., they can be considered excess returns) and are gross of transaction costs and fees. The sample period is January 1960 to December 2015.

well when general equity and bond markets are at their worst, giving credence to a claim that trend following provides equity and bond crisis alpha. Performance is also strong in the best equity and bond market environments, giving rise to a well-known "equity smile" and a lesser-known but even more pronounced "bond smile."[18]

We also decompose the strategy returns into the performance from the four different asset classes: bonds, commodities, currencies, and equities.[19] Interestingly, equities, bonds, and currencies all show both an equity and bond smile. The performance of commodities displays more of a left skew, with performance particularly strong during the worst periods for equities and bonds.

We performed the following sensitivity checks: (i) using a 12-month rolling performance evaluation window (rather than 3 months) and (ii) starting the analysis in 1974, when we have data for currencies. In both cases, we find that the *momCTA* strategy does well in both the worst equity and worst bond market environments. We also analyzed the *mom(1,4)*, *mom(5,8)*, and *mom(9,11)* strategies. *Mom(1,4)* stands out by providing such crisis alpha, which is in line with the skewness results presented in the previous section. Further details, including figures illustrating *mom(1,4)*, *mom(5,8)*, and *mom(9,11)*, can be found in the chapter appendix.

Next, we explore how we might further enhance the crisis alpha characteristic of trend-following strategies. Specifically, we run versions of the *momCTA* strategy where positions in equities are capped at zero. This will ensure that the strategy is well-positioned during periods of equity market decline (as it can never be long). Obviously, this will also ensure that during an equity bull market the strategy can only be flat or short (i.e., erroneously positioned in equities). We repeat this exercise for bonds. We scale the restricted returns to have (ex-post) the same volatility as the baseline (unrestricted) case, so as to facilitate a comparison between the two versions.

Figure 1.7 shows the annualized average *momCTA* return for rolling three-month windows, with and without a restriction to hold no long positions in equities (left panel) or bonds (right panel). We scale the restricted returns to have (ex-post) the same volatility as the baseline case, so as to facilitate the comparison between the two versions. In the left panel, the results are reported for equity market quintiles, with quintile 1 corresponding to the worst three-month S&P 500 returns and quintile 5 to the best. The rightmost bar corresponds to the average return across all periods. Similarly, the right panel shows results for different bond market (U.S. Treasury) quintiles. Returns do not include interest income (i.e., they can be considered

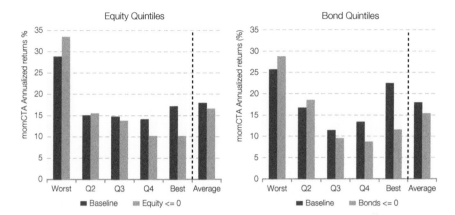

FIGURE 1.7 *momCTA* **performance, equity and bond quintiles, rolling three-month window (restrictions).** In Figure 1.7, we compare the performance for our baseline (unrestricted) case to that of using the no-long-equity restriction for equity quintiles (left panel) and no-long-bond restriction for bond quintiles (right panel). Quintile 1 corresponding to the worst three-month returns and quintile 5 to the best. The rightmost bar corresponds to the average return across all periods. Returns do not include interest income (i.e., they can be considered excess returns) and are gross of transaction costs and fees. The sample period is January 1960 to December 2015.

excess returns) and are gross of transaction costs and fees. Different columns correspond to different sets of securities to which the strategy is applied. The sample period is January 1960 to December 2015.

In both cases, the position capping further improves the already good performance in quintile 1 while reducing the performance in quintiles 3, 4, and 5. Also the average performance (averaged over all quintiles) goes down, which can be seen as the price one pays for the enhanced crisis alpha return profile.

For an investor who cares about both the equity and bond crisis alpha return profile, the situation is more nuanced, however, due to an unfavorable cross-effect. As we show in Figure 1.8, a no-long-bond restriction worsens the return in all equity quintiles (left panel), and similarly a no-long-equity restriction worsens the return in all bond quintiles (right panel). In particular, the worst performance in quintile 1 is an undesirable cross-effect and may at first sight be surprising, given that common fundamental factors would typically imply a positive equity–bond correlation (Baele, Bekaert, and Inghelbrecht 2010). However, at times of severe stock market uncertainty, the equity–bond correlation has empirically turned very negative, which is often ascribed to a flight-to-safety effect (Connolly, Stivers, and Sun 2005).

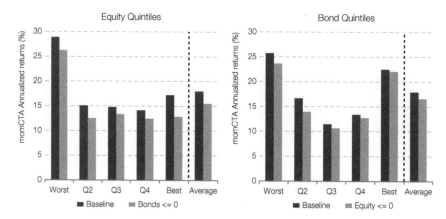

FIGURE 1.8 momCTA performance, equity and bond quintiles, rolling three-month window (cross-restrictions). Figure 1.8 shows the annualized average *momCTA* return for rolling three-month windows, with and without a cross-restriction to hold no long positions in bonds (left panel) or equities (right panel). We scale the restricted returns to have (ex-post) the same volatility as the baseline case, so as to facilitate the comparison between the two versions. In the left panel, the results are reported for equity market quintiles, with quintile 1 corresponding to the worst three-month S&P 500 returns and quintile 5 to the best. The rightmost bar corresponds to the average return across all periods. Similarly, the right panel shows results for different bond market (U.S. Treasury) quintiles. Returns do not include interest income (i.e., can be considered excess returns) and are gross of transaction costs and fees. Different columns correspond to different sets of securities to which the strategy is applied. The sample period is January 1960 to December 2015.

CONCLUDING REMARKS

In this chapter, we have introduced a key component of strategic risk management: identification of active strategies that serve to cushion portfolios in times of stress. Trend-following strategies theoretically have such a property in that they resemble the dynamic replication of long straddles—but without the cost of initiating such an option position. In this sense, we refer to this particular strategy as generating crisis alpha.

While the track record of live trend-following strategies has been impressive, that record only begins in the late 1980s. An obvious question is whether the recent experience has been special. Indeed, during this time period, interest rates have declined from very high levels to historically low levels. As such, we evaluate these strategies between 1960 and 2015, a time period that includes extended bull and bear markets for both equities and bonds. The strategy that we construct closely matches the BTOP50 (over the period the BTOP50 is available) and the strategy has performed consistently over the full 56-year period. It also has a number of compelling risk characteristics: positively skewed returns and strong performance in the worst equity and bond market environments, which we refer to as equity and bond market crisis alpha, respectively.

Despite 56 years of supportive empirical evidence, it is natural to ask whether momentum strategies will continue to be profitable. In this respect, it is worth noting that academic papers on the topic date back to at least Jegadeesh and Titman (1993) and performance has persisted since then. While a meaningful amount of capital is dedicated to exploiting the momentum phenomenon, there is evidence that there are very large players that have a tendency to take the other side (knowingly or unknowingly), possibly addressing concerns that too much capital is chasing momentum profits. For example, Lou, Polk, and Skouras (2016) present evidence that stock momentum is different from other trading strategies in that professional, institutional investors tend to "trade against the momentum characteristic."

We should emphasize that the design of our momentum strategy was deliberately barebones, as any frills added would call into question whether the risk-and-return characteristics identified are general effects or specific to the chosen formulation. Many additional considerations play an important role when running a live momentum strategy on futures, including fine-tuning the trading signal definition, portfolio construction, risk management, and execution.

While time-series momentum strategies tend to do well, on average, in periods of poor equity and bond performance, there are key questions that remain unanswered, in particular:

1. Are the strategies providing consistent performance when we drill down to specific drawdown episodes (this chapter only reported averages)?
2. How do these strategies perform in recessions (periods that are especially sensitive to investors because of losses in income from human capital)?
3. How do trend-following methods compare to alternative protective strategies such as buying put options or investing in gold?

These questions are addressed in the next chapter.

APPENDIX 1A: SENSITIVITY ANALYSES FOR EQUITY AND BOND CRISIS ALPHA AND SMILES

We find that for rolling 12-month evaluation windows, the equity smile becomes a full-on left-skew with *momCTA* doing best in quintile 1 (the worst equity markets) and worst in quintile 5. The bond smile flattens somewhat but the *momCTA* performance continues to be strong in quintile 1. See Figure 1A.1.

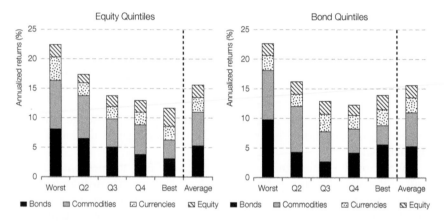

FIGURE 1A.1 *momCTA* performance, equity and bond quintiles, rolling 12-month window. The figure shows the annualized average *momCTA* return for rolling 12-month windows, attributed to the four asset classes covered. In the left panel the results are reported for equity market quintiles, with quintile 1 corresponding to the worst 12-month S&P 500 returns and quintile 5 to the best. The rightmost bar corresponds to the average return across all periods. Similarly, the right panel shows results for quintiles from a different bond market (U.S. Treasury). Returns do not include interest income (i.e., can be considered excess returns) and are gross of transaction costs and fees. Different columns correspond to different sets of securities to which the strategy is applied. The measurement period is January 1960 to December 2015.

When we start our analysis in 1974, post Bretton Woods, and when we have currency data, the bond and equity smiles still remain. See Figure 1A.2.

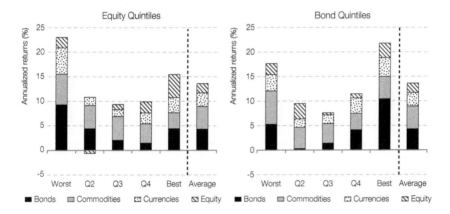

FIGURE 1A.2 *momCTA* performance, equity and bond quintiles, rolling three-month window, post-1974. The figure shows the annualized average *momCTA* return for rolling three-month windows, post-1974, attributed to the four asset classes covered. In the left panel the results are reported for equity market quintiles, with quintile 1 corresponding to the worst three-month S&P 500 returns and quintile 5 to the best. The rightmost bar corresponds to the average return across all periods. Similarly, the right panel shows results for different bond market (U.S. Treasury) quintiles. Returns do not include interest income (i.e., can be considered excess returns) and are gross of transaction costs and fees. Different columns correspond to different sets of securities to which the strategy is applied. The measurement period is January 1974 to December 2015.

We find that equity and bond smiles are obtained for *mom(1,4)* but are less clear for *mom(5,8)* and *mom(9,11)* that use more distant past returns. See Figure 1A.3.

mom(1,4)

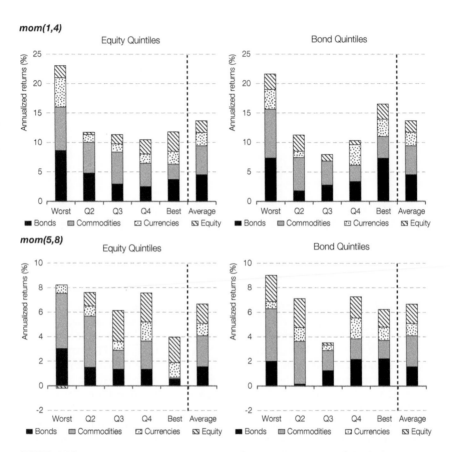

FIGURE 1A.3 *mom(1,4)*, *mom(5,8)*, *mom(9,11)* **performance, equity and bond quintiles, rolling three-month window.** Figure 1A.3 shows the annualized average *mom(1,4)*, *mom(5,9)*, and *mom(9,11)* return for rolling three-month windows, attributed to the four asset classes covered. In the left panel the results are reported for equity market quintiles, with quintile 1 corresponding to the worst three-month S&P 500 returns and quintile 5 to the best. The rightmost bar corresponds to the average return across all periods. Similarly, the right panel shows results for different bond market (U.S. Treasury) quintiles. Returns do not include interest income (i.e., can be considered excess returns) and are gross of transaction costs and fees. Different columns correspond to different sets of securities to which the strategy is applied. The measurement period is January 1960 to December 2015.

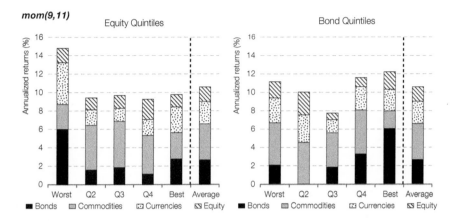

mom(9,11)

FIGURE 1A.3 (*Continued*)

REFERENCES

Baele, L., G. Bekaert, and K. Inghelbrecht (2010). "The Determinants of Stock and Bond Return Comovements," *Review of Financial Studies*, 23(6), 2374–2428.

Baltas, N., and R. Kosowski (2013). "Momentum Strategies in Futures Markets and Trend-Following Funds," working paper.

Connolly, R., C. Stivers, and L. Sun (2015). "Stock Market Uncertainty and the Stock-Bond Return Relation," *Journal of Financial and Quantitative Analysis*, 40(1), 161–194.

Fung, W., and D. Hsieh (2001). "The Risk In Hedge Fund Strategies: Theory and Evidence from Trend Followers," *Review of Financial Studies*, 14(2), 313–341.

Goyal, A., and S. Wahal (2015). "Is Momentum an Echo?," *Journal of Financial and Quantitative*, 50(6), 1237–1267.

Greyserman, A. (2012). "The Multi-Centennial View of Trend Following," ISAM whitepaper.

Hamill, Carl, Sandy Rattray, and Otto Van Hemert (2016, August 30). "Trend Following: Equity and Bond Crisis Alpha." Available at SSRN: https://ssrn.com/abstract=2831926.

Hurst, B., Y. Ooi, and L. Pedersen (2012). "A Century of Evidence on Trend-Following Investing," AQR white paper.

Jegadeesh, N., and S. Titman (1993). "Returns to Buying Winners and Selling Losers: Implications for Stocks Market Efficiency," *Journal of Finance*, 48(1), 65–91.

Kaminski, K. (2011). "In Search of Crisis Alpha: A Short Guide to Investing in Managed Futures," working paper.

Lempérière, Y., C. Deremble, P. Seager, M. Potters, and J. Bouchaud (2014). "Two Centuries of Trend Following," CFM whitepaper.

Lou, D., C. Polk, and S. Skouras (2016). "A Tug of War: Overnight versus Intraday Expected Returns," working paper.

Martin, R., and D. Zou (2012). "Momentum Trading: Skews Me," *Risk*, 25(8), 52–57.

Moskowitz, T., Y. Ooi, and L. Pedersen (2012). "Time Series Momentum," *Journal of Financial Economics*, 104(2), 228–250.

Novy-Marx, R. (2012). "Is Momentum Really Momentum?," *Journal of Financial Economics*, 103(3), 429–453.

CHAPTER 2

Can Portfolios Be Crisis Proofed?

INTRODUCTION

In the previous chapter, we introduced a key concept in strategic risk management: integrating strategies that have favorable risk management characteristics into the asset selection process. We did a deep dive on trend-following strategies and showed that they exhibit positive convexity—a much desired property in risk management. Further, we showed that this protective property appeared robust to different economic environments since 1960. However, trend following is only one possible strategy that has protective characteristics. Further, it is important to diagnose the performance of various strategies in specific economic episodes. This is what we endeavor to do in this chapter.[1]

Indeed, in the late stages of long bull markets, a common question arises: What steps can an investor take to mitigate the impact of the inevitable large equity correction? Hedging equity portfolios is notoriously difficult and expensive. We analyze the performance of different tools that investors could deploy. For example, continuously holding short-dated S&P 500 put options is the most reliable defensive method but also the costliest strategy. Holding "safe-haven" U.S. Treasury bonds produces a positive carry, but may be an unreliable crisis-hedge strategy, as the post-2000 negative bond–equity correlation is a historical rarity. Long gold and long credit protection portfolios sit in between puts and bonds in terms of both cost and reliability. Dynamic strategies that performed well during past drawdowns include futures time-series momentum (as detailed in Chapter 1) and a quality strategy that takes long/short positions in the highest-/lowest-quality company stocks (which benefits from a "flight-to-quality" effect during crises). We examine both large equity drawdowns and recessions. We also provide some out-of-sample evidence of the defensive performance of these strategies relative to an earlier, related paper.

The typical investment portfolio is highly concentrated in equities, leaving investors vulnerable to large drawdowns. We examine the performance of a number of candidate defensive strategies, both active and passive, between 1985 and 2018, with a particular emphasis on the eight worst drawdowns (the instances where the S&P 500 fell by more than 15%) and three U.S. recessions. To guard against overfitting, we provide out-of-sample evidence of the performance of these strategies in the 2018Q4 drawdown that occurred after we wrote an earlier, related paper.[2] (Chapter 7 looks at the COVID-19 drawdown as further out-of-sample validation.)

We begin with two passive strategies that benefit directly from a falling equity market. The first is a strategy that buys, and then rolls, one-month S&P 500 put options. This performs well in each of the eight equity drawdown periods, but it is very costly during more typical times, which constitute 86 percent of our sample, and expansionary (non-recession) times, which constitute 93 percent of our observations. As such, passive option protection seems too expensive to be a viable crisis hedge. The second passive strategy is long credit protection (short credit risk). This one also benefits during each of the eight equity drawdown periods, but in a more uneven manner. It does particularly well during the 2007–2009 Financial Crisis, which was a credit crisis. Despite its more erratic performance, the credit protection strategy is less costly during normal times and non-recessions than the put-buying strategy.

Next, we consider so-called safe-haven investments. For this, we choose a strategy that holds long positions in 10-year U.S. Treasuries. It performed well in the post-2000 equity drawdowns, but is less effective during earlier equity selloffs. This is consistent with the negative bond–equity correlation we observe after 2000, which is atypical when considered from the longer historical perspective. As we move beyond the extreme monetary easing that has characterized the post–Financial Crisis period, it is possible that the bond–equity correlation may revert to its previous norm, rendering a long bond strategy potentially unreliable as a crisis hedge. A long gold strategy generally performs better during crisis periods than at normal times, consistent with its reputation as a safe-haven security. However, its appeal as a crisis hedge is diminished by the fact that its long-run return, measured over the 1985–2018 period, is close to zero and that it carries substantial idiosyncratic risk unrelated to equity markets. In addition, extended historical evidence presented in Erb and Harvey (2013) suggests that gold is an unreliable equity and business cycle hedge.

We then turn our attention to dynamic strategies. Certain active strategies—such as shorting currency carry or taking long positions in on-the-run Treasury bonds against short positions in off-the-run bonds—may perform well during crisis periods, but they are expensive in the long term. Given the costs of managing active strategies, we choose to focus only on those that are, at the least, positive in expectation before costs: time-series momentum and a long-short quality strategy.

Time-series momentum strategies add to winning positions and reduce losing positions, much like a dynamic replication of an option straddle strategy (see discussion in Chapter 1).[3] We show that such strategies performed well over the eight equity drawdowns and three recessions. We also explore limiting the equity exposure (i.e., no long positions allowed), which we find enhances the crisis performance.

Next, we consider long-short U.S. equity strategies. The factors proposed in the academic literature suggest that taking long positions in high-quality companies and short positions in low-quality companies is most promising as a crisis hedge. This is because such long-short U.S. equity strategies benefit from flights to quality when panic hits markets. The definition of a high-quality business is, of course, open to debate. However, broadly speaking, such companies will be profitable and growing, have safer balance sheets, and run investor-friendly policies in areas such as payout ratios. We examine a host of quality metrics, and illustrate the importance of a beta-neutral rather than a dollar-neutral portfolio construction. (Beta-neutral construction is more common in practice, while dollar-neutral is more common in academic study.)

Finally, we show that futures time-series momentum strategies and quality long-short equity strategies are not only conceptually different, but also have historically uncorrelated returns, meaning that they can act as complementary crisis-hedge components within a portfolio. We demonstrate the efficacy of the dynamic hedges through some portfolio simulations.

CRISIS PERFORMANCE OF PASSIVE INVESTMENTS

We begin by identifying the eight worst equity drawdowns and three recessions for the United States in the 34-year period from 1985 to 2018. Next, we consider a number of passive, buy-and-hold strategies, including ones that hold futures contracts that are rolled according to some predefined schedule. We first analyze strategies that should logically benefit from falling firm valuations, such as a long put option and a short credit investment, and explore how they perform during these crises. This is followed by a discussion of how a long safe-haven (bond or gold) position fares during equity crises, which includes an analysis of the bond–equity correlation since 1900 and the gold–equity correlation post–Bretton Woods.[4]

We do not include transaction costs or fees in the tables and figures in the initial analysis, but we do comment on the approximate cost of implementation. We explicitly account for transaction costs in the section on crisis proofing, where we evaluate the effectiveness of dynamic strategies.

Crisis Definitions

Figure 2.1 shows the cumulative total return of the S&P 500 (top line) using daily data from 1985 to 2018.[5] A log scale is used, so a straight line corresponds to a constant rate of return, aiding the comparison of the severity of drawdown periods at different points in time. We focus on the eight periods in which the S&P 500 lost more than 15 percent from its peak, with the corresponding peak-to-trough periods shown in Figure 2.1. We also mark the three U.S. recessions that occur during our sample as defined by the NBER.

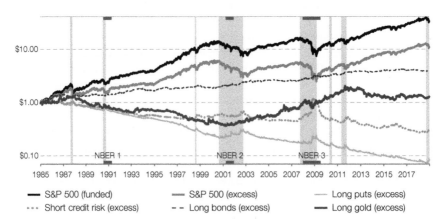

FIGURE 2.1 Passive investment total returns over time. We show the cumulative return of the S&P 500 (funded and in excess of cash), as well as the excess return of long puts (one-month, at-the-money S&P 500 puts), short credit risk (duration-matched U.S. Treasuries over U.S. investment-grade corporate bonds), long bonds (U.S. 10-year Treasuries), and long gold (futures). We highlight the eight worst drawdowns for the S&P 500. National Bureau of Economic Research (NBER) recessions are indicated by darker marks at the top and bottom edges of the figure. The data are from 1985 to 2018.

Table 2.1 provides a more detailed analysis, which includes returns, peak and trough dates, lengths of the drawdowns, and whether the peak was

TABLE 2.1 **Performance over drawdown periods.** We report the total return of the S&P 500 and various strategies during the eight worst drawdowns of the S&P 500, the annualized (geometric) return during drawdown, normal, all periods, and the hit rate (percentage of drawdowns with positive return). The annualized standard deviation ranges between 6.4 percent for bonds to 16.5 percent for the S&P 500, with dynamic strategies all scaled to 10 percent. The row "Peak = HWM" indicates whether the index was at an all-time high before the drawdown began. The data are from 1985 to 2018.

	Black Monday	Gulf War	Asian crisis	Tech burst	Financial crisis	Euro crisis I	Euro crisis II	2018Q4	Draw-down (14%)	Normal (86%)	All (100%)	Hit rate %
Peak day	25-Aug-87	16-Jul-90	17-Jul-98	1-Sep-00	9-Oct-07	23-Apr-10	29-Apr-11	20-Sep-18				
Trough day	19-Oct-87	11-Oct-90	31-Aug-98	9-Oct-02	9-May-09	2-Jul-10	3-Oct-11	20-Dec-18				
Weekdays count	39	63	31	548	369	50	111	67				
Peak = HWM?	Yes	Yes	Yes	Yes	Yes	No	No	Yes				
Strategy												
				Total return						Annualized return		%
S&P 500 (funded)	−32.9%	−19.2%	−19.2%	−47.4%	−55.2%	−15.6%	−18.6%	−19.4%	−44.3%	24.4%	10.8%	n.a.
SSP 500 (excess)	−33.5%	−20.7%	−19.7%	−51.0%	−56.3%	−15.7%	−18.6%	−19.8%	−45.8%	20.3%	7.3%	n.a.
Long puts (excess)	38.0%	12.4%	15.5%	44.7%	40.5%	15.8%	13.4%	18.0%	42.4%	−14.2%	−7.4%	100%
Short credit risk (excess)	7.6%	3.3%	12.1%	17.0%	127.7%	11.7%	26.1%	9.5%	39.6%	−9.8%	−3.6%	100%
Long bonds (excess)	−8.3%	−2.7%	3.0%	24.2%	20.4%	5.7%	10.1%	2.5%	10.6%	3.1%	4.1%	75%
Long gold (excess)	4.4%	5.5%	−6.9%	7.5%	18.9%	4.6%	6.3%	4.5%	9.0%	−0.6%	0.7%	88%

(*Continued*)

TABLE 2.1 (*Continued*)

Strategy	Black Monday	Gulf War	Asian crisis	Tech burst	Financial crisis	Euro crisis I	Euro crisis II	2018Q4	Draw-down (14%)	Normal (86%)	All (100%)	Hit rate %
				Total return					Annualized return			
1m MOM unconstrained	5.6%	19.3%	9.0%	31.3%	28.6%	2.7%	4.9%	8.1%	22.5%	6.2%	8.4%	100%
1m MOM EQ position cap	9.5%	22.8%	12.5%	37.4%	34.3%	4.8%	8.4%	9.7%	29.0%	3.1%	6.5%	100%
3m MOM unconstrained	10.3%	10.5%	9.3%	50.7%	32.6%	0.5%	10.9%	0.8%	25.1%	6.2%	8.7%	100%
3m MOM EQ position cap	15.4%	18.7%	14.4%	61.3%	41.4%	4.7%	13.7%	2.7%	35.1%	3.5%	7.6%	100%
12m MOM unconstrained	0.4%	12.2%	7.7%	52.3%	17.3%	-4.0%	-4.1%	-2.8%	14.5%	11.2%	11.6%	63%
12m MOM EQ position cap	8.3%	18.7%	16.2%	71.7%	23.7%	2.1%	0.2%	-0.9%	27.0%	8.2%	10.7%	88%
Profitability, dollar-neutral	-1.6%	-2.1%	3.0%	161.9%	33.9%	10.5%	10.9%	4.5%	35.7%	1.2%	5.5%	75%
Profitability, beta-neutral	2.3%	2.9%	9.1%	160.7%	21.2%	2.4%	3.3%	1.7%	32.1%	1.7%	5.6%	100%
Payout, dollar neutral	0.1%	6.3%	9.1%	178.6%	20.5%	7.0%	5.0%	7.6%	37.3%	0.3%	4.9%	100%
Payout, beta-neutral	-2.8%	8.0%	11.9%	196.1%	13.1%	1.2%	1.2%	5.1%	34.3%	3.2%	7.2%	88%
Growth, dollar-neutral		-6.6%	-9.6%	-8.6%	9.0%	10.8%	9.8%	-1.3%	0.2%	1.2%	1.0%	43%
Growth, beta-neutral		-3.0%	-5.7%	-16.2%	12.4%	3.1%	2.8%	1.4%	-1.6%	-0.1%	-0.3%	57%
Safety, dollar-neutral	5.0%	9.5%	9.1%	90.7%	12.2%	7.9%	13.6%	9.9%	30.0%	-4.3%	0.0%	100%
Safety, beta-neutral	-3.5%	4.8%	0.8%	96.9%	-9.1%	1.8%	4.2%	1.9%	14.9%	4.5%	5.9%	75%
Quality All, dollar-neutral	4.3%	7.3%	8.2%	142.9%	26.3%	10.2%	15.2%	4.5%	38.5%	-1.5%	3.5%	100%
Quality All, beta-neutral	-3.3%	7.0%	6.6%	164.9%	9.6%	2.4%	4.6%	1.7%	29.1%	5.0%	8.2%	88%

at the highwater mark (HWM) before the drawdown began. The HWM is the highest point reached so far, and one that could be surpassed in the future. The bursting of the 2000–2001 tech bubble and the Financial Crisis are the most severe equity crises, resulting in the S&P 500 losing about half of its value. The drawdown around 1987's Black Monday was also severe, with a return of –32.9 percent in less than two months. The remaining equity selloffs are associated with the first Gulf War, the Asian financial crisis (along with the ruble devaluation and LTCM collapse), two episodes of the eurozone sovereign debt crisis, and the 2018Q4 selloff.[6]

Based on these eight drawdowns, 14 percent of days since 1985 are equity drawdown days and 86 percent are normal days. The annualized S&P 500 return during equity crises and normal periods is –44.3 percent and 24.4 percent, respectively, and it is 10.8 percent overall. Both the total return and annualized return take into account the effect of compounding.[7] We also report the S&P 500 return above that of one-month Treasury bills, which provides an apples-to-apples comparison to the defensive strategies.

In Table 2.2, we report results for recessions, which do not overlap exactly with S&P 500 drawdown periods. For the Gulf War period, the recession includes the stock market rebound, and the S&P 500 is actually up over the full recession period. For the tech bubble burst, the recession period just covers a small part of the lengthy S&P 500 drawdown period. Only for the 2007–2009 Financial Crisis do the recession and stock market drawdown periods mostly overlap.

Using the National Bureau of Economic Research definitions, only 8 percent of the sample is in recession. The annualized S&P 500 return during recessions is –12.1 percent; during expansions it is 13.2 percent. Not surprisingly, the return difference between recessions and expansions is a lot less than the difference segregated by large drawdowns. Does this mean that hedging recessions is less important than protecting against drawdowns? Probably not. Both are important. While the drawdowns during recessions are less, recessions are often accompanied by painful negative shocks to investors' incomes.[8]

We report the following for the various strategies that we will detail later:

- The total return of the S&P 500 and various strategies during the three NBER recession periods
- The annualized (geometric) return during recession, expansion, and all periods
- The hit rate (percentage of recessions with positive return)

TABLE 2.2 Performance over recession periods. The annualized standard deviation of the various strategies ranges between 6.4 percent for bonds to 16.5 percent for the S&P 500, with dynamic strategies all scaled to 10 percent. The data run from 1985 to 2018.

	Gulf War recession	Tech burst recession	Financial crisis recession	Recession (8%)	Expansion (92%)	All (100%)	Hit rate %
Peak day	1-Aug-90	1-Apr-01	1-Jan-08				
Trough day	31-Mar-91	30-Nov-01	30-Jun-09				
Weekdays count	172	174	390				
Strategy	Total return				Annualized return		
S&P 500 (funded)	7.9%	−0.9%	−35.0%	−12.1%	13.2%	10.8%	n.a.
S&P 500 (excess)	3.2%	−3.1%	−36.1%	−14.6%	9.5%	7.3%	n.a.
Long puts (excess)	−3.7%	9.1%	9.7%	5.2%	−8.5%	−7.4%	67%
Short credit risk (excess)	−3.6%	−3.7%	26.0%	5.7%	−4.5%	−3.6%	33%
Long bonds (excess)	2.2%	3.5%	11.1%	5.8%	4.0%	4.1%	100%
Long gold (excess)	−7.6%	4.3%	7.0%	1.1%	0.7%	0.7%	67%

Strategy	Total return			Annualized return			%
1m MOM unconstrained	20.4%	2.7%	26.3%	17.0%	7.7%	8.4%	100%
1m MOM EQ position cap	18.9%	2.6%	28.4%	17.2%	5.5%	6.5%	100%
3m MOM unconstrained	9.4%	2.1%	26.8%	13.1%	8.4%	8.7%	100%
3m MOM EQ position cap	10.5%	3.2%	31.9%	15.5%	6.9%	7.6%	100%
12m MOM unconstrained	−2.5%	11.0%	3.0%	3.9%	12.4%	11.6%	67%
12m MOM EQ position cap	−1.6%	13.1%	4.7%	5.6%	11.2%	10.7%	67%
Profitability, dollar-neutral	8.3%	12.7%	6.9%	9.8%	5.2%	5.5%	100%
Profitability, beta-neutral	11.9%	13.2%	6.9%	11.3%	5.1%	5.6%	100%
Payout, dollar neutral	−3.4%	7.9%	6.9%	3.9%	5.0%	4.9%	67%
Payout, beta-neutral	−3.5%	12.7%	5.5%	5.0%	7.4%	7.2%	67%
Growth, dollar-neutral	10.2%	0.1%	−8.4%	0.4%	1.1%	1.0%	67%
Growth, beta-neutral	13.4%	−3.5%	−2.4%	2.4%	−0.6%	−0.3%	33%
Safety, dollar-neutral	−4.6%	1.5%	−3.1%	−2.2%	0.2%	0.0%	33%
Safety, beta-neutral	−3.6%	6.7%	−9.1%	−2.4%	6.7%	5.9%	33%
Quality All, dollar-neutral	1.2%	6.6%	3.0%	3.8%	3.5%	3.5%	100%
Quality All, beta-neutral	5.0%	11.4%	0.1%	5.7%	8.4%	8.2%	100%

Hedging with Passive Short Firm-Value Strategies: Long Puts and Short Credit Risk

In this subsection, we consider passive hedging strategies that directly benefit when equity value decreases: a long put option strategy and a short credit risk strategy.

A rolling long put option strategy is perhaps the most direct hedge against equity drawdowns because it protects against the risk of a sudden, severe equity market selloff. Various other equity derivatives may also be usefully considered for crisis hedges—most notably variance and volatility swaps, due to the inverse relationship between equity returns and equity volatility. Although only traded over-the-counter, these swaps can be liquid and can also be entered on a forward-starting basis (see, for example, Demerterfi, Derman, Kamal, and Zou 1999). However, as these are all somewhat related, we have focused only on the most straightforward option-based strategy, buying put options, for this analysis.

To evaluate how a long put investment performs during the eight drawdowns we identified, as well as in normal times, we look at the CBOE S&P 500 PutWrite Index, for which we have daily returns starting in 1986. The index tracks the performance of selling one-month at-the-money S&P 500 put options each month and holds them until expiry, at which point new options are sold. Positions are sized such that the options are fully collateralized at all times. Then even if the S&P 500 goes to zero, the obligation to the put option buyer can be honored. Since we are interested in the returns of *buying* puts, we use the negative of the index's excess returns.[9] We also examine a shorter sample of how out-of-the-money puts perform.

Figure 2.1 and Table 2.1 show that the long put strategy performs well in all eight large equity drawdowns; however, the performance is not evenly spread over these episodes. Instead, it appears earned in short periods of time, like October 2008, when the equity selloff suddenly accelerated. Once a drawdown has begun, the subsequent rolls of the options become more expensive as implied volatility rises, increasing the cost of the hedge. This effect then requires accelerated price decreases to produce the same hedge return.

Table 2.2 details the performance of the long put strategy during the three recessions in our sample. This strategy's returns during recession periods are lower mainly because equity returns in the Gulf War recession were positive.

The main concern with this strategy is its long-term overall cost. When applied to the whole sample (equity crisis and normal), the long put strategy's annualized excess return is −7.4 percent. An equal-weighted combination of a long S&P 500 investment and the long put strategy has a negative excess return in each of the eight crises, as well as a negative overall excess return. Including the transaction costs of trading options (which are relatively high) would make the return of this strategy even more negative, underlining our observation that it is an expensive strategy.[10]

As a robustness check, we show in Appendix 2A that using monthly data since 1996 from a leading broker for over-the-counter S&P 500 puts leads to similar results. These additional data also allow us to study 5 percent and 10 percent out-of-the-money put options. While out-of-the-money puts are cheaper than at-the money puts on a per-unit basis, they provide a worse cost-benefit tradeoff if you factor in that they do not provide much of a payoff during more gradual, prolonged drawdowns.

Long credit protection strategies have generally benefited during drawdowns as the spreads between corporate and Treasury bond yields widen. It is generally more difficult, in the case of credit strategies, to accurately simulate historical returns going back to 1985, as many reliable indices were only introduced later in our sample. We use the Bank of America Merrill Lynch U.S. Corporate Master Total Return index, which tracks the performance of U.S. investment-grade corporate bonds. Index returns in excess of duration-matched Treasury bonds are available from 1997. Our passive investment again uses the negative of these returns. For earlier years, using a rolling one-year window, we measured the beta of the index to 10-year U.S. Treasury futures. The excess returns of this strategy are the beta-adjusted returns of the Treasury futures minus the excess returns of the credit index. As a final step, we scaled the returns ex-post to achieve a volatility of 10 percent across the whole sample. This is based on what we feel is the reasonable assumption that leverage can be applied, without capital borrowing requirements.[11]

From a practical point of view, while it may be hard to short a large number of corporate bonds (particularly during a crisis), one may instead obtain a short credit risk exposure using credit default swaps, for instance with the synthetic CDX index.[12] One consideration that we do not attempt to address here is that during a major crisis there may be other risks that affect any credit strategy, such as the reliability of mark-to-market pricing and heightened counterparty risk.

Similar to the put strategy, the credit strategy appears to have had negative returns on average, outside of equity market drawdown periods. Drawdown period returns in Table 2.1 are on a similar scale to the put strategy. The 2007–2009 Financial Crisis, which was primarily a credit crisis, was a particularly profitable episode for the strategy (128% return). Unfortunately, the subsequent drawdown was equally large and swift. Over the whole sample, the credit strategy generated a small negative return. It is somewhat surprising that the full-period return is not more negative because the strategy is short the credit risk premium (see also Luu and Yu 2011). It is noted, however, that Figure 2.1 shows that the strategy has been on a pronounced downward drift since 2000.[13]

Table 2.2 shows that the credit strategy produced a large positive return in the 2007–2009 recession and small negative returns in the other two recessions. Comparing the long put option and short credit-risk strategies, long puts should intuitively be more reliable, because they are more directly linked to the equity value they aim to hedge. However, the long put strategy appears to come at a higher cost in terms of negative long-term returns. In other words, investors face a tradeoff between reliability and cost of the hedge.

Hedging with Safe-Haven Assets: Long Bonds and Long Gold

Government bonds and gold are often described as safe-haven assets, meaning they are expected to maintain their value, or increase in value, during volatile periods or drawdowns.[14] A long bond position is sometimes viewed as a crisis hedge, possibly based upon the perception that the government bonds of advanced economies are safe-haven securities. We show the performance of a long 10-year U.S. Treasury investment in Figure 2.1 and Tables 2.1 and 2.2. Returns are based on 10-year Treasury futures contracts.[15]

Over the period 1985–2018, bonds performed well, helped by the compression in 10-year yields, from double-digit levels in the mid-1980s to around 2 percent in 2018. The annualized return over cash for equity drawdown periods is 10.6 percent in Table 2.1, which exceeds the value of 3.1 percent for normal periods. However, it is only during the drawdowns after 2000 that bonds performed well. During the earlier drawdowns, the performance of bonds was mixed, and over the Black Monday period, the bond return was −8.3 percent. The bond performance is consistently positive during the three recessions detailed in Table 2.2.

The shift in bond–equity return correlations over the past 20 years is consistent with the fact that that the recent performance of bonds during equity drawdown periods exceeds that of earlier times. That is to say, since 2000, when stock prices have fallen, Treasuries have rallied. To explore further the long-term evidence for this, we looked at monthly returns for the U.S. equity index and Treasury bond returns extending our sample using returns from Global Financial Data. Figure 2.2 (Panel A) shows the rolling five-year bond–equity correlation. We see that, although post-2000 the correlation was negative, it was positive for most of the 100 years before that. This is in line with studies that argue that common fundamental factors typically imply a positive bond–equity correlation (see, for example, Baele, Bekaert, and Inghelbrecht 2010). Funnell (2017) provides a similar long-term perspective of the bond–equity relationship for the UK.

Panel A: Rolling five-year correlation

Panel B: Bond returns by three-month equity return quintile

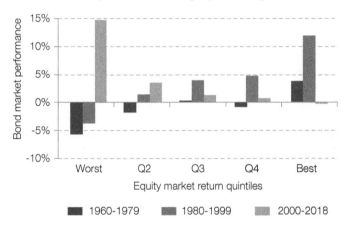

FIGURE 2.2 Time varying co-movement between equity and bond returns. In Panel A, we plot the rolling five-year correlation between monthly U.S. equities and U.S. Treasury bond excess returns from 1900 to 2018. In Panel B, we plot the annualized bond returns by three-month equity quintiles and for different sub-periods. The data are from Global Financial Data, Bloomberg, and Man-AHL.

Another approach to analyzing the shifting bond–equity relationship is to take three subsamples of the 1960–2018 period, each of length around 20 years, and then sort the three-month bond returns into quintiles based on the equity return.[16] Quintile one represents the periods with the worst equity returns; quintile five denotes the periods with the best equity returns. Figure 2.2 (Panel B) plots the annualized average bond return for the five quintiles. Consistent with the positive bond–equity correlation before 2000, a long bond position does not provide a drawdown hedge before 2000. In fact, bond returns are negative in quintile one (the worst periods for equities) for both the 1960–1979 and 1980–1999 periods. Given that stocks and bonds have common fundamental drivers, and that before 2000 stock and bond returns have generally been positively correlated, investors should take pause. It is not clear that in the future bonds will deliver the type of hedge they provided in the 2007–2009 Financial Crisis.

Gold has long been viewed as the original safe-haven asset, a source of absolute value in an uncertain world, whose price rises with increased risk aversion in markets. It does not provide a dividend, but, as a real asset, it can help offer protection against certain sources of long-term inflation. Gold is typically priced in U.S. dollars (and all subsequent analyses follow this convention), and so its price is partly driven by fluctuations in foreign exchange rates. This links gold to U.S. monetary policy. For example, a hawkish shift in policy may lead to a rise in the dollar on a trade-weighted basis and a subsequent fall in the price of gold. A related scenario under which gold may benefit is a significant loss of confidence in fiat currencies, a tail risk in the true sense of the expression. However, gold is also subject to significant idiosyncratic risk; for example, miners' strikes and political instability in mining regions could make gold an unreliable hedge under many circumstances.

We use gold futures for the excess returns shown in Tables 2.1 and 2.2. Gold shows positive returns in seven of the eight equity drawdowns, with an annualized return of 9.0 percent during equity market drawdowns. Outside of equity drawdown periods, gold returns were negative on average, leading to a full-sample performance that is marginally better than flat. Gold's hedging ability is less clear for recessions; positive returns are recorded for only two of the three in Table 2.2.

Based on our trading experience, we expect the annual transaction costs for maintaining a bond or gold exposure through futures to be below 0.1 percent per year.

In Appendix 2B, we take a longer view of gold, as we did with bonds in Figure 2.2, and find that from 1972 (the end of Bretton Woods) to 1984 the gold–equity correlation is slightly positive. From 1985 gold has performed well during the worst equity market environments. Indeed, during this period, there is a strong correlation between gold and bonds. Erb and Harvey (2013) extend the analysis back hundreds of years. Their evidence suggests that gold is an unreliable crisis hedge and an unreliable unexpected inflation hedge. While gold has kept its buying power over millennia, the large amount of idiosyncratic noise means that holding periods need to be measured not in years but in centuries.

ACTIVE HEDGING STRATEGIES: TIME-SERIES MOMENTUM

We now examine the performance of an active strategy, time-series momentum, applied to 50 futures and forward markets, during equity market drawdown and recession periods.[17] We explore both an unconstrained strategy and one where equity exposures are capped at zero (i.e., no long equity positions), given that a long equity position will not be a useful hedge in an equity drawdown. As before, the performance is reported gross of transaction costs. We estimate the combined transaction and slippage costs of implementing a three-month momentum strategy to be 0.6–0.8 percent per annum.[18]

A Simple Time-Series Momentum Strategy

We introduce a simple futures time-series momentum signal, like we did in Chapter 1, as the compound return over the past N days, scaled by volatility:

$$\text{mom}_{t-1}^k(N) = \frac{\prod_{i=1}^{N}(1 + R_{t-i}^k) - 1}{\sigma_{t-1}^k \sqrt{N}} \tag{2.1}$$

where R_{t-i}^k is the daily return of security k at time $t - i$, σ_{t-1}^k is the standard deviation of the past 100 daily returns for security k, observed at time $t - 1$, which is multiplied by $\sqrt{N}$ to achieve an approximate unit standard deviation for the signal.[19]

For the purpose of analysis, we consider 1-, 3-, and 12-month momentum strategies to capture short-, medium-, and long-term momentum trading. That is, N in Equation 1.1 is set to 22, 65, and 261 days, respectively.

We divide the momentum score by the rolling standard deviation of security returns to calculate a risk-adjusted market target allocation. The strategy performance is then given by multiplying the market target allocations by a gearing factor and the next period's return, and then summing across securities:

$$\text{Performance}_t(N) = \sum_k \text{Gearing}_{t-1}^k \frac{\text{mom}_{t-1}^k}{\sigma_{t-1}^k} R_t^k \tag{2.2}$$

The gearing factor is chosen such that we target an annualized volatility of 10 percent and allocate risk to six groups as follows: 25 percent currencies, 25 percent equity indices, 25 percent fixed income, and 8.3 percent to each of agricultural products, energies, and metals. Within each group, markets are allocated equal risk. Gearing factors are calculated at the group-level using an expanding window.

In order to prevent the strategy from increasing overall portfolio equity beta, we follow our procedure in Chapter 1 and consider an extension of the strategy, whereby positions in each equity market are capped at zero. (Only zero or short equity positions are acceptable.) Like Chapter 1, we rescale the position-capped strategy return series to achieve the same realized volatility as the unconstrained strategy and, as such, effectively redistribute some of the equity risk allocation to the other asset classes. That is, we consider:

- **Unconstrained.** As defined in Equation 2.1 with no further limits to the equity exposure.
- **Equity position cap.** Positions in equities are capped at zero.

We scale the returns of each strategy (ex-post) to 10 percent annualized volatility to allow for fair comparison.[20]

Securities Included

We study the empirical performance of the different strategies using the 50 liquid futures and forwards listed in Table 2.3. While we evaluate strategy returns from only 1985 onwards, where possible we use data from 1980 to compute risk estimates. Prior to its introduction in 1999, the euro (EUR/USD) is replaced with the deutsche mark.

Performance of Futures Time-Series Momentum Strategies

We report the total return of the time-series strategies for equity drawdowns in Table 2.1 and for recessions in Table 2.2. The one- and three-month unconstrained strategies have tended to perform well during equity crises, consistent with the results in Chapter 1, which show that faster trend strategies are particularly good at providing potential crisis alpha, and during recessions.

On the other hand, the 12-month unconstrained strategy has negative returns during the three most recent equity drawdowns (where the 2018 fourth-quarter selloff can be considered out-of-sample, per our discussion before) and performs notably less well during recessions.

The equity position cap strategy performs better during equity drawdowns. In the cases of 3- and 12-month momentum, this comes at the cost of a 1.1 percent and 0.9 percentage points lower overall performance (per annum) respectively, compared to the unconstrained strategy.

In Table 2.4, we report the average 5-, 22-, 65-, and 261-day return (not annualized) of three-month momentum strategies for different equity

TABLE 2.3 Data for futures time-series momentum analysis. This table lists the 50 futures and forward markets used for evaluating the times-series momentum strategies. Data are from Bloomberg and Man Group.

Name	Exchange	Start date	Name	Exchange	Start date	Name	Exchange	Start date
COMMODITIES - AGRICULTURALS			CURRENCIES (AGAINST USD)			FIXED INCOME - BONDS		
Corn	CBOT	Jan-80	Australian dollar	OTC forward	Jan-80	2-year Germany	Eurex	Mar-97
Soybeans	CBOT	Jan-80	Canadian dollar	OTC forward	Jan-80	5-year Germany	Eurex	Oct-91
Wheat	CBOT	Jan-80	Euro (D-Mark)	OTC forward	Jan-80	10-year Germany	Eurex	Jun-83
Cocoa	ICE - US	Jan-80	Norwegian krone	OTC forward	Dec-88	10-year Japan	TSE	Mar-83
Coffee	ICE - US	Jan-80	New Zealand dollar	OTC forward	Dec-88	10-year UK	LIFFE	Nov-82
Sugar	ICE - US	Jan-80	Swiss franc	OTC forward	Jan-80	30-year US	CBOT	Jan-80
			Swedish krona	OTC forward	Dec-88	2-year US	CBOT	Jul-05
COMMODITIES - ENERGIES			British pound	OTC forward	Jan-80	5-year US	CBOT	Oct-91
Crude oil - Brent	ICE - Europe	Jun-88	Japanese yen	OTC forward	Jan-80	10-year US	CBOT	May-82
Crude oil - WTI	NYMEX	Oct-83						
Heating oil	NYMEX	Jan-80	EQUITIES			FIXED INCOME - INTEREST RATE		
Natural gas	NYMEX	Apr-90	CAC 40	Euronext	Nov-88	Eurodollar	CME	Feb-82
Gas oil	ICE - Europe	Apr-81	DAX	Eurex	Nov-90	Euribor	LIFFE	Apr-89
Gasoline	NYMEX	Dec-84	Nasdaq	CME	Apr-96	Short sterling	LIFFE	Nov-82
			Russell	ICE - US	Sep-00			

(Continued)

TABLE 2.3 (*Continued*)

Name	Exchange	Start date	Name	Exchange	Start date
COMMODITIES - METALS			**EQUITIES**		
Aluminium	LME	Jan-80	S&P 500	CME	Apr-82
Copper	COMEX	Jan-80	EuroSTOXX	Eurex	Jun-00
Gold	COMEX	Jan-80	FTSE	LIFFE	May-84
Lead	LME	Jun-89	Hang Seng	HKFE	Jan-87
Nickel	LME	Jan-80	KOSPI	KSE	Sep-00
Silver	COMEX	Jan-80	Nikkei	SGX	Mar-87
Zinc	LME	Jan-80			

TABLE 2.4 Average return three-month futures times-series momentum for equity quintiles. We report the average rolling 5-, 22-, 65-, and 261-day return of the S&P 500 and unconstrained and equity position cap futures times-series momentum strategies by S&P 500 return quintiles. The momentum strategies are scaled to 10 percent annualized volatility (ex-post). The data are from 1985 to 2018.

5-day equity quintiles

	Worst	Q2	Q3	Q4	Best	ALL
S&P500 (excess)	-3.00%	-0.67%	0.30%	1.17%	3.01%	0.16%
3m MOM (unconstrained)	0.30%	0.00%	0.16%	0.27%	0.13%	0.17%
3m MOM (EQ position cap)	0.79%	0.17%	0.09%	0.00%	-0.29%	0.15%

22-day equity quintiles

	Worst	Q2	Q3	Q4	Best	ALL
S&P500 (excess)	-5.64%	-0.92%	1.10%	2.83%	6.12%	0.70%
3m MOM (unconstrained)	1.25%	0.13%	0.63%	0.72%	0.98%	0.74%
3m MOM (EQ position cap)	2.28%	0.50%	0.41%	0.12%	-0.05%	0.65%

65-day equity quintiles

	Worst	Q2	Q3	Q4	Best	ALL
S&P500 (excess)	-8.73%	-0.36%	2.77%	5.63%	11.08%	2.08%
3m MOM (unconstrained)	3.73%	0.59%	1.26%	1.84%	3.64%	2.21%
3m MOM (EQ position cap)	5.61%	0.93%	0.82%	0.87%	1.49%	1.94%

261-day equity quintiles

	Worst	Q2	Q3	Q4	Best	ALL
S&P500 (excess)	-16.22%	4.11%	10.83%	17.55%	27.64%	8.78%
3m MOM (unconstrained)	14.39%	6.27%	7.49%	7.92%	10.29%	9.27%
3m MOM (EQ position cap)	18.18%	5.60%	6.57%	5.21%	4.89%	8.09%

quintiles based on 5-, 22-, 65-, and 261-day windows. These statistics were derived without reference to our equity drawdown periods, and so offer additional insight into the strategies' performance when equity markets fall. Unsurprisingly, the equity position cap strategy outperforms the unconstrained strategy in the worst equity market quintile and underperforms in the best equity market quintile.

Summarizing, medium-term time-series momentum strategies have performed well during recent crisis periods (including 2018Q4), as well as over our full sample. Restricting the long equity exposures seems to increase the crisis performance potential of these strategies, but comes at a cost in terms of overall performance.

ACTIVE HEDGING STRATEGIES: QUALITY STOCKS

We now turn to a second active strategy, long-short U.S. equity strategies that use quality metrics. Performance is reported gross of transaction costs. Based on our live experience, we estimate that the combined transaction, slippage, and financing costs of implementing the composite quality strategies amounts to around 1.0–2.0 percent per annum.

Motivation to Look at Quality Stocks

Asness, Frazzini, and Pedersen (2019, henceforth AFP) argue that although quality stocks logically deserve a higher price-to-book ratio, in reality they do not always exhibit such a premium. In particular, toward the end of equity bull markets, quality stocks have often looked underpriced. Then, when the market has a drawdown, these stocks have relatively outperformed, benefiting from the so-called flight-to-quality effect.

Using the Gordon growth model, AFP derive the following formula for the price-to-book (P/B) ratio:[21]

$$\frac{P}{B} = \frac{\text{Profitability} \times \text{Payout Ratio}}{\text{Required Return} - \text{Growth}} \qquad (2.3)$$

Each of the four components on the right-hand side of Equation 2.3 is a quality metric that can be measured in several ways, such as:

1. **Profitability:** profits (gross profits, earnings, cash flows) scaled by an accounting value (book equity, book assets, sales)
2. **Growth:** trailing five-year growth of a profitability measure

3. **Safety (required return):** safer companies command lower required returns; return-based measures include market beta and volatility and fundamental-based measures include low leverage, low volatility of profitability and low credit risk
4. **Payout:** the fraction of profits paid out to shareholders, which can be seen as a measure of the "shareholder friendliness" of management

The literature suggests that many of these metrics have some ability to predict cross-sectional stock returns.

Evidence from Other Popular Factors

We start our analysis by using publicly available daily returns to evaluate the performance of factors documented in the literature. In Table 2.5, we present results for the Fama and French (2015) five-factor model (the first five factors), as well as factor returns based on AFP and other researchers (the last three factors).[22] Only U.S. stocks are considered in each case.

Quality and profitability (in itself a component of quality) stand out in terms of their performance over equity market drawdown periods (Panel A) and recessions (Panel B). It is important to note that these factors are constructed in a dollar-neutral way, which is common practice in the literature. In the case of the quality factor, however, this leads to a negative correlation of –0.48 to the S&P 500, based on five-day overlapping returns. This raises the question of whether the positive drawdown-period performance is simply explained by the negative equity exposure.[23] We will present evidence that suggests this is not the case.

Also noteworthy for its return during equity drawdowns is the stock momentum factor, which in this case is traded at the stock level and in a cross-sectional (dollar-neutral) fashion, and so differs from the futures time-series momentum discussed in a previous section. However, some of the intuition behind why futures trend-following provides crisis alpha (see Chapter 1) may also come from stock momentum. For example, stock momentum may pick up sector trends that reflect the broader macro movements, which are also picked up by futures trend following. The investment factor, which goes long the stock of conservative companies with low growth in book assets while shorting aggressive, high-asset-growth companies, performs about as well as the cross-sectional stock momentum factor during equity drawdowns.

In contrast, the value factor has been much less effective as an equity market drawdown hedge than the quality and profitability factors over our sample. In general, a profitability factor is the ratio of two accounting values,

TABLE 2.5 Equity factor performance over drawdown and recession periods. We report the total return of various long-short U.S. equity strategies with publicly available return data. In Panel A, we report the total return over the eight worst drawdowns for the S&P 500, the annualized (geometric) return during equity market drawdown, normal, and all periods, and the correlation to the S&P 500. In Panel B, we report the same statistics for recessions and expansions. Strategies are scaled to a dollar long-short. The data are from 1985 to 2018.

Panel A (Drawdowns)

Factor	Total return								Annualized return			Correlation
	Black Monday	Gulf War	Asian crisis	Tech burst	Financial crisis	Euro crisis I	Euro crisis II	2018Q4	Drawdown (14%)	Normal (86%)	All (100%)	Correl. to S&P500
Market (NYSE, AMEX, NASDAQ)	−30.1%	−22.2%	−21.3%	−51.8%	−55.8%	−16.1%	−20.3%	−21.0%	−46.2%	20.4%	7.2%	0.99
Size	9.5%	−11.0%	−8.6%	29.4%	−5.5%	−3.8%	−10.1%	−9.0%	−3.1%	0.3%	−0.2%	−0.02
Value	4.4%	7.3%	5.6%	72.0%	−23.2%	−8.9%	−7.7%	0.8%	5.9%	1.4%	2.0%	−0.11
Profitability (Robust - Weak)	−2.3%	−1.0%	5.2%	123.4%	31.5%	2.2%	13.3%	0.7%	29.1%	0.5%	4.2%	−0.27
Investment (Conservative - Aggressive)	4.0%	12.3%	9.8%	61.2%	0.2%	−1.9%	−4.7%	5.4%	15.7%	0.7%	2.8%	−0.35
Cross-sectional momentum	−7.9%	10.0%	2.3%	39.3%	35.7%	−5.4%	1.3%	0.7%	13.9%	5.0%	6.2%	−0.13
Quality (Quality- Junk)	1.5%	7.7%	9.1%	101.9%	67.3%	7.6%	24.1%	8.3%	43.3%	0.1%	5.4%	−0.48
Low risk (Bet-against-Beta)	3.1%	−1.3%	−0.1%	115.3%	−32.0%	3.8%	5.3%	0.8%	10.7%	8.5%	8.8%	−0.36

Panel B (Recessions)

Factor	Total return			Annualized return			Correlation
	Gulf War recession	Tech burst recession	Financial crisis recession	Recession (8%)	Expansion (92%)	All (100%)	Correl. to S&P500
Market (NYSE, AMEX, NASDAQ)	3.9%	–2.3%	–34.7%	–13.5%	9.4%	7.2%	0.99
Size	–2.6%	7.6%	9.0%	4.8%	–0.6%	–0.2%	–0.02
Value	–5.6%	0.5%	–7.4%	–4.5%	2.7%	2.0%	–0.11
Profitability (Robust - Weak)	7.5%	9.7%	21.5%	13.5%	3.3%	4.2%	–0.27
Investment (Conservative - Aggressive)	–5.2%	2.9%	–1.7%	–1.5%	3.1%	2.8%	–0.35
Cross-sectional momentum	2.5%	–0.4%	–39.9%	–15.8%	8.5%	6.2%	–0.13
Quality (Quality - Junk)	9.4%	10.3%	29.6%	17.1%	4.4%	5.4%	–0.48
Low risk (Bet-against-Beta)	–16.3%	12.1%	–23.9%	–11.2%	10.8%	8.8%	–0.36

for example, the ratio of net income to the book value of equity. As such, the factor's positioning is unaffected by the short-term gyrations of the equity market. In contrast, value factor is also a ratio, but it compares an accounting value to a market value, for example, the ratio of net income to the market value of equity. Hence a value metric will change more favorably for stocks that underperform the market, causing the factor to increase its exposure to such stocks.

Individual Quality Factor Performance

In this section, we evaluate various quality metrics. Table 2.6 lists all the signals we consider, which form a subset of AFP's signals, as we omit Ohlson's O and Altman's Z (which are more highly parameterized than the others) and instead focus on return- and leverage-based safety measures.[24]

At each date, the raw signal value, s, is ranked cross-sectionally, $r(s) = rank\ s$. Then, a cross-sectional z-score is determined, $z(r) = (r - \mu_r)/\sigma_r$, where μ_r is the cross-sectional mean and σ_r is the cross-sectional standard deviation. The key purpose of this ranking step is to reduce the impact of outliers. This robustness step can be a relevant precaution when working with accounting data. Denoting the signal arising from this first step time at t for stock i as $\text{Signal}_{t,i}$, we form a beta-neutral portfolio by defining a neutral signal as:

$$\text{Signal}_{t,i}^{\text{Neutral}} = \begin{cases} \frac{\text{Signal}_{t,i}}{\text{BetaLong}}, & \text{if } \text{Signal}_{t,i} \geq 0 \\ \frac{\text{Signal}_{t,i}}{\text{BetaShort}}, & \text{if } \text{Signal}_{t,i} < 0 \end{cases} \quad (2.4)$$

where

$$\text{BetaLong} = \sum_j I\{\text{Signal}_{t,j} > 0\}\ \text{Signal}_{t,j}\beta_{t,j}$$

$$\text{BetaShort} = \sum_j I\{\text{Signal}_{t,j} < 0\}\ \text{Signal}_{t,j}\beta_{t,j}$$

The beta is computed with respect to the S&P 500 using five-day overlapping returns over the past three years. Strategy returns are obtained by multiplying the final signal values, lagged by a day, with stock returns:

$$\text{Performance}_t = \sum_k \text{Signal}_{t-1,k}^{\text{Neutral}} R_{t,k} \quad (2.5)$$

In the final step, we scale strategy returns (ex-post) such that the full-sample realized volatility is 10 percent, merely to aid comparison across various definitions of quality and with the futures time-series momentum strategies.

TABLE 2.6 Quality factor definitions. We list the various quality factors used in our strategies. All fundamental data are from Worldscope.

Category	Name	Description
Profitability	Cash flow over assets	(net income + depreciation − change working capital − capital expenditures) / total assets
Profitability	Gross margin	(revenue − cost of goods sold) / net sales
Profitability	Gross profits over assets	(revenue − cost of goods sold) / total assets
Profitability	Low accruals	(depreciation − change working capital) / total assets
Profitability	Return on assets	Net income / total assets
Profitability	Return on equity	Net income / book equity
Payout	Net debt issuance	− log(total debt current / total debt one year ago)
Payout	Net equity issuance	− log(outstanding number of shares current / outstanding number of shares one year ago)
Payout	Total net payouts over profits	Total net payouts / profits
Growth	Cash flow over assets (5y change)	Five-year change corresponding profitability metric, i.e. $(\text{CashFlow}_t - \text{CashFlow}_{t-5})$ / TotalAssets_{t-5}
Growth	Gross margin (5y change)	Five-year change corresponding profitability metric
Growth	Gross profits over assets (5y change)	Five-year change corresponding profitability metric
Growth	Low accruals (5y change)	Five-year change corresponding profitability metric
Growth	Return on assets (5y change)	Five-year change corresponding profitability metric
Growth	Return on equity (5y change)	Five-year change corresponding profitability metric
Safety	Low beta	Minus realized beta to S&P 500 Index based on weekly returns over a rolling three-year window
Safety	Low idiosyncratic volatilty	Minus standard deviation of the daily market-adjusted returns over the past year
Safety	Low leverage	Total debt / total assets

We evaluate the performance of the quality factors in a universe of mid- and large-cap U.S. stocks. Each month, we define a market cap threshold. Those stocks that exceed it are defined as large-cap, and those that do not are mid-cap. This threshold is set equal to $2 billion at the end of 2016 onward, and for earlier dates is suitably deflated.[25] As an example, the threshold in 1986 was about $200 million. This results in a sample with lower turnover, with the number of constituents ranging between 951 and 1,611 over our analysis.

Table 2.7, Panel A, reports the drawdown- and normal-period performance for the different quality factors. As a result of data availability, some factors have returns missing for the first one or two equity drawdowns. For most factors, the annualized drawdown-period return is higher than the return during normal periods, suggesting a crisis-hedge property. A notable exception, however, is the category of growth factors where, in three out of six cases, the drawdown-period performance is worse than the normal performance and, moreover, the overall performance is around zero for all six growth factors.

A second exception is the low beta factor. A beta-neutral implementation of the low beta factor effectively means leveraging the long positions in low beta stocks. This tends to lead to better overall performance but worse drawdown-period performance due to the fact that strategies with embedded leverage underperform when funding constraints tighten (Frazzini and Pedersen 2014). This often occurs at times of market stress (such as in the 2007–2009 Financial Crisis). In contrast, a beta-neutral, low-idiosyncratic-volatility strategy does not involve as much leveraging of the long positions, and indeed still historically performs well during crises.

During recession periods, reported in Table 2.7, Panel B, results are a bit more mixed, but some profitability and payout factors show a notable stronger performance during recessions compared to expansionary periods.

In Appendix 2C, Table 2C.1, we report results for dollar-neutral versions of the strategies, which can be constructed by setting all beta estimates to unity in Equation 2.4. Constructing the strategies in this way can lead to negative correlations with the S&P 500. The low beta factor provides an extreme example with a correlation of –0.73. Dollar-neutral implementations are commonplace in many published papers (e.g., see AFP), but they leave open the possibility that a good performance over equity drawdown periods can be attributed to the negative equity exposure, rather than performance being a "positive convex" function of the equity market return. We are mostly interested in positive convexity, with a factor performing well during equity bear markets, without performing badly during equity bull markets.

TABLE 2.7 Quality factor performance, beta-neutral. We report the total return of various quality factors, where portfolios are constructed to be beta-neutral. In Panel A, we report the total return over the eight worst drawdowns for the S&P 500, the annualized (geometric) return during equity market drawdown, normal, and all periods, and the correlation to the S&P 500. In Panel B, we report the same statistics for recessions and expansions. All strategies are scaled to 10 percent annualized volatility (ex-post). The data are from 1985 to 2018.

Panel A (Drawdowns)

Category	Name	Total return									Annualized return			Correlation
		Black Monday	Gulf War	Asian crisis	Tech burst	Financial crisis	Euro crisis I	Euro crisis II	2018Q4	Drawdown (14%)	Normal (86%)	All (100%)	Correl. to S&P500
Profitability	Cash flow over assets		11.7%	6.5%	113.5%	8.9%	1.1%	2.8%	1.6%	25.4%	3.0%	6.3%	−0.14
Profitability	Gross margin	4.7%	2.4%	8.1%	−25.9%	12.8%	4.6%	4.7%	3.5%	1.9%	3.0%	2.8%	0.03
Profitability	Gross profits over assets	0.5%	−3.7%	5.6%	132.5%	13.8%	−0.8%	2.9%	3.1%	23.8%	1.9%	4.8%	−0.18
Profitability	Low accruals		−5.3%	4.0%	68.4%	0.7%	0.0%	−1.9%	−3.1%	10.3%	1.1%	2.5%	−0.11
Profitability	Return on assets	0.1%	7.4%	5.7%	122.8%	21.3%	2.3%	2.9%	2.1%	27.6%	−0.3%	3.3%	−0.16
Profitability	Return on equity	1.5%	1.3%	6.1%	138.0%	8.4%	2.0%	3.1%	0.1%	24.9%	1.1%	4.2%	−0.14
Payout	Net debt issuance	0.2%	6.5%	15.5%	130.7%	22.8%	−1.3%	2.9%	5.3%	30.9%	5.3%	8.7%	−0.18
Payout	Net equity issuance	−2.9%	3.5%	7.4%	159.7%	5.5%	0.2%	2.5%	3.8%	26.5%	2.2%	5.4%	−0.18
Payout	Total net payouts over profits	11.7%		9.8%	56.2%	8.7%	3.9%	−2.6%	2.1%	17.5%	0.0%	2.6%	0.01

(Continued)

TABLE 2.7 (*Continued*)

Category	Name	Total return								Annualized return			Correlation
		Black Monday	Gulf War	Asian crisis	Tech burst	Financial crisis	Euro crisis I	Euro crisis II	2018Q4	Drawdown (14%)	Normal (86%)	All (100%)	Correl. to S&P500
Growth	Cash flow over assets (5y change)			0.1%	37.6%	5.3%	1.4%	2.3%	−0.1%	9.5%	−0.6%	1.2%	−0.03
Growth	Gross margin (5y change)		−4.7%	−5.4%	−39.9%	4.7%	3.0%	2.1%	3.2%	−9.7%	1.4%	−0.4%	0.12
Growth	Gross profits over assets (5y change)		−4.6%	−4.9%	−32.8%	9.6%	1.5%	1.1%	3.3%	−7.0%	0.2%	−0.9%	0.07
Growth	Low accruals (5y change)			−2.7%	−32.8%	1.9%	0.6%	−0.1%	0.9%	−8.3%	−0.1%	−1.7%	0.06
Growth	Return on assets (5y change)		2.7%	−3.0%	12.9%	13.7%	3.5%	2.2%	−0.1%	6.5%	−1.1%	0.0%	0.00
Growth	Return on equity (5y change)		−4.7%	−4.5%	21.4%	12.9%	3.9%	4.5%	−1.1%	6.4%	−0.7%	0.3%	0.01
Safety	Low beta	−6.5%	−4.7%	−7.1%	77.7%	−16.6%	1.0%	3.1%	−0.5%	5.0%	9.5%	8.8%	0.24
Safety	Low idiosyncratic volatility	−0.2%	10.1%	8.2%	99.1%	3.6%	1.3%	4.5%	3.4%	22.3%	1.4%	4.3%	−0.19
Safety	Low leverage	−2.4%	4.9%	−2.4%	49.1%	−13.4%	1.6%	0.6%	−0.1%	5.8%	−0.3%	0.6%	−0.04

Panel B (Recessions)

Category	Name	Total return			Annualized return		
		Gulf War recession	Tech burst recession	Financial crisis recession	Recession (8%)	Expansion (92%)	All (100%)
Profitability	Cash flow over assets		12.1%	1.0%	10.2%	5.9%	6.3%
Profitability	Gross margin	8.0%	-3.7%	13.3%	6.0%	2.5%	2.8%
Profitability	Gross profits over assets	18.3%	12.9%	10.9%	14.9%	3.9%	4.8%
Profitability	Low accruals		0.3%	4.8%	-3.7%	3.2%	2.5%
Profitability	Return on assets	8.1%	13.0%	1.0%	7.7%	2.9%	3.3%
Profitability	Return on equity	3.8%	6.2%	-4.2%	2.0%	4.4%	4.2%
Payout	Net debt issuance	-3.2%	26.8%	14.3%	12.7%	8.3%	8.7%
Payout	Net equity issuance	-3.4%	9.0%	6.3%	4.1%	5.5%	5.4%
Payout	Total net payouts over profits		-3.0%	-9.6%	-4.5%	3.3%	2.6%
Growth	Cash flow over assets (5y change)			0.7%	3.9%	0.9%	1.2%
Growth	Gross margin (5y change)		-7.6%	0.4%	1.5%	-0.6%	-0.4%
Growth	Gross profits over assets (5y change)		-3.2%	4.0%	6.2%	-1.6%	-0.9%
Growth	Low accruals (5y change)			1.9%	-2.0%	-1.6%	-1.7%
Growth	Return on assets (5y change)		2.6%	-6.8%	2.1%	-0.2%	0.0%
Growth	Return on equity (5y change)		0.5%	-6.2%	1.1%	0.3%	0.3%
Safety	Low beta	-3.8%	9.3%	-16.8%	-4.6%	10.2%	8.8%
Safety	Low idiosyncratic volatility	-0.4%	5.6%	-1.0%	1.4%	4.5%	4.3%
Safety	Low leverage	-7.7%	-2.3%	-5.5%	-5.5%	1.2%	0.6%

TABLE 2.8 Average return beta-neutral quality composites for equity quintiles. We report the average 5-, 22-, 65-, and 261-day return of the S&P 500 and various beta-neutral quality composites by S&P 500 return quintiles. All strategies are scaled to 10 percent annualized volatility (ex-post). The data are from 1985 to 2018.

5-day equity quintiles

	Worst	Q2	Q3	Q4	Best	ALL
S&P500 (excess)	-3.00%	-0.67%	0.30%	1.17%	3.01%	0.16%
Profitability	0.62%	0.11%	0.06%	0.00%	-0.10%	0.14%
Payout	0.70%	0.24%	0.12%	-0.07%	-0.12%	0.17%
Growth	-0.14%	-0.04%	0.02%	0.10%	0.08%	0.00%
Safety	0.26%	0.20%	0.15%	0.03%	0.08%	0.14%
Quality All	0.56%	0.22%	0.18%	0.03%	0.01%	0.20%

22-day equity quintiles

	Worst	Q2	Q3	Q4	Best	ALL
S&P500 (excess)	-5.64%	-0.92%	1.10%	2.83%	6.12%	0.70%
Profitability	2.18%	0.40%	0.22%	0.30%	0.03%	0.63%
Payout	2.36%	0.80%	0.35%	0.14%	0.22%	0.77%
Growth	-0.07%	-0.14%	-0.05%	0.29%	0.05%	0.01%
Safety	0.97%	0.69%	0.70%	0.42%	0.46%	0.65%
Quality All	2.09%	0.79%	0.62%	0.51%	0.48%	0.90%

65-day equity quintiles

	Worst	Q2	Q3	Q4	Best	ALL
S&P500 (excess)	-8.73%	-0.36%	2.77%	5.63%	11.08%	2.08%
Profitability	6.01%	1.79%	0.88%	0.86%	-0.17%	1.87%
Payout	6.26%	2.60%	1.30%	0.95%	0.41%	2.30%
Growth	-0.25%	0.02%	0.12%	0.41%	-0.03%	0.06%
Safety	2.91%	2.35%	1.60%	1.54%	1.40%	1.96%
Quality All	5.67%	3.00%	1.84%	1.78%	1.16%	2.69%

261-day equity quintiles

	Worst	Q2	Q3	Q4	Best	ALL
S&P500 (excess)	-16.22%	4.11%	10.83%	17.55%	27.64%	8.78%
Profitability	27.97%	5.92%	1.93%	3.89%	0.94%	8.13%
Payout	31.03%	4.19%	3.97%	5.51%	6.57%	10.25%
Growth	-0.81%	3.70%	0.11%	0.78%	-2.18%	0.43%
Safety	15.76%	4.43%	7.32%	5.33%	9.36%	8.44%
Quality All	28.91%	6.75%	6.23%	7.28%	9.18%	11.67%

Composite Quality Factor Performance

Tables 2.1 and 2.2 present the performance of composite factors for both dollar-neutral and beta-neutral portfolios. Dollar neutral is common in academia and so is included to facilitate comparison with academic studies. Beta neutral is more common in practice as it fully neutralizes the correlation of the long-short portfolio with the overall market. Composites are determined at each point in time, by averaging the ranked and z-scored score of a stock across multiple factors, and then re-ranking and z-scoring these averages across stocks.

In Table 2.1, we see that profitability, payout, safety, and a grand composite of the four quality composites (labeled "quality all") performed well during equity market drawdowns and for the full sample. Only the growth composite stands out as performing poorly during both equity market drawdown and normal periods. In Table 2.2, we see that the annualized performance during recessions is strong for profitability, but not for safety.

In Appendix 2C, Table 2C.2, we report the output of a regression of the different quality composites on the market, size, value, and momentum factors. The main result is that quality composites capture anomalies beyond these control factors. Also noteworthy is that, except for growth, all composites have a negative beta to the size factor.[26] Profitability and growth have a negative beta to the value factor while payout and safety have a positive beta to value. The exposure to the cross-sectional equity momentum factor is small in all cases.

In Table 2.8, we report the return (not annualized) of quality composites for different equity quintiles based on 5-, 22-, 65-, and 261-day windows, as we did previously for the futures time-series momentum strategies. The quintile analysis does not depend on our choice of equity drawdown periods, so it provides an alternative view of the defensive property. Profitability, payout, safety, and quality all perform best in the worst equity quintile for each of the four horizons.

CAN PORTFOLIOS BE CRISIS PROOFED?

In Table 2.9, we present correlations between a selected subset of the strategies considered before. The futures time-series momentum strategies (1-, 3-, and 12-month momentum with equity positions capped at zero) demonstrate negligible correlation with any of the quality stock strategies (profitability, payout, growth, safety, and the grand quality composite). Hence time-series momentum and quality stocks are complementary defensive strategies.[27]

TABLE 2.9 Correlation between strategies considered in this chapter. We report the correlations between the five-day overlapping returns of various strategies considered. From "Hedging with Passive Short Firm-Value Strategies: Long Puts and Short Credit Risk": S&P 500 (excess), long puts (one-month, at-the-money S&P 500 puts), short credit risk (duration-matched U.S. Treasuries over U.S. investment-grade corporate bonds), long bonds (U.S. 10-year Treasuries), and long gold (futures). From "Active Hedging Strategies: Time-Series Momentum": 1-, 3-, and 12-month futures time-series momentum with equity positions capped at zero. From "Active Hedging Strategies: Quality Stocks": the different beta-neutral quality stock composites. The data are from 1985 to 2018.

	S&P 500	Long puts	Short credit risk	Long bonds	Long gold	1m MOM: EQ pos. cap	3m MOM: EQ pos. cap	12m MOM: EQ pos. cap	Profitability, beta-neutral	Payout, beta neutral	Growth, beta-neutral	Safety, beta-neutral	Quality All, beta-neutral
S&P 500		-0.86	-0.35	-0.05	-0.03	-0.36	-0.36	-0.23	-0.18	-0.18	0.05	-0.01	-0.12
Long puts			0.35	0.11	0.05	0.42	0.39	0.22	0.18	0.15	-0.04	-0.01	0.10
Short credit risk				0.17	0.05	0.24	0.24	0.17	0.16	0.11	0.03	0.00	0.09
Long bonds					0.04	0.13	0.20	0.29	0.08	0.05	-0.01	0.16	0.14
Long gold						0.04	0.09	0.12	-0.08	-0.05	0.08	-0.03	-0.04
1m MOM: EQ pos. cap							0.73	0.45	0.06	0.10	-0.06	0.01	0.04
3m MOM: EQ pos. cap								0.68	0.07	0.11	-0.05	0.03	0.07
12m MOM: EQ pos. cap									0.04	0.07	0.02	0.06	0.07
Profitability, beta-neutral										0.66	0.20	0.39	0.79
Payout, beta neutral											-0.38	0.74	0.88
Growth, beta-neutral												-0.54	-0.17
Safety, beta-neutral													0.83
Quality All, beta-neutral													

TABLE 2.10 Effectiveness of dynamic hedges. We simulated portfolios with varying allocations to the S&P 500, three-month momentum with no long equity positions, and the quality composite factor strategy. Transaction costs for the dynamic strategies are included. A hedge proportion of 30 percent implies a 70 percent allocation to the S&P 500 and a 30 percent allocation to the hedge portfolio. In Panel A, we report the total return during the eight worst drawdowns for the S&P 500 and the annualized (geometric) return during equity market drawdown, normal, and all periods. In Panel B, we report the same statistics for recessions and expansions. The data are from 1985 to 2018.

Panel A (Drawdowns)

Portfolio											
Hedge Proportion	Total return								Annualized return		
	Black Monday	Gulf War	Asian crisis	Tech burst	Financial crisis	Euro crisis I	Euro crisis II	2018Q4	Drawdown (14%)	Normal (86%)	All (100%)
0%	−32.9%	−19.2%	−19.2%	−47.4%	−55.2%	−15.6%	−18.6%	−19.4%	44.3%	24.4%	10.8%
10%	−29.1%	−15.1%	−15.7%	−33.0%	−48.6%	−13.5%	−15.4%	−17.1%	−36.8%	23.5%	12.2%
20%	−25.1%	−10.9%	−12.0%	−14.9%	−41.1%	−11.4%	−12.0%	−14.9%	−28.4%	22.6%	13.5%
30%	−21.0%	−6.4%	−8.2%	7.7%	−32.8%	−9.2%	−8.6%	−12.6%	−19.0%	21.6%	14.7%
40%	−16.8%	−1.8%	−4.2%	35.9%	−23.6%	−7.0%	−5.1%	−10.2%	−8.6%	20.6%	15.9%
50%	−12.4%	3.0%	−0.1%	70.9%	−13.3%	−4.8%	−1.5%	−7.8%	2.9%	19.6%	17.0%

(*Continued*)

59

TABLE 2.10 (*Continued*)

Panel B (Recessions)

Portfolio	Total return			Annualized return		
Hedge Proportion	Gulf War recession	Tech burst recession	Financial crisis recession	Recession (8%)	Expansion (92%)	All (100%)
0%	7.9%	-0.9%	-35.0%	-12.1%	13.2%	10.8%
10%	9.7%	1.3%	-29.3%	-8.2%	14.2%	12.2%
20%	11.4%	3.5%	-23.4%	-4.2%	15.2%	13.5%
30%	13.2%	5.7%	-17.2%	-0.3%	16.2%	14.7%
40%	14.9%	7.8%	-10.8%	3.6%	17.1%	15.9%
50%	16.5%	9.9%	-4.3%	7.4%	17.9%	17.0%

To investigate the effectiveness of dynamic strategies in providing returns during equity market drawdown periods and recessions, we simulate portfolios with varying allocations to the S&P 500, three-month momentum with no long equity positions, and the quality composite factor strategy. In the first step, we deduct transaction costs from the time-series momentum as well as the quality strategies. We assume the midpoints of our earlier estimates: 0.7 percent per annum for momentum and 1.5 percent per annum for quality. Second, we scale up returns (after costs) of the hedge strategies so that they achieve 15 percent volatility when combined. This higher volatility is closer to the long-run historical volatility of equities. Based on the authors' experience, the combined hedge portfolio can be implemented at this leverage without any additional funding.

The simulated portfolios allocate some proportion of capital to the combined hedge portfolio, and the remaining capital to the S&P 500. Hence, a hedge proportion of 30 percent implies a 70 percent allocation to the S&P 500 and a 30 percent allocation to the hedge portfolio. Statistics for these portfolios are shown in Table 2.10, Panel A (for equity drawdowns) and Panel B (for recessions). Although a 50 percent allocation to the hedge strategy is required to achieve a positive return over the equity-market drawdown periods in our simulations, a 10 percent allocation improves the return in each of the eight historical equity-market drawdown periods, resulting in an 8 percentage point improvement in the annualized drawdown-period return (from –44.3% to –36.8%).

CONCLUDING REMARKS

This chapter had multiple goals. With strategic risk management, certain strategies are blended into a portfolio that lessen the pain in negative market environments. Ideally, these strategies have positive convexity (payoff in down markets) and are not so expensive as to wipe out the excess returns in good times. Our goals were to detail a range of candidate strategies and to assess their benefit and costs. Importantly, rather than just looking at average performance, we dissected the performance of each strategy in both individual drawdown episodes and recessions.

Can a portfolio be crisis proofed? Possibly, but at a very high cost. We show that a passive strategy that continually holds put options on the S&P 500 is prohibitively expensive, leading to a return drag of more than 7 percent per year. A strategy that passively holds 10-year U.S. Treasuries is an unreliable crisis hedge, given that the post-2000 negative bond–equity correlation is historically atypical. Over our sample, long gold and short credit risk sit in between puts and bonds in terms of both cost and reliability according to our research.

To reduce the cost of crisis protection, we evaluated a number of dynamic strategies for their potential to perform well during the worst equity market drawdowns as well as recessions.

Two conceptually different classes of strategies emerge as credible candidates in our view. First, the futures time-series momentum strategies studied in Chapter 1, which resemble a dynamic replication of long straddle positions, performed well during both severe equity market drawdowns and recessions. Restricting these strategies from taking long equity positions further enhances their protective properties, but the cost is lower overall performance.

Second, strategies that take long and short positions in single stocks, using quality metrics to rank companies cross-sectionally, have also historically performed well in equity-market selloffs and in recessions, likely a result of a flight-to-quality effect. We analyzed a host of different quality metrics, and point out the importance of a beta-neutral portfolio construction, rather than the dollar-neutral formulation that is more common in most published papers.

In the late stages of a bull market, it is prudent for investors to plan for the inevitable drawdown that might be accompanied by a recession. We analyze a number of passive and active strategies and detail the effectiveness of these strategies across various crises. However, investors need to be careful in defining "best" when selecting the best of strategies in the worst of times. It is essential to understand not only the performance but also the overall cost of implementing various protective measures.

Every crisis is different. For each one, some defensive strategies will turn out to be more helpful than others. Therefore, diversification across a number of promising defensive strategies may be most prudent.

So far, we have considered a range of candidate strategies that are useful for strategic risk management. These can be considered inputs to the portfolio. However, there is another crucial aspect of design—how these inputs are combined into a portfolio. That is, the portfolio construction method itself is of vital importance. Also, the sizing of positions matters, and in the next chapter we show that downsizing at times of increased volatility provides another tool for managing risk.

APPENDIX 2A: LONG PUTS USING OTC PUT OPTION DATA FROM A BROKER

Earlier we used the CBOE S&P 500 PutWrite Index, for which we have daily at-the-money (ATM) S&P 500 put returns starting in 1986. As a robustness check, here we also use mid-quote data for over-the-counter (OTC) S&P 500 put options from a large broker, which are available since 1996, and include 5 percent and 10 percent out-of-the money (OTM) put data. Because the OTC put data are monthly, we extend our drawdown periods to span whole calendar months.

The passive strategy based on these OTC options initiates a long 1-month put position at month-end and the puts are held until expiry at the subsequent month-end. In contrast, the PutWrite Index positions are initiated and expire on the third Friday of the month, and the payoff at expiry is based on the special open quotation (SOQ).

We first consider the strategy of holding one put option (i.e., the return is the net payoff of one option, divided by the index level at option initiation). This mimics the PutWrite Index methodology. The return of passively investing in the OTC one-month ATM S&P 500 puts correlates 0.85 to the short PutWrite Index returns and the all-period return is similarly negative (see Table 2A.1). Both ATM option strategies generate positive returns for all drawdown periods (100% hit rate), though during the tech bubble burst, shorting the PutWrite Index performs notably better.

Turning to 5 percent and 10 percent OTM options, one can see from Table 2A.1 that the all-period return is less negative, which is intuitive given the lower premium relative to an ATM put. However, the drawdown period performance is not consistently positive anymore, and mostly negative in the case of 10 percent OTM puts. The reasoning is that these OTM puts do not pay off when there is a more gradual decline (and monthly returns do not exceed −5 percent and −10 percent respectively).

Rather than buying a fixed number of puts, one can also spend a fixed fraction of wealth on option premiums. We consider the case of spending 1 percent per month. This arguably creates a more like-for-like comparison between ATM and OTM options. Also, such a strategy naturally buys fewer options when they are expensive. From the bottom rows of Table 2A.1, we see that the ATM option strategy provides the best cost-benefit tradeoff. This should come as no surprise, as insurance against only the worst states of the world commands a disproportionately high risk premium.

TABLE 2A.1 **Long puts.** We report the total return of the S&P 500 and various long put strategies during drawdown periods of the S&P 500, the annualized (geometric) return during drawdown, normal, all periods, and the hit rate (percentage of drawdowns with positive return). We consider both buying one put and spending 1 percent of wealth on puts each month. The index data are as before and based on the CBOE S&P 500 PutWrite Index. The OTC data are from a large broker. The data are monthly from 1996 to 2018.

	Asian crisis	Tech burst	Financial crisis	Euro crisis I	Euro crisis II	2018Q4	Drawdown (14%)	Normal (86%)	All (100%)	Hit rate %
Starting month	Jul-98	Sep-00	Oct-07	Apr-10	Apr-11	Sep-18				
Ending month	Aug-98	Oct-02	Mar-09	Jul-10	Oct-11	Dec-18				
Strategy							Annualized return			
S&P 500 (funded)	−15.4%	−39.9%	−45.8%	−5.2%	−7.1%	−13.0%	−26.7%	20.6%	8.2%	n.a.
S&P 500 (excess)	−16.1%	−44.1%	−47.1%	−5.3%	−7.1%	−13.6%	−28.4%	18.1%	5.9%	n.a.
ATM puts (index, as before)	14.9%	32.8%	19.5%	3.7%	1.4%	12.2%	16.6%	−12.7%	−7.0%	100%
ATM puts (OTC), 1 unit	11.6%	17.3%	20.2%	2.6%	2.8%	10.2%	12.8%	−13.0%	−7.9%	100%
5% OTM puts (OTC), 1 unit	7.8%	−3.1%	2.4%	−1.6%	−4.0%	4.3%	1.1%	−7.3%	−5.5%	50%
10% OTM puts (QTC), 1 unit	3.8%	−11.2%	−7.5%	−2.6%	−3.4%	−0.7%	−4.4%	−3.1%	−3.4%	17%
ATM puts (OTC), 1% pm	5.0%	10.8%	7.8%	1.4%	1.6%	8.2%	7.0%	−6.9%	−4.1%	100%
5% OTM puts (OTC), 1% pm	7.0%	1.2%	3.8%	−0.1%	−4.1%	11.8%	3.8%	−10.9%	−7.9%	67%
10% OTM puts (OTC), 1% pm	6.7%	−22.3%	−11.3%	−3.9%	−5.9%	−3.9%	−8.6%	−11.4%	−10.8%	17%

APPENDIX 2B: LONGER VIEW OF GOLD

In this appendix, we take a longer view of gold. The analysis of gold prices prior to 1972 is complicated by the Bretton Woods system, which tied major currencies to gold. In Figure 2B.1, we show the five-year rolling correlation of monthly gold spot returns with U.S. equities. Between 1976 and 1985

Panel A: Rolling five-year correlation

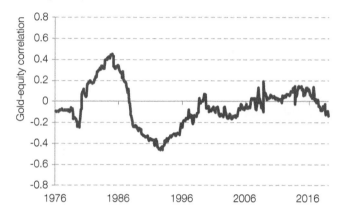

Panel B: Gold returns by three-month equity return quintile

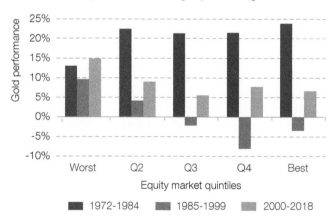

FIGURE 2B.1 Time varying co-movement between equity and gold returns (funded). In Panel A, we plot the rolling five-year correlation between monthly U.S. equities and gold spot returns from 1977–2018. In Panel B, we plot the annualized gold returns by three-month equity quintiles and for three sub-samples of 1972–2018. The gold data are from Bloomberg, and the equity data are from Global Financial Data and Bloomberg.

gold was moderately positively correlated with equities. In the subsequent 10 years, the correlation was moderately negative and since the mid-1990s it has been close to zero. We split the period 1972–2018 into three sub-samples and, for each subsample, calculated the mean return of gold by three-month equity quintile. Pre-1985, the returns of gold were strong and appear largely indifferent to equity returns. The positive equity correlation is perhaps evident in the relatively weaker performance of gold during the worst three-month periods for equities. In the period 1985 to 1999, when the gold–equity correlation was mostly negative, we see gold performing relatively well during the worst equity quintile. This outperformance dur-ing difficult periods for equities was carried into the 2000s, but without the negative returns during best equity months.

APPENDIX 2C: ADDITIONAL RESULTS FOR QUALITY STOCKS

Table 2C.1 reports the quality factor performance based on a dollar-neutral portfolio construction, rather than the beta-neutral portfolio construction used in Table 2.7.

In Table 2C.2, we show the output of the following regression, per-formed using five-day returns, and as before defining the information ratio as the regression alpha divided by the standard deviation of the error.

$$R_t^{\text{strategy}} = \alpha + \beta^{\text{Market}} R_t^{\text{Market}} + \beta^{\text{Size}} R_t^{\text{Size}} + \beta^{\text{Value}} R_t^{\text{Value}} + \beta^{\text{Mom}} R_t^{\text{Mom}} + \varepsilon_t \tag{2.6}$$

$$IR = \frac{\alpha}{\sigma(\varepsilon)} \sqrt{261/5}$$

As dependent variables we use the different quality composites reported on in Tables 2.1 and 2.2, and as independent variables we use the market, size, value, and momentum factors used before in Table 2.5.

TABLE 26.1 Quality factor performance, dollar-neutral. We report the total return for various quality factors, where portfolios are constructed to be dollar-neutral. We report the total return during the eight worst drawdowns for the S&P 500, the annualized (geometric) return during equity market drawdown, normal, and all periods, and the correlation to the S&P 500. All strategies are scaled to 10 percent annualized volatility (ex-post). The data are from 1986 to 2018.

Category	Name	Total return								Annualized return			Correlation
		Black Monday	Gulf War	Asian crisis	Tech burst	Financial crisis	Euro crisis I	Euro crisis II	2018Q4	Drawdown (14%)	Normal (86%)	All (100%)	Correl. to S&P500
Profitability	Cash flow over assets		0.3%	4.2%	171.9%	20.2%	7.7%	11.9%	5.9%	36.4%	-1.2%	4.0%	-0.40
Profitability	Gross margin	0.9%	0.7%	3.3%	-28.0%	33.1%	11.7%	12.8%	2.8%	5.5%	1.7%	2.2%	-0.03
Profitability	Gross profits over assets	-2.4%	-5.2%	-1.1%	109.8%	19.7%	2.7%	10.2%	2.6%	22.2%	3.5%	6.0%	-0.11
Profitability	Low accruals		0.1%	3.4%	90.6%	4.1%	-4.4%	-9.9%	-0.1%	12.8%	0.9%	2.7%	-0.10
Profitability	Return on assets	-2.9%	0.4%	2.8%	128.5%	29.9%	10.4%	9.4%	6.0%	31.5%	-1.2%	3.0%	-0.26
Profitability	Return on equity	-0.7%	-2.0%	1.0%	155.1%	14.0%	9.2%	8.6%	1.1%	28.7%	0.2%	3.9%	-0.24
Payout	Net debt issuance	2.9%	9.4%	10.7%	96.2%	29.2%	-7.0%	-4.7%	3.0%	24.2%	6.5%	8.9%	-0.12
Payout	Net equity issuance	-0.7%	2.2%	7.0%	137.2%	12.4%	5.2%	9.1%	7.0%	29.6%	0.0%	3.8%	-0.36
Payout	Total net payouts over profits		6.9%	4.2%	62.0%	10.8%	14.1%	-1.1%	4.9%	19.9%	-3.7%	-0.4%	-0.23

(Continued)

TABLE 2C.1 (*Continued*)

Category	Name	Total return								Annualized return			Correlation
		Black Monday	Gulf War	Asian crisis	Tech burst	Financial crisis	Euro crisis I	Euro crisis II	2018Q4	Drawdown (14%)	Normal (86%)	All (100%)	Correl. to S&P500
Growth	Cash flow over assets (5y change)			−0.5%	42.1%	1.6%	11.9%	16.7%	−1.9%	14.5%	−0.2%	2.4%	−0.13
Growth	Gross margin (5y change)		−6.1%	−8.8%	−35.4%	1.4%	8.4%	7.5%	−0.5%	−8.7%	2.7%	0.9%	0.28
Growth	Gross profits over assets (5y change)		−5.8%	−8.1%	−32.6%	5.3%	6.1%	6.8%	−1.0%	−7.5%	2.2%	0.6%	0.29
Growth	Low accruals (5y change)			−2.7%	−41.0%	15.0%	3.3%	0.8%	3.7%	−7.3%	−1.7%	−2.8%	0.20
Growth	Return on assets (5y change)		−4.1%	−6.6%	18.4%	9.3%	12.0%	8.9%	−0.7%	7.4%	−0.5%	0.7%	0.02
Growth	Return on equity (5y change)		−7.3%	−8.8%	24.1%	10.7%	14.2%	13.8%	−2.6%	8.5%	−0.1%	1.2%	0.04
Safety	Low beta	7.6%	9.2%	8.2%	81.6%	15.0%	9.8%	18.0%	12.0%	31.7%	−5.3%	−0.5%	−0.73
Safety	Low idiosyncratic volatility	2.9%	9.0%	10.1%	93.7%	18.8%	6.3%	10.8%	7.5%	29.9%	−3.5%	0.8%	−0.55
Safety	Low leverage	0.0%	3.9%	3.0%	69.0%	−15.0%	−0.4%	−0.1%	2.7%	9.7%	−2.4%	−0.7%	−0.22

TABLE 2C.2 Quality composites four-factor regression analysis. We report the output of running the regression given in Equation 2.6 for various quality composites. T-statistics are based on Newey-West corrected errors (25 lags). We consider both dollar-neutral and beta-neutral versions. All strategies are scaled to 10 percent annualized volatility (ex-post). The data are from 1986–2018.

Category	Construction	IR	Alpha (ann.)		Market factor		Size factor		Value factor		Mom. factor	
		Estimate	Estimate	[t-stat]	Estimate	[t-stat]	Estimate	[t-stat]	Estimate	[t-stat]	Estimate	[t-stat]
Profitability	Dollar-neutral	0.85	8.4%	[4.34]	−0.20	[−9.10]	−0.36	[−3.92]	−0.22	[−3.48]	0.10	[2.05]
Profitability	Beta-neutral	0.74	8.2%	[3.76]	−0.15	[−5.14]	−0.34	[−3.16]	−0.05	[−0.64]	0.07	[1.21]
Payout	Dollar-neutral	0.79	6.9%	[4.23]	−0.26	[−9.61]	−0.41	[−5.21]	0.40	[5.86]	0.06	[1.27]
Payout	Beta-neutral	0.88	8.6%	[4.63]	−0.12	[−4.15]	−0.43	[−4.40]	0.49	[6.42]	0.05	[0.89]
Growth	Dollar-neutral	0.24	1.8%	[1.28]	0.11	[4.29]	0.02	[0.66]	−0.67	[−19.98]	0.07	[2.25]
Growth	Beta-neutral	0.08	0.6%	[0.45]	0.04	[1.61]	0.12	[5.32]	−0.64	[−16.76]	0.09	[2.45]
Safety	Dollar-neutral	0.38	2.5%	[2.05]	−0.40	[−20.66]	−0.37	[−7.30]	0.32	[7.68]	0.09	[2.83]
Safety	Beta-neutral	0.54	5.4%	[2.87]	0.01	[0.35]	−0.37	[−4.46]	0.55	[7.82]	0.10	[1.90]
Quality All	Dollar-neutral	0.84	6.6%	[4.34]	−0.37	[−18.53]	−0.45	[−5.66]	0.15	[2.68]	0.10	[2.40]
Quality All	Beta-neutral	0.90	9.6%	[4.55]	−0.08	[−2.66]	−0.47	[−4.06]	0.33	[4.06]	0.11	[1.80]

REFERENCES

AQR whitepaper. "Good Strategies for Tough Times," Alternative Thinking 2015Q3, 2015.

Arnott, R., C.R. Harvey, V. Kalesnik, and J. Linnainmaa (2019). "Alice's Adventures in Factorland: Three Blunders that Plague Factor Investing," *Journal of Portfolio Management*, 45(4), 18–36.

Asness, C., A. Frazzini, R. Israel, T. Moskowitz, and L. Pedersen (2018). "Size Matters, If You Control Your Junk," *Journal of Financial Economics*, 129(3), 479–509.

Asness, C., A. Frazzini, and L. Pedersen (2019). "Quality Minus Junk," *Review of Accounting Studies*, 24(1), 34–112.

Asvanunt, A., L. Nielsen, and D. Villalon (2015). "Working Your Tail Off: Active Strategies versus Direct Hedging," *Journal of Investing*, 24(2), 134–145.

Baele, L., G. Bekaert, and K. Inghelbrecht (2010). "The Determinants of Stock and Bond Return Comovements," *Review of Financial Studies*, 23(6), 2374–2428.

Cook, M., E. Hoyle, M. Sargaison, D. Taylor, and O. Van Hemert (2017). "The Best Strategies for the Worst Crises," Man Group working paper.

Demeterfi, K., E. Derman, M. Kamal, and J. Zou (1999). "More Than You Ever Wanted to Know About Volatility Swaps," Goldman Sachs Quantitative Strategies Research Notes.

Erb, C.B., and C.R. Harvey (2013). "The Golden Dilemma," *Financial Analyst Journal*, 69(4), 10–42.

Fama, E., and K. French (2015). "A Five-Factor Asset Pricing Model," *Journal of Financial Economics*, 116(1), 1–22.

Frazzini, A., and L. Pedersen (2014). "Betting Against Beta." *Journal of Financial Economics*, 111(1), 1–25.

Funnell, B. (2017). "Fire, Then Ice," Man GLG Views.

Harvey, C., E. Hoyle, S. Rattray, M. Sargaison, D. Taylor, and O. Van Hemert (2019). "The Best of Strategies for the Worst of Times: Can Portfolios Be Crisis Proofed?," *Journal of Portfolio Management*, 45(5), 7–28. DOI: https://doi.org/10.3905/jpm.2019.45.5.007.

Kaminski, K. (2011). "In Search of Crisis Alpha: A Short Guide to Investing in Managed Futures," RPM working paper.

Levine, A., and L. Pedersen (2015). "Which Trend Is Your Friend?" *Financial Analyst Journal*, 72(3), 51–66.

Liang, C., Z. Tang, and X. Xu (2019). "Uncertainty, Momentum, and Profitability," *Journal of Portfolio Management, forthcoming*.

Luu, B.V., and P. Yu (2011). "The Credit Risk Premium: Should Investors Overweight Credit, When, and by How Much?," *Journal of Investing*, 20(4), 132–130.

Shephard, N., and K. Sheppard (2010). "Realising the Futures: Forecasting with High-Frequency-Based Volatility (HEAVY) Models," *Journal of Applied Econometrics*, 25, 197–231.

CHAPTER 3

Risk Management via Volatility Targeting

INTRODUCTION

In the first two chapters, we explored the performance of various types of investments during equity market drawdown periods and recessions. Understanding the historical track record of these investments is an essential component of strategic risk management. However, there are other tools in the investor's arsenal that positively contribute to risk management, including rebalancing strategies (Chapter 4), drawdown strategies (Chapter 5), as well as the subject of this chapter, volatility targeting.[1]

A portfolio strategy that targets certain levels of volatility may act similarly to the positive convexity strategies that we discussed in the first chapter. For example, research has documented two features of volatility. First, volatility is persistent (sometimes described as *clustering*). High volatility over the recent past tends to be followed by high volatility in the near future. This observation underpins Engle's (1982) pioneering work on ARCH models.[2] Second, for equity markets there is a negative relation between volatility and return realizations. As a result, a portfolio strategy that targets a certain level of volatility will be reducing weights in assets where volatility is spiking, which naturally reduces the severity of drawdown.

In this chapter, we focus on a portfolio strategy that is designed to counter the fluctuations in volatility. We achieve this by leveraging the portfolio at times of low volatility, and scaling down at times of high volatility. Effectively, the portfolio is targeting a constant level of volatility rather than a constant level of notional exposure.

Conditioning portfolio choice on volatility has attracted considerable recent attention. The financial media has zoomed in on the increasing popularity of risk parity funds.[3] Recent studies show that a constant-volatility approach results in higher Sharpe ratios than a constant notional exposure. In recent work, Moreira and Muir (2017) find that volatility-managed portfolios increase the Sharpe ratios in the case of the broad equity market and a number of dynamic, mostly long-short stock strategies. While most of the existing studies have concentrated on equity markets, we investigate the impact of volatility targeting across more than 60 assets, with daily data beginning as early as 1926. We find that Sharpe ratios are higher with volatility scaling for risk assets (equities and credit), as well as for portfolios that have a substantial allocation to these risk assets, such as a balanced (60–40 equity-bond) portfolio and a risk parity (equity-bond-credit-commodity) portfolio.

Risk assets exhibit a so-called leverage effect (i.e., a negative relation between returns and volatility), and so volatility scaling effectively introduces some momentum into strategies. As previously mentioned, periods of high volatility are associated with negative returns and volatility scaling reduces losing positions—the same type of effect that one would expect from a time-series momentum strategy. Historically, such a momentum strategy has performed well (see Chapters 1 and 2) and offered protection in down markets. We will show for other assets, such as bonds, currencies, and commodities, volatility scaling has a negligible effect on realized Sharpe ratios.

The impact of volatility targeting goes beyond the Sharpe ratio; we find that it reduces the likelihood of extreme returns (and the volatility of volatility) across our 60+ assets. Particularly relevant for investors, left-tail events tend to have a less severe effect, as they typically occur at times of elevated volatility, when a target-volatility portfolio has a relatively small notional exposure. Under reasonable investor preferences, a thinner left tail is much preferred (for a given Sharpe ratio).[4] Volatility targeting also reduces the maximum drawdowns for both the balanced and risk parity portfolios.

In this chapter, we first discuss the data, volatility-scaling methods, and statistics used for comparing the performance of unscaled and volatility-scaled portfolios. Then, we focus on U.S. equities, for which we have data starting in 1926. After that, we study U.S. bonds and credit, and we look at 50 global equity indices, fixed income, currency, and commodity futures and forwards. Following this are the analyses for the multi-asset balanced and risk parity portfolios. Finally, we discuss the leverage effect to provide further insights as to why the Sharpe ratio of risk assets is improved by volatility scaling. We offer some concluding remarks in the final section and comment on methods other than volatility scaling that may improve the Sharpe ratio and left-tail risk of a long-only portfolio.

OUR APPROACH

There are three main inputs needed to study the impact of volatility scaling: (1) securities return data, (2) methods for volatility scaling, and (3) performance statistics used to compare the unscaled and volatility-scaled investment returns.

Data

Our study relies on daily return data as a starting point. Often monthly data are available for longer histories, but these data are less suitable for obtaining responsive volatility estimates. Table 3.1 provides an overview.

TABLE 3.1   Securities and sample periods.In all cases, the frequency of the data used is at least daily. For S&P 500 and 10-year Treasury futures we also use five-minute intraday data. Data before the start of sample periods, where available, are used to initialize volatility measures.

Asset class	Sample period		Source
Equities (all U.S.)	Full	1927–2017	K. French website
Equities (all U.S.)	I	1928–1957	K. French website
Equities (all U.S.)	II	1958–1987	K. French website
Equities (all U.S.)	III	1988–2017	K. French website
Equities (S&P 500 futures)	III	1988–2017	Man AHL data
Equities (10 industries U.S.)	Full	1927–2017	K. French website
Bonds (U.S., proxied from yield data)	II/III	1962–2017	FRB of St. Louis
Bonds (10y Treasury future)	III	1988–2018	Man AHL data
Credit (BoA ML U.S. Corp. Credit Index, hedged with Treasuries)	III	1988–2018	Bloomberg, Man AHL data
Commodity futures (6 ags, 6 energies, 7 metals)	III	1988–2018	Man AHL data
Currencies forwards (9 crosses against the U.S. dollar)	III	1988–2018	Man AHL data
Equity index futures (10)	III	1988–2018	Man AHL data
Fixed income futures (9 bonds, 3 interest rate)	III	1988–2018	Man AHL data
Balanced (60–40 equity-bond)	III	1988–2018	Man AHL data
Risk parity (25-25-25-25 equities-bonds-credit-commodities.)	III	1988–2018	Man AHL data

Table 3.1 presents the data in the order it will be discussed in this chapter. First, we will consider U.S. equity data. The earliest daily return dataset available to us is from July 1, 1926, and is obtained from Kenneth French's website.[5] It is the value-weighted returns of firms listed on the NYSE, AMEX, and NASDAQ, henceforth referred to as "Equities All U.S." We will also use the returns of the 10 industry portfolios, available from the same source and start date. We additionally use S&P 500 futures data from 1988, which allows us to estimate volatility based on intraday data.

Then, we focus our attention on fixed income. For U.S. Treasury bonds, daily yields are available from the Federal Reserve since 1962.[6] We construct proxy daily returns by assuming that 10-year yields are par yields, and computing the return of par coupon bonds.[7] We additionally use 10-year Treasury futures data from 1988, which will again allow us to evaluate volatility estimates based on intraday data. We also explore credit returns, hedged with Treasuries, creating a long time series for an exposure that should resemble the synthetic CDX investment-grade index that is available today. To this end, we use the Bank of America Merrill Lynch U.S. Corporate Master Total Return index, and the hedging methodology follows Cook et al. (2017).

Finally, we use daily futures and forwards data for 50 liquid securities from Cook et al. (2017). This dataset covers commodities (six agricultural, six energy, and seven metal contracts), nine currencies (all against the U.S. dollar), 10 equities, nine bonds, and three interest rate contracts.

Volatility Scaling

We focus on excess returns, as they capture the compensation for bearing risk, not the time value of money. Excess returns are a type of "unfunded" returns, for example, a long equities position financed by borrowing at the risk-free Treasury bill rate. The unfunded nature of excess returns makes evaluating scaled position returns particularly straightforward. That is, volatility-scaled returns are simply inversely proportional to a conditional volatility estimate that is known a full 24 hours ahead of time, using returns up to $t-2$.[8] That is,

$$r_t^{\text{scaled}} = r_t \times \frac{\sigma^{\text{target}}}{\sigma_{t-2}} \times k^{\text{scaled}} \tag{3.1}$$

where we added a constant k (approximately 1), chosen such that ex post, over the full sample period, the target volatility is realized. We do this to facilitate comparison across different securities, methods, and sample periods. That is, the value of k does not change the results qualitatively, but a value that leads to 10 percent realized volatility facilitates comparison with other strategies. We will set the volatility target to 10 percent annualized throughout.

Unscaled returns involve no conditional volatility estimate, just a constant to achieve the same ex post 10 percent realized volatility as scaled returns:

$$r_t^{\text{unscaled}} = r_t \times k^{\text{unscaled}} \tag{3.2}$$

Notice that futures and forwards trade on margin, so their returns are already essentially unfunded, and so the risk-free rate is not deducted. In addition, the Treasury-hedged credit returns are unfunded by construction.

To estimate volatility, we use the standard deviation of daily returns, with exponentially decaying weights to returns at different lags.[9] We find similar results when using equal weights to returns over a rolling window of fixed length, or using estimates based on three- or five-day overlapping returns (not reported).

As volatility may be more precisely estimated with higher-frequency data, we also examine the effects of scaling by intraday volatility for the S&P 500 and 10-year Treasury futures since 1988.[10] We obtain a volatility estimate from five-minute returns over the liquid 9:15am to 2:00pm (Central time) time window.[11] We aggregate squared returns to a daily realized variance value, average these daily values with exponentially decaying weights, and then take the square root.

For the Equities All U.S. data, we work with calendar-day data to account for Saturday returns before 1952.[12] For other assets, we work with weekday data. In all cases, we annualize the volatility estimate, adjusting for the number of data points, to ensure comparability.

Performance Statistics

In Table 3.2, we list the performance statistics that we focus on. In most cases, we evaluate these statistics at the monthly frequency, which we believe is more relevant to investors than, for example, the daily frequency. More precisely, we use 30 calendar days (in the case of Equities All U.S.) or 21-weekday overlapping returns. Only the mean and turnover of the notional exposure are evaluated using daily data.

Throughout the tables in this chapter, we report the Sharpe ratio both gross and net of transaction costs. We use the following transaction cost estimates, expressed as fraction of the notional value traded: 1.0bp (basis point, or 0.01 percent) for equities, 0.5bp for bonds, 0.5bp for credit, 1.0 for gold, 2.0bp for oil, and 3.5bp for copper.[13] In the figures, we show returns gross of transaction costs, but results are very similar on a net basis.

TABLE 3.2 Performance statistics. As a default, we compute the Sharpe ratio, volatility of volatility (vol of vol), mean shortfall, and mean exceedance using a one-month (21 weekdays or 30 calendar days) evaluation frequency. The mean and turnover of the notional exposure are evaluated using daily data.

Statistic	Description
Sharpe ratio	Ratio of the mean and standard deviation of the excess returns (annualized)
Mean notional exposure	Mean daily exposure
Turnover notional exposure	Mean absolute daily exposure change, annualized, and divided by twice the mean exposure (to count round-trip trades)
Vol of vol	Standard deviation of the rolling one-year standard deviation of 21-weekday or 30–calendar day overlapping returns
Mean shortfall (left tail)	Mean of returns below the pth percentile ($p = 1$ and 5 will be considered)
Mean exceedance (right tail)	Mean of returns above the pth percentile ($p = 95$ and 99 will be considered)

The amount of trading needed to implement the volatility scaling can be inferred from the mean notional exposure multiplied by the turnover of the notional exposure. The latter is obtained as the mean absolute daily exposure change, annualized, and divided by twice the mean exposure. That is, turnover is expressed as the annual number of round trips of the mean exposure. Notice that an unscaled position in a particular asset will have a zero turnover. We do not consider turnover incurred from rolling futures or forwards contracts.

The volatility of the rolling one-year realized volatility (i.e., vol of vol) is the statistic that most directly measures the extent to which the volatility scaling results in more constant risk exposure.

The mean shortfall is the realized counterpart of expected shortfall, also known as the conditional value at risk. In contrast, the usual value-at-risk metric simply measures how bad the pth percentile of the returns distribution is; that is, it ignores returns below the pth percentile. The mean shortfall is often preferred because it uses all the returns below the pth percentile.

The mean shortfall measures left-tail behavior, which is most relevant for investors. However, we will also show the mean exceedance, the equivalent metric for the right tail, to illustrate how volatility scaling cuts both the left and the right tails.

While skewness and kurtosis are commonly reported, we have omitted them from our main analysis for two reasons. The first is that skewness and kurtosis measures are very sensitive to outliers, as their computation involves taking the third and fourth power of returns, respectively. Second, skewness is impacted by both left- and right-tail behavior, while investors are likely much more concerned with the left tail of the return distribution. Readers interested in more detail can refer to Appendix A, where we also discuss tail skewness, tail kurtosis, and (maximum) drawdown (which is studied in much more detail in Chapter 5).

U.S. EQUITIES

In this section we look at U.S. equities, for which we have the longest history of daily data available.

Unscaled Equity Returns Since 1926

The top three panels of Figure 3.1 present daily, monthly, and annual excess equity returns. It is evident that volatility tends to cluster. In our data from 1926–2017, volatility is persistently high during the 1930s (Great Depression), the early 2000s (following the bursting of the tech bubble), and 2007–2009 (Global Financial Crisis). The most negative day, October 19, 1987 (Black Monday), is also clearly visible.

The bottom panel of Figure 3.1 contrasts nominal, excess, and real cumulative returns, with the nominal return markedly higher during the high-inflation 1970s and 1980s. Notice that the excess returns (the focus in this chapter) are slightly below real returns. This is intuitive because the short-rate deducted to arrive at excess returns captures both an inflation component (the larger effect empirically) and a real rate component.[14]

Persistence of Equity Volatility

In Figure 3.2, we sort returns into quintiles based on the previous month's volatility. The left panel shows the mean excess return and the right panel the volatility (both annualized) for the subsequent month. The persistence of volatility is evident in the right panel. However, the mean return shows no clear predictive pattern across different volatility quintiles (left panel). So expected returns do not seem to reflect the persistence in volatility; that is, they do not provide a substantially higher reward in the case of predictably higher volatility. This is a first indication that volatility scaling may improve

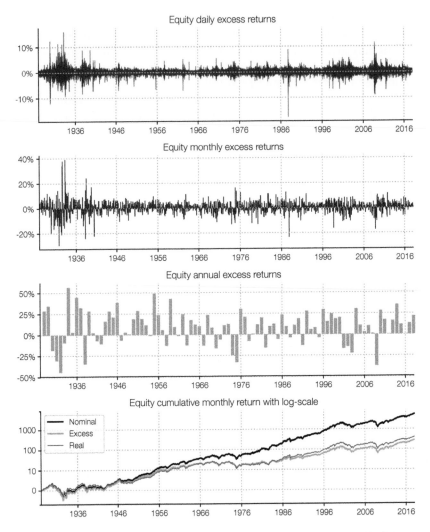

FIGURE 3.1 Equities All U.S. returns (1926–2017). The first three panels of the figure are daily, monthly, and annual U.S. equity returns in excess of the T-bill rate for the 1926–2017 period. No volatility scaling has been applied. The bottom panel shows cumulative (nominal, excess, and real) returns on a log-scale.

the Sharpe ratio of a long equities investment, as we will establish in the next subsection.

To further illustrate that equity volatility clusters, we show in Appendix B the autocorrelation of the monthly squared volatility (i.e., variance) of daily returns.

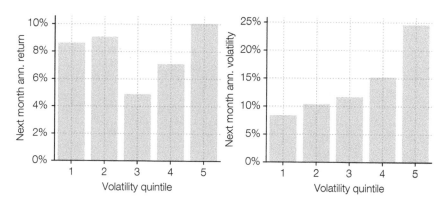

FIGURE 3.2 Quintile analysis for Equities All U.S. (1926–2017). The left panel shows the mean excess return and the right panel the volatility (both annualized) when sorting on the previous month's return for Equities All U.S. over the 1926–2017 period.

Performance of Volatility-Scaled Equity Returns

In Table 3.3, we show performance statistics for unscaled (top row) and volatility-scaled (other rows) "Equities All U.S." investments (1927–2017). We use exponentially decaying weights for the volatility estimate with a half-life indicated in parentheses in the first column of the table.

The Sharpe ratio improves from 0.40 (unscaled) to between 0.48 and 0.51 (volatility scaled) and is not very sensitive to the choice of volatility estimate.[15,16] The gross and net Sharpe ratios are the same for the reported precision, so we add the caveat that we use transaction cost estimates reflective of the current environment and apply this to the full history.[17] As described in the section about our approach, we use a rolling one-month (30 calendar days) evaluation frequency. We find very similar results for a rolling three-month (90 calendar days) evaluation frequency, although those results are not reported in this chapter.

The mean exposure is higher with volatility scaling. In order to achieve the same 10 percent full sample realized volatility, larger exposures (additional investments) are taken during low-volatility episodes. The turnover is zero for the unscaled investment and ranges from about five times a year for the most responsive and reactive volatility estimates, to less than once a year for the least responsive volatility estimates.

Both the vol of vol and left tail (mean shortfall) materially improve with volatility scaling, and the improvement is greatest for the most responsive volatility estimates.[18] The right tail (mean exceedance) is also, not surprisingly, reduced with volatility scaling. Hence, volatility scaling cuts both the

TABLE 3.3 Performance statistics Equities All U.S. (1927–2017). The table reports the performance statistics detailed in Table 3.2 for Equities All U.S. (1927–2016). The gross and net (of estimated costs) Sharpe ratio, volatility of volatility (vol of vol), mean shortfall (left tail), and mean exceedance (right tail) use a rolling one-month (30–calendar day) evaluation frequency. To facilitate comparison, both the unscaled and volatility-scaled returns are shown at 10 percent full-sample volatility.

Scaling	Sharpe ratio		Notional exposure		Vol of vol	Left tail		Right tail	
	Gross	Net	Mean[a]	Turn-over[b]		1%	5%	95%	99%
Unscaled	0.40	0.40	52%	0.00	4.6%	−11.4%	−6.9%	6.3%	11.8%
Scaled (10-day half-life)	0.48	0.48	71%	4.66	1.7%	−8.3%	−6.1%	5.8%	7.3%
Scaled (20-day half-life)	0.49	0.49	70%	2.39	1.8%	−9.0%	−6.4%	5.8%	7.3%
Scaled (40-day half-life)	0.50	0.50	69%	1.22	1.9%	−9.6%	−6.5%	5.8%	7.4%
Scaled (60-day half-life)	0.51	0.51	68%	0.82	2.1%	−9.9%	−6.6%	5.9%	7.5%
Scaled (90-day half-life)	0.51	0.51	67%	0.56	2.2%	−10.1%	−6.7%	5.9%	7.7%

[a]Mean notional exposure is simply the dollar investment (as percentage of one's wealth) to achieve the 10% full-sample volatility.
[b]Turnover is the number of trading round trips per year.

left and right tails. Consistent with this, in Appendix 3.A, we show that kurtosis is much reduced when volatility scaling is used. Its effect on skewness is more ambiguous, as both the left and right tails are cut. The maximum drawdown is also lower with volatility scaling.

For reporting purposes, we have ex post scaled the volatility to be exactly 10 percent. This makes it easy to calculate Sharpe ratios by inspection. However, this ex post scaling (which uses the full sample) has little to no impact on our results. The ex ante scaling is very close to the ex post 10 percent. Notice that the ex post scaling to 10 percent is purely to facilitate the reader's interpretation (no need to report Sharpe ratios because you can do them in your head). The ex ante value is very close to 10 percent, differing on average by only 43bp on an absolute basis.[19] To be clear, the volatility scaling implemented on the ex ante basis has no look-ahead bias.

We report ex post scaling that is very similar to the ex ante scaling for ease of interpretation.

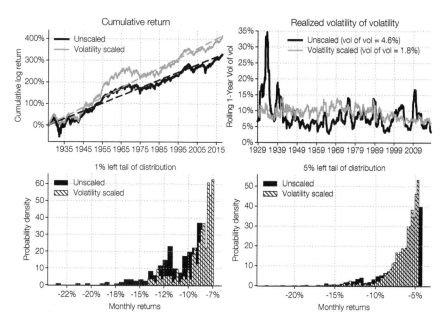

FIGURE 3.3 Cumulative returns, realized volatility, left and right tail for Equities All U.S. (1927–2017). This figure compares unscaled and volatility-scaled (exponentially weighted, 20-day half-life) Equities All U.S. excess returns for the 1927–2017 period. The top-left panel shows the cumulative return. The top-right panel shows the rolling one-year standard deviation of one-month (30 calendar days) overlapping returns. The standard deviation of the rolling one-year standard deviation is reported in parentheses in the legend. The bottom-left and bottom-right panels show the lowest 1 percent and 5 percent of the rolling one-month (30 calendar days) return distribution. To facilitate comparison, both the unscaled and volatility-scaled returns are shown at 10 percent full-sample volatility.

In Figure 3.3, we further compare unscaled and volatility-scaled returns, where the latter uses a volatility estimate based on a half-life of 20 days. In the top-left panel, we plot the cumulative return, which shows that the volatility-scaled investment generally outperformed, except during the middle part of the sample period. The impact of volatility scaling is illustrated in the top-right panel, where we depict the rolling one-year realized volatility for both unscaled and volatility-scaled 30-day overlapping returns. The realized volatility of volatility-scaled returns is much more stable over time. This is also evident from the vol of vol metric (i.e., the standard deviation of the rolling one-year realized volatility) reported in the legend: 4.6 percent for unscaled returns versus 1.8 percent for volatility-scaled returns. Finally, in the bottom-left and bottom-right panels we show the lowest 1 percent and 5 percent of the one-month (30 calendar days) return distribution.[20] Very negative returns of, say, –10 percent or worse are more common for unscaled returns.

To summarize, Figure 3.3 illustrates the two main ways volatility scaling has helped an Equities All U.S. investment: First, it improves the risk-adjusted performance, and second, it reduces the left tail.

Performance of Volatility-Scaled Equity Returns and Robustness across Subsamples and Industries

In Figure 3.4, we show the key statistics visually. We include equities broadly over the full sample period (1927–2017), equities broadly over three 30-year

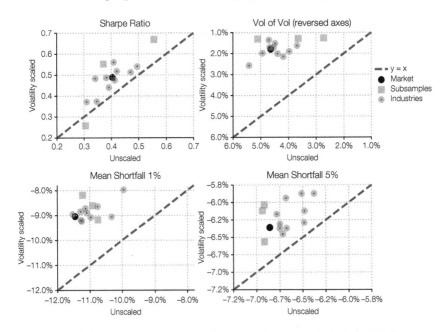

FIGURE 3.4 Performance statistics for Equities All U.S. (1927–2017). This figure compares unscaled and volatility-scaled (exponentially weighted, 20-day half-life) excess returns for Equities All U.S. full sample (black dots), subsamples (grey squares), and 10 industries full sample (grey dots). For all four statistics, observations above the dashed diagonal line correspond to a situation where volatility scaling improves the statistic (using reversed axes for vol of vol). All statistics are based on a rolling one-month (30 calendar days) evaluation frequency. To facilitate comparison, both the unscaled and volatility-scaled returns are shown at 10 percent full-sample volatility.

subsample periods, and 10 industry portfolios over the full sample period. Subplots are such that in all cases observations above the dashed diagonal correspond to situations where volatility scaling improves the statistic.

The Sharpe ratio improves in all cases, except during the 1957–1987 subsample period. The vol of vol and mean shortfall consistently and materially improve with volatility scaling.

Performance of Volatility-Scaled S&P 500 Futures Returns and the Use of Intraday Data

Table 3.4 explores the benefit of using higher frequency S&P 500 futures data (five-minute intervals from 1988) to estimate volatility. The top panel uses daily data and the bottom panel uses the 5-minute bars. The Sharpe ratio, vol of vol, and left tail (mean shortfall) all slightly improve when using intraday data (and comparing versions with a similar turnover value).

TABLE 3.4 Performance statistics S&P 500 futures (1988–2017) using intraday vol estimates. The table reports the performance statistics detailed in Table 3.2 for S&P 500 futures (1988–2016). We consider volatility estimates based on daily data (top panel) and five-minute intraday data (bottom panel). The gross and net (of estimated costs) Sharpe ratio, vol of vol, mean shortfall (left tail), and mean exceedance (right tail) use a rolling one-month (21 weekdays) evaluation frequency. To facilitate comparison, both the unscaled and volatility-scaled returns are shown at 10 percent full-sample volatility.

	Sharpe ratio		Notional exposure			Left tail		Right tail	
Scaling	Gross	Net	Mean[a]	Turn-over[b]	Vol of vol	1%	5%	95%	99%
Unscaled	0.50	0.50	68%	0.00	3.8%	−11.2%	−6.9%	6.2%	9.1%
Volatility used for scaling based on daily data									
Scaled (10-day half-life)	0.57	0.56	85%	4.56	1.1%	−7.8%	−6.0%	5.9%	7.6%
Scaled (20-day half-life)	0.59	0.59	84%	2.31	1.2%	−8.4%	−6.1%	6.0%	7.7%
Scaled (40-day half-life)	0.60	0.60	83%	1.17	1.5%	−9.0%	−6.3%	6.0%	7.9%
Scaled (60-day half-life)	0.60	0.59	82%	0.78	1.8%	−9.3%	−6.4%	6.0%	8.1%
Scaled (90-day half-life)	0.59	0.59	80%	0.53	2.1%	−9.6%	−6.5%	6.1%	8.2%

(*Continued*)

TABLE 3.4   (*Continued*)

Scaling	Sharpe ratio		Notional exposure			Left tail		Right tail	
	Gross	Net	Mean[a]	Turn-over[b]	Vol of vol	1%	5%	95%	99%
Volatility used for scaling based on 5-minute data									
Scaled (intraday, 5-day)	0.60	0.59	86%	3.96	1.3%	−7.5%	−5.7%	6.0%	7.4%
Scaled (intraday, 15-day)	0.62	0.62	85%	1.52	1.4%	−8.3%	−6.1%	5.9%	7.5%
Scaled (intraday, 25-day)	0.63	0.63	84%	0.97	1.5%	−8.7%	−6.2%	6.0%	7.6%
Scaled (intraday, 40-day)	0.63	0.62	83%	0.64	1.6%	−9.1%	−6.3%	6.0%	7.8%
Scaled (intraday, 60-day)	0.62	0.62	81%	0.45	1.8%	−9.4%	−6.4%	6.0%	8.0%

[a]Mean notional exposure is simply the dollar investment (as percentage of one's wealth) to achieve the 10% full-sample volatility.
[b]Turnover is the number of trading round trips per year.

U.S. BONDS AND CREDIT

In this section we study U.S. bonds and long credit risk positions.

Unscaled Bond Returns Since 1926

As we did for equities, we start by examining bond returns since 1926, with (proxy) daily returns starting in 1962. In Figure 3.5, top three panels, we plot the daily, monthly, and annual excess returns.

Returns were less volatile pre-1980, and much less so pre-1967. Hence it seems that bond markets have gone through different volatility regimes, lasting multiple decades. In contrast to the equity market, the bond market looks structurally different before and after the 1970s. This reflects the fact that, for much of the pre-1970s sample, this market was actively managed by the Federal Reserve. Indeed, the Fed was not independent of the Treasury until the Treasury–Federal Reserve Accord in March 1951. Importantly, structural breaks may render the evaluation of a bond volatility-targeting strategy

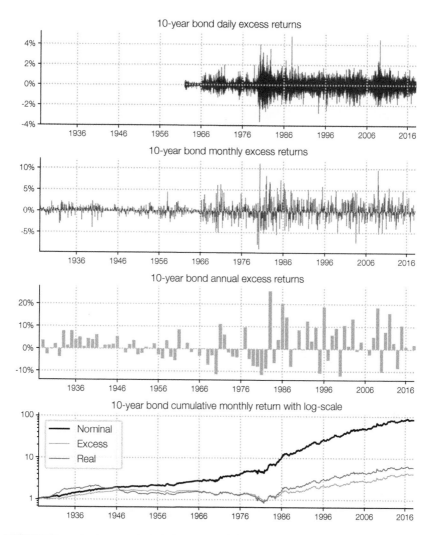

FIGURE 3.5 U.S. bond returns (1926–2017). The top three panels of the figure show (proxy) daily, monthly, and annual U.S. bonds returns in excess of the T-bill rate for the 1926–2017 period. No volatility scaling has been applied. The bottom panel shows cumulative (nominal, excess, and real) returns against a log-scale.

that includes data from before the mid-1980s less appropriate. In contrast, equity markets experienced clusters of volatility, but without clear structural breaks. From the bottom panel of Figure 3.5, we can see that excess returns were relatively flat for the first 55 years of our sample period and experienced a 40-year drawdown, ending in the 1980s.

Persistence of Bond Volatility

As we did for Figure 3.2, in Figure 3.6 we sort returns into quintiles based on the previous month's volatility. The left panel shows the mean excess return and the right panel shows the volatility (annualized), both for the subsequent month. Volatility is persistent (right panel). However, in contrast to equities in Figure 3.2, the mean bond returns are not similar across different quintiles (left panel), but rather the returns are much higher in the high-volatility quintile. So it is not obvious that volatility scaling will impact the Sharpe ratio of a long bond investment.

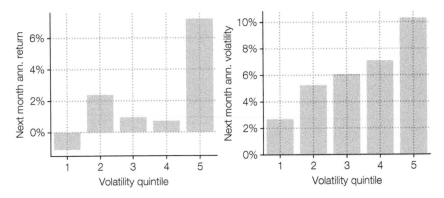

FIGURE 3.6 Quintile analysis for U.S. bonds (1962–2017). The left panel shows the mean excess return and the right panel the volatility (both annualized) when sorting on the previous month's return for U.S. bonds over the 1962–2017 period.

To further illustrate that bond volatility clusters, we show in Appendix 3.B the autocorrelation of the monthly squared volatility (i.e., variance) of daily returns.

Performance of Volatility-Scaled Bond Returns (Since 1963)

In Table 3.5, we report the performance statistics for U.S. bonds over the 1963–2017 period. Consistent with the quintile analysis displayed in Figure 3.6, volatility scaling decreases the Sharpe ratio over this period. The reason is straightforward: the 1960–1980 period was characterized by both negative returns and low volatility. So a volatility-targeting approach would lead to relatively large exposures during this extended bond bear market. Notice that the notional exposure is always above 100 percent. This reflects the fact that bond volatility on average is less than 10 percent. Volatility targeting does lead to a lower vol of vol during this period, as it did for equities.

TABLE 3.5   Performance statistics U.S. bonds (1963–2017). The table reports the performance statistics detailed in Table 3.2 for U.S. bonds, proxied from daily yield data (1963–2016). The gross and net (of estimated costs) Sharpe ratio, volatility of volatility (vol of vol), mean shortfall (left-tail), and mean exceedance (right-tail) use a rolling one-month (21 weekdays) evaluation frequency. To facilitate comparison, both the unscaled and volatility-scaled returns are shown at 10 percent full-sample volatility.

Scaling	Sharpe ratio		Notional exposure		Vol of vol	Left tail		Right tail	
	Gross	Net	Mean[a]	Turn-over[b]		1%	5%	95%	99%
Unscaled	0.25	0.25	127%	0.00	3.9%	−8.4%	−5.9%	7.1%	11.7%
Scaled (10-day half-life)	0.05	0.04	180%	4.96	2.1%	−8.6%	−6.3%	6.0%	8.2%
Scaled (20-day half-life)	0.06	0.06	179%	2.51	2.1%	−8.9%	−6.3%	6.1%	8.4%
Scaled (40-day half-life)	0.08	0.08	177%	1.27	2.2%	−9.0%	−6.4%	6.2%	8.5%
Scaled (60-day half-life)	0.08	0.08	174%	0.86	2.4%	−9.2%	−6.4%	6.2%	8.5%
Scaled (90-day half-life)	0.09	0.09	170%	0.58	2.6%	−9.5%	−6.4%	6.2%	8.6%

[a]Mean notional exposure is simply the dollar investment (as percentage of one's wealth) to achieve the 10 percent full-sample volatility.
[b]Turnover is the number of trading round trips per year.

In Figure 3.7, we contrast the cumulative return, realized volatility, and 1 percent and 5 percent left tail of the return distribution for an unscaled and volatility-scaled bond investment. In all cases, the volatility-scaling is done using exponentially decaying weights with a half-life of 20 days. Visible from the top-right panel is that the unscaled bond investment indeed has a low realized volatility during the 1964–1980 period. The underperformance of the volatility-scaled investment occurs only in the pre-1980 period.

One could argue that bond markets underwent a structural change in the mid-1980s when monetary policy became more geared toward inflation targeting. Hence, the post-1988 sample period considered in the next subsection may be more representative of today's bond markets.

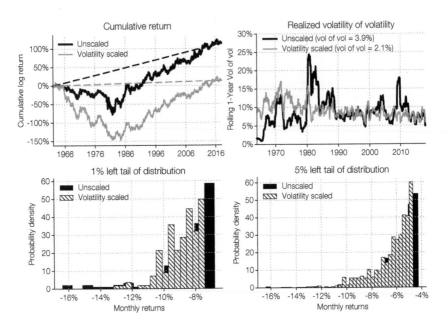

FIGURE 3.7 Cumulative returns, realized volatility, left and right tail for U.S. bonds (1963–2017). This figure compares unscaled and volatility-scaled (exponentially weighted, 20-day half-life) U.S. bond returns (proxied from daily yield data) for the 1963–2017 period. The top-left panel shows the cumulative return. The top-right panel shows the rolling one-year standard deviation of one-month (21 weekdays) overlapping returns. The standard deviation of the rolling one-year standard deviation is reported in parentheses in the legend. The bottom-left and bottom-right panel show the lowest 1 percent and 5 percent of the rolling one-month (21 weekdays) return distribution. To facilitate comparison, both the unscaled and volatility-scaled returns are shown at 10 percent full-sample volatility.

Performance of Volatility-Scaled Bond Returns (Since 1988)

In Table 3.6, we report the performance statistics over 1988–2017, for which we have U.S. 10-year Treasury futures data, both daily and intraday. We see that, in general, the vol of vol is much lower with volatility scaling, but the Sharpe ratio and mean shortfall (left tail) are similar. Using intraday data for the volatility estimate produces a slight improvement in all metrics.

In Figure 3.8, we contrast the cumulative return, realized volatility, and 1 percent and 5 percent left tail of the return distribution for an unscaled and volatility-scaled bond investment. In all cases, the volatility scaling is done using exponentially decaying weights with a half-life of 20 days. Consistent with Table 3.6, the main difference between unscaled and scaled returns for Treasuries over the 1988–2017 period is the lower vol of vol when volatility scaling (top-right panel).

TABLE 3.6 Performance statistics 10-year Treasury futures (1988–2017), also using intraday vol estimates. The table reports the performance statistics detailed in Table 3.2 for U.S. 10-year Treasury futures (1988–2016). We consider volatility estimates based on daily data (top panel) and five-minute intraday data (bottom panel). The gross and net (of estimated costs) Sharpe ratio, vol of vol, mean shortfall (left tail), and mean exceedance (right tail) use a rolling one-month (21 weekdays) evaluation frequency. To facilitate comparison, both the unscaled and volatility-scaled returns are shown at 10 percent full-sample volatility.

	Sharpe ratio		Notional exposure			Left tail		Right tail	
Scaling	Gross	Net	Mean[a]	Turn-over[b]	Vol of vol	1%	5%	95%	99%
Unscaled	0.64	0.64	171%	0.00	2.5%	−7.3%	−5.5%	6.7%	10.1%
Volatility used for scaling based on daily data									
Scaled (10-day half-life)	0.63	0.62	182%	4.33	1.2%	−7.5%	−5.6%	6.3%	7.9%
Scaled (20-day half-life)	0.63	0.63	182%	2.19	1.2%	−7.5%	−5.6%	6.3%	8.1%
Scaled (40-day half-life)	0.63	0.63	182%	1.11	1.4%	−7.5%	−5.6%	6.4%	8.4%
Scaled (60-day half-life)	0.63	0.63	181%	0.74	1.5%	−7.5%	−5.6%	6.5%	8.6%
Scaled (90-day half-life)	0.63	0.63	180%	0.49	1.6%	−7.5%	−5.6%	6.5%	8.8%
Volatility used for scaling based on 5-minute data									
Scaled (intraday, 5-day)	0.66	0.65	186%	3.80	1.1%	−7.4%	−5.4%	6.2%	7.6%
Scaled (intraday, 15-day)	0.64	0.64	186%	1.39	1.1%	−7.4%	−5.5%	6.3%	7.7%
Scaled (intraday, 25-day)	0.64	0.64	186%	0.87	1.2%	−7.5%	−5.5%	6.3%	7.9%
Scaled (intraday, 40-day)	0.63	0.63	185%	0.56	1.3%	−7.5%	−5.5%	6.4%	8.1%
Scaled (intraday, 60-day)	0.63	0.63	184%	0.38	1.4%	−7.6%	−5.5%	6.4%	8.3%

[a]Mean notional exposure is simply the dollar investment (as percentage of one's wealth) to achieve the 10 percent full-sample volatility.
[b]Turnover is the number of trading round trips per year.

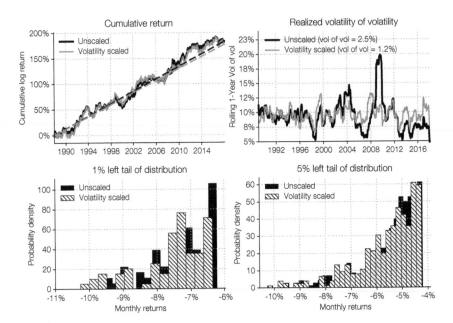

FIGURE 3.8 Cumulative returns, realized volatility, left and right tail for Treasury futures (1988–2017). This figure compares unscaled and volatility-scaled (exponentially weighted, 20-day half-life) 10-year Treasury futures returns for the 1988–2017 period. The top-left panel shows the cumulative return. The top-right panel shows the rolling one-year standard deviation of one-month (21 weekdays) overlapping returns. The standard deviation of the rolling one-year standard deviation is reported in parentheses in the legend. The bottom-left and bottom-right panel show the lowest 1 percent and 5 percent of the rolling one-month (21 weekdays) return distribution. To facilitate comparison, both the unscaled and volatility-scaled returns are shown at 10 percent full-sample volatility.

Performance of Volatility-Scaled Credit Returns

Moving on to credit, we see in Table 3.7 a substantial increase in the Sharpe ratio when using a relatively fast volatility (10-day half-life) estimate. For slower estimates (longer half-lives) the situation reverses. Also, the mean shortfall (left tail) is similar to unscaled for fast volatility estimates, but worse otherwise. The vol of vol is reduced for all volatility scaling cases considered. Credit is related to equities in the sense that both are exposed to firms' cash flow risk (i.e., both are risk assets), and so it is intuitive we see some similarities with the previously discussed results for equities (e.g., the improvement of the Sharpe ratio for relatively fast volatility estimates).

TABLE 3.7 Performance statistics for U.S. Credit (1988–2017). The table reports the performance statistics detailed in Table 3.2 for U.S. credit, hedged with Treasuries (1988-2017). The gross and net (of estimated costs) Sharpe ratio, vol of vol, mean shortfall (left-tail), and mean exceedance (right-tail) use a rolling one-month (21 weekdays) evaluation frequency. To facilitate comparison, both the unscaled and volatility-scaled returns are shown at 10 percent full-sample volatility.

Scaling	Sharpe ratio		Notional exposure			Left tail		Right tail	
	Gross	Net	Mean[a]	Turn-over[b]	Vol of vol	1%	5%	95%	99%
Unscaled	0.30	0.30	273%	0.00	6.7%	−14.5%	−7.2%	6.9%	13.5%
Scaled (10-day half-life)	0.49	0.46	510%	4.79	4.1%	−11.8%	−7.1%	5.8%	7.2%
Scaled (20-day half-life)	0.41	0.39	486%	2.49	4.3%	−13.3%	−7.6%	5.6%	7.1%
Scaled (40-day half-life)	0.30	0.30	458%	1.30	4.6%	−14.9%	−8.0%	5.3%	6.7%
Scaled (60-day half-life)	0.24	0.23	439%	0.89	4.9%	−15.7%	−8.2%	5.1%	6.6%
Scaled (90-day half-life)	0.18	0.17	415%	0.61	5.2%	−16.4%	−8.4%	5.1%	6.9%

[a]Mean notional exposure is simply the dollar investment (as percentage of one's wealth) to achieve the 10% full-sample volatility.
[b]Turnover is the number of trading round trips per year.

FUTURES AND FORWARDS

In this section, we study 50 futures and forwards across global equities, fixed income, currencies (all against the USD), and commodities.

Persistence of Futures Volatility

In Figure 3.9, we show the autocorrelation of the monthly variance of daily returns for the 50 futures and forwards markets in light gray. The average for different sectors is superimposed in darker shades. Persistence in variance is ubiquitous with a remarkably similar autocorrelation pattern across the 50 markets and seven sectors considered. Each of the seven sectors has an autocorrelation of around 0.5 for consecutive monthly variances, which then gradually decreases to 0.1–0.2 for the autocorrelation at a lag of 12 months.

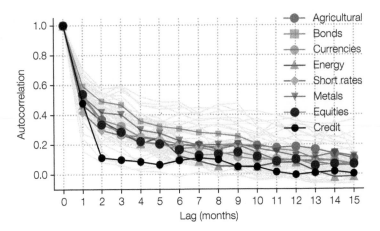

FIGURE 3.9 Autocorrelation of futures and forwards variance (1988–2017). The figure shows the autocorrelation of the monthly variance of 50 daily futures and forwards returns for the 1988–2017 period.

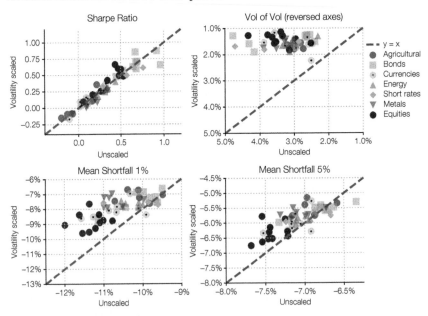

FIGURE 3.10 Performance statistics for futures and forwards (1988–2017). This figure compares unscaled and volatility-scaled (exponentially weighted, 20-day half-life) returns for 50 global futures and forwards markets, where different sectors are represented by different colors. For all four statistics, observations above the dashed diagonal line correspond to a situation where volatility scaling improves the statistic (using reversed axes for the volatility of volatility). All statistics are based on a rolling one-month (21 weekdays) evaluation frequency. To facilitate comparison, both the unscaled and volatility-scaled returns are shown at a 10 percent full-sample volatility.

Performance of Volatility-Scaled Futures Returns

The performance of the 50 futures and forwards markets is depicted in Figure 3.10. The Sharpe ratio improves slightly for equity indices when volatility scaling, but is similar for other assets. The vol of vol and mean shortfall improve materially for almost all assets with volatility scaling.

PORTFOLIOS

So far, we have considered single-asset investments. In this section, we turn our attention to two popular multi-asset portfolios: the 60–40 equity-bond "balanced portfolio" and a 25-25-25-25 equity-bond-credit-commodity "risk parity" portfolio.

We will contrast three ways to implement such a portfolio:

1. Unscaled at both the asset and portfolio level
2. Volatility scaling at the asset level only
3. Volatility scaling at both the asset and portfolio level

In all cases, the asset-level returns are subject to the full-sample scaling to 10 percent discussed earlier, which means that, as a starting point, the allocation to the different asset classes is in proportion to full-sample volatility, and thus we can sensibly compare the different cases. As we have previously mentioned, in practice we use the ex ante volatility to avoid any look-ahead bias. The difference between the ex ante and ex post results is minor.

For simplicity, we assume portfolios are rebalanced to the target asset allocation mix each day.[21]

Balanced 60–40 Equity-Bond Portfolio

In Table 3.8, we report the performance statistics for the balanced 60–40 equity-bond portfolio, based on S&P 500 and 10-year Treasury futures return data.[22] Because of the aforementioned asset-level scaling to 10 percent volatility in all cases, the 60–40 split here is in risk terms. That is, 60 percent of the risk will be allocated to equities rather than 60 percent of the capital. This implies a dollar allocation lower than 60 percent given that equities are riskier than bonds. The Sharpe ratio, vol of vol, and expected shortfall (left tail) all improve from asset-level volatility scaling. A portfolio of assets that are volatility-scaled individually may still display time-varying portfolio volatility, as the correlation between the assets and thus the dampening effect of diversification can vary over time. When we

TABLE 3.8 Performance statistics for the balanced portfolio (1988–2017). The table reports the gross and net (of estimated costs) Sharpe ratio, vol of vol, mean shortfall (left tail), and mean exceedance (right tail) statistics described in Table 3.2 for the 60–40 equity-bond balanced portfolio. We contrast an unscaled portfolio with, first, a portfolio with volatility scaling at the asset level only, and then a portfolio with volatility scaling at both the asset and portfolio levels. The volatility-scaling is done using exponentially decaying weights with a half-life of 20 days. We use a rolling one-month (21 weekdays) evaluation frequency. To facilitate comparison, both the unscaled and volatility-scaled returns are shown at 10 percent full-sample volatility.

Asset scaling	Portfolio scaling	Sharpe ratio		Notional exposure			Left tail		Right tail	
		Gross	Net	Mean[a]	Turn-over[b]	Vol of vol	1%	5%	95%	99%
Unscaled	Unscaled	0.80	0.80	153%	0.00	3.4%	−9.7%	−6.0%	6.8%	9.7%
Scaled (20-day half-life)	Unscaled	0.87	0.87	179%	2.24	2.2%	−8.0%	−5.6%	6.6%	8.7%
Scaled (20-day half-life)	Scaled (20-day half-life)	0.91	0.90	183%	3.95	1.3%	−7.3%	−5.5%	6.5%	8.0%

[a]Mean notional exposure is simply the dollar investment (as percentage of one's wealth) to achieve the 10% full-sample volatility.
[b]Turnover is the number of trading round trips per year.

apply a second volatility-scaling step at the portfolio level to adjust for time variation in the correlation between different assets, the Sharpe ratio, vol of vol, and expected shortfall (left tail) further improve. Also, the improvement in left-tail returns is greater than the reduction in right-tail returns.

In Figure 3.11, we contrast the cumulative return, realized volatility, and 1 percent and 5 percent left tail of the return distribution for an unscaled and volatility-scaled (at both the asset and portfolio level) balanced portfolio. Volatility-scaling is done using exponentially decaying weights with a half-life of 20 days. Consistent with the results of Table 3.8, both the cumulative return and left tail improve with volatility scaling.

Risk Parity Portfolio

We now turn our attention to the 25-25-25-25 equity-bond-credit-commodity, or risk parity portfolio.[23] The equity, bond, and credit assets

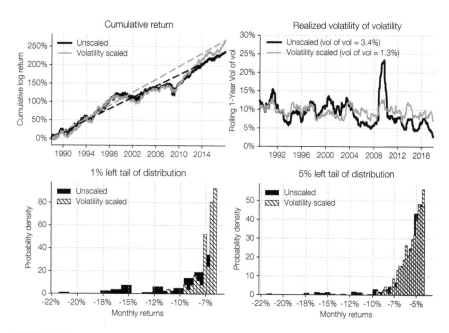

FIGURE 3.11 Cumulative returns, realized volatility, left and right tail returns for balanced portfolio (1988–2017). This figure compares unscaled and volatility-scaled (exponentially weighted, 20-day half-life) 60–40 equity-bond "balanced" portfolio returns for the 1988–2017 period. The top-left panel shows the cumulative return. The top-right panel shows the rolling one-year standard deviation of one-month (21 weekdays) overlapping returns. The standard deviation of the rolling one-year standard deviation is reported in parentheses in the legend. The bottom-left and bottom-right panels show the lowest 1 percent and 5 percent of the rolling one-month (21 weekdays) return distribution. To facilitate comparison, both the unscaled and volatility-scaled returns are shown at 10 percent full-sample volatility.

are for the United States (S&P 500, 10-year Treasury, and the credit index hedged with Treasuries, as used in the earlier section on U.S. bonds and credit). The commodity component is equally split between gold, copper, and crude oil (which some consider macro commodities or securities that may serve as a partial inflation hedge). The diversifying potential of commodities is particularly relevant in this context, as a main motivation to invest in a risk parity portfolio is that its returns may be more consistent across different macro environments, including inflationary environments, than a more traditional balanced portfolio.

Our 25 percent allocation to commodities is a simplification of what asset managers do in practice. First, they often augment the commodity exposure with inflation-indexed bonds. Second, because commodity futures may not earn a passive risk premium over the long run (it is, *a priori*, not obvious if a premium is earned on the long or the short side), some asset managers supplement the passive long commodity exposure with dynamic overlays based on momentum or carry, for example.

In Table 3.9, we report the performance statistics for the illustrative risk parity portfolio. We again find that volatility scaling is useful at both the asset and portfolio level, and generally all the performance statistics improve compared to an unscaled portfolio.

TABLE 3.9   Performance statistics for the risk parity portfolio (1988–2017). The table reports gross and net (of estimated costs) Sharpe ratio, vol of vol, mean shortfall (left tail), and mean exceedance (right tail) statistics described in Table 3.2 for the 25-25-25-25 equity-bond-credit-commodity risk parity portfolio. We contrast an unscaled portfolio with: (1) a portfolio with volatility scaling at the asset level only and (2) a portfolio with volatility scaling at both the asset and portfolio level. The volatility-scaling is done using exponentially decaying weights with a half-life of 20 days. We use a rolling one-month (21 weekdays) evaluation frequency. To facilitate comparison, both the unscaled and volatility-scaled returns are shown at 10 percent full-sample volatility.

Asset scaling	Portfolio scaling	Sharpe ratio Gross	Net	Notional exposure Mean[a]	Turn-over[b]	Vol of vol	Left tail 1%	5%	Right tail 95%	99%
Unscaled	Unscaled	0.80	0.80	268%	0.00	4.3%	−12.8%	−6.1%	6.5%	9.4%
Scaled (20-day half-life)	Unscaled	0.89	0.88	412%	2.39	1.7%	−8.8%	−6.0%	5.9%	7.0%
Scaled (20-day half-life)	Scaled (20-day half-life)	0.91	0.89	402%	3.95	1.7%	−8.2%	−5.7%	6.2%	7.9%

[a]Mean notional exposure is simply the dollar investment (as percentage of one's wealth) to achieve the 10% full-sample volatility.
[b]Turnover is the number of trading round trips per year.

In Figure 3.12, we contrast the cumulative return, realized volatility, and 1 percent and 5 percent left tail of the return distribution for an unscaled and volatility-scaled (at both the asset and portfolio level) risk parity portfolio. Volatility scaling is done using exponentially decaying weights with a half-life of 20 days. Both the cumulative return and left tail improve with volatility scaling.

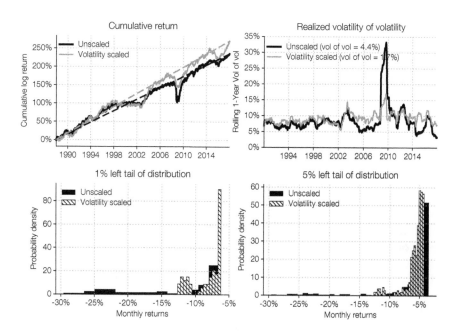

FIGURE 3.12 Cumulative returns, realized volatility, left and right tail for the risk parity portfolio (1988–2017). This figure compares unscaled and volatility-scaled (exponentially weighted, 20-day half-life) 25-25-25-25 equity-bond-credit-commodities risk parity portfolio returns for the 1988-2017 period. The top-left panel shows the cumulative return. The top-right panel shows the rolling one-year standard deviation of one-month (21 weekdays) overlapping returns. The standard deviation of the rolling one-year standard deviation is reported in parentheses in the legend. The bottom-left and bottom-right panels show the lowest 1 percent and 5 percent of the rolling one-month (21 weekdays) return distribution. To facilitate comparison, both the unscaled and volatility-scaled returns are shown at 10 percent full-sample volatility.

VOLATILITY SCALING AND THE SHARPE RATIO OF RISK ASSETS

In this section, we examine possible explanations for why volatility scaling improves the Sharpe ratio for risk assets, such as equities and credit, but has no effect on the Sharpe ratio of other assets. Our analysis suggests an answer that can be split into three parts: (1) only risk assets empirically display a so-called leverage effect, (2) the leverage effect effectively introduces some momentum, and (3) such a momentum overlay is beneficial for the Sharpe ratio. Indeed, we will show that the tendency of volatility scaling to introduce some momentum empirically explains much of the cross-sectional variation in the Sharpe ratio improvement when volatility scaling.

Leverage Effect Is Confined to Risk Assets

Equities and credit display a leverage effect, which is the tendency of returns to have a negative contemporaneous correlation to changes in volatility. The classic explanation by Black (1976) is that a negative equity return leads to a higher firm-value–to–equity ratio (more leverage in the capital structure of the firm), which in turn means equity volatility should increase (holding constant the firm's cash flow volatility).[24]

In Figure 3.13, we indeed observe this leverage effect empirically for equities and credit, but not for other assets. The top panels show results for Equities All U.S. (1926–2017), the three subsamples, and the 10 industry portfolios considered in Figure 3.4. The bottom panels show results for credit and the 50 futures and forwards for the 1988–2017 sample period. The right panels show the leverage effect: a negative correlation between monthly observations of the return and the change in variance. The left panels show a very similar picture for the correlation between monthly observations of return and the level of the variance.

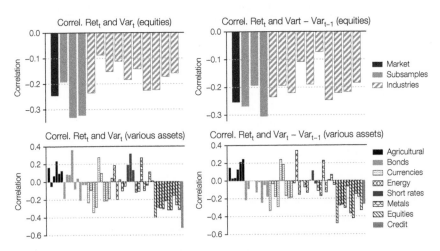

FIGURE 3.13 Leverage effect for various assets. This figure shows the contemporaneous correlation of monthly observations for asset returns and variance (left panels) and change in variance (right panels). The variance estimate is based on intra-month daily data. The top panels show results for Equities All U.S. (1926–2017), the three subsamples, and the 10 industry portfolios considered. The bottom panels show results for credit and the 50 futures and forwards for the 1988–2017 sample period.

Leverage Effect Introduces Some Momentum

When applied to assets exhibiting the leverage effect, volatility scaling effectively introduces some time-series momentum into strategies. That is, negative returns tend to be followed by a reduction in the position size (as volatility is higher in that case) and positive returns tend to be followed by an increase in the position size (as volatility is lower in that case).

In Figure 3.14, we show more explicitly for which assets volatility scaling leads to changes in position sizes that are in the momentum direction (i.e., smaller after negative returns, bigger after positive returns). Specifically, we show the correlation between the reciprocal of the volatility estimate (which is proportional to position sizing when volatility scaling is applied) and the past 21-, 65-, 130-, and 260-day returns (1-, 3-, 6-, 12-month momentum) in the four panels respectively. Here we consider a 20-day half-life for the volatility estimate. Mirroring the results for the leverage effect in Figure 3.13, we see in Figure 3.14 that only risk assets consistently show a positive correlation between position sizing (reciprocal volatility) and momentum (past returns). In fact, for other assets the correlation is predominantly negative, introducing a bet on mean reversion.

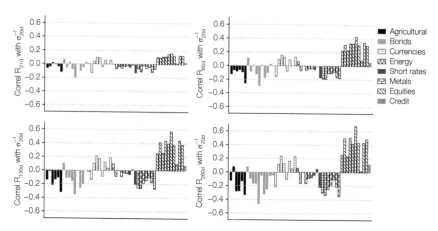

FIGURE 3.14 Correlation past returns and 1/vol for various assets. This figure shows the correlation between the reciprocal of the volatility estimate (which is proportional to position sizing when volatility scaling is applied) and the past 21-, 65-, 130-, and 260-day returns (1-, 3-, 6-, 12-month momentum) in the four panels respectively. The volatility estimate is based on exponentially weighted returns with a 20-day half-life. We consider credit and the 50 futures and forwards for the 1988–2017 sample period.

Momentum and the Impact of Volatility Scaling on the Sharpe Ratio

The final part of our investigation is to link directly cross-sectional differences in the impact of volatility scaling on the Sharpe ratio and asset return properties.

The evidence suggests that time-series momentum strategies have historically performed well (see Chapter 1).[25] In Figure 3.15, we show that it is indeed the "momentum-ness" of volatility scaling that explains a large part of the cross-sectional variation in the Sharpe ratio improvement when volatility scaling for the various assets considered. We find the shorter-term, one-month, momentum of returns to be most relevant here. Using a 20-day half-life for volatility scaling, the R-squared is 45 percent. For a slower volatility estimate using a 90-day half-life, the R-squared is even higher at 60 percent.

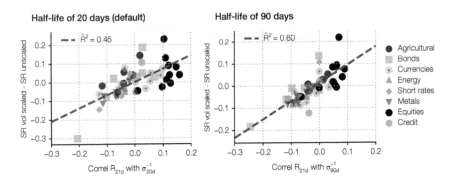

FIGURE 3.15 Improvement Sharpe Ratios when volatility scaling versus correlation (past returns, 1/vol) for various assets, 1988–2017. This figure plots the improvement from volatility scaling (vertical axis) versus the "momentum-ness" of volatility scaling, determined as the correlation between the past 21-day returns and the reciprocal of the volatility estimate (horizontal axis). The volatility estimate is based on exponentially weighted returns with a 20-day half-life (left panel) and 90-day half-life (right panel).

CONCLUDING REMARKS

In the first two chapters, we explored specific assets and investment strategies that might be useful in limiting downside risk in portfolios. In contrast, this chapter has focused on portfolio management strategies—that is, the dynamic management of the assets in the portfolio. The initial strategy we examined is volatility targeting investment weights rather than focusing on dollar weights.

We contrasted the performance of both individual assets and portfolios with a constant notional exposure (unscaled) to strategies that target a constant level of volatility (scaled or volatility targeted). Our initial evidence, consistent with recent studies, indicates that volatility scaling helps to boost Sharpe ratios. However, most recent research has focused on equities. Our results show that this boost is specific to so-called risk assets (e.g., equity and credit) or portfolios that have a sizable allocation to these risk assets. That is, for other assets, such as fixed income, currencies, and commodities, the effect of a simple volatility scaling on the Sharpe ratio is negligible.

While the Sharpe ratio is important, most investors have broader investment objectives. We show that volatility scaling has one unambiguous effect across assets and asset classes: It reduces the likelihood of extreme returns (and the volatility of volatility). In particular, the lower probability of very negative returns (left-tail events) is valuable for investors.

While we provided a detailed historical account of the impact of volatility targeting across 60+ assets and two multi-asset portfolios, some topics are beyond the scope of this chapter. We will comment on three.

First, the detailed analysis for equity and bonds was done for U.S. assets, for which we have the longest daily return history. A caveat of this approach is that the U.S. is an ex post winner in the sense that, over the past century it had robust economic growth and no major war on its own soil. This may particularly matter for bonds, which can start to resemble a credit investment when the creditworthiness of a government is questioned by investors. As such, our finding that volatility scaling does not meaningfully improve the Sharpe ratio of a bond investment should also come with a caveat and, going forward, volatility scaling may improve the Sharpe ratio of bonds that unexpectedly start to behave in a more credit-like manner.

Second, while the focus in this chapter was on volatility scaling, there are other methods with the potential to improve the risk management of a long portfolio. Chapter 1 shows that trend-following strategies tend to work particularly well at times of equity and bond market sell-offs. Hence a trend-following overlay may further improve the risk and return of a long portfolio. Indeed, Haydon (2018) illustrates the benefits of such an overlay for a balanced 60–40 equity-bond portfolio.

Finally, while we explored intraday data for S&P 500 and Treasury futures and found some benefits vis-à-vis daily data, we believe this chapter only scratches the surface of this topic. More assets now have good-quality intraday data, and for more hours of the day. In addition, advances in statistical modeling may help us to use the intraday data to get more timely estimates (see, e.g., Noureldin, Shephard, and Sheppard [2012] for a discussion of multivariate high-frequency-based volatility [HEAVY] models).

We have made the case in this chapter that the method of forming a portfolio is as important as the assets that compose it. Volatility scaling for risk assets provides a type of protection that is similar to investing directly in positive-convexity dynamic strategies like trend following. Next, we consider another portfolio strategy that many incorrectly believe they fully understand: rebalancing a portfolio. We will argue there is a big gap between the beliefs of the benefits of rebalancing and what actually happens. Unbeknownst to many, rebalancing is an active strategy that buys losers and sells winners. Mechanical rebalancing increases—not decreases—the risk of a portfolio. Rebalancing is an essential component of strategic risk management.

APPENDIX 3A: OTHER RISK METRICS

In this appendix, we explore the following additional risk metrics to contrast unscaled and volatility-scaled returns: skewness, kurtosis, tail skewness, tail kurtosis, and (maximum) drawdown. Throughout, we use a volatility estimate based on exponentially decaying weights (20-day half-life). As before, we evaluate these statistics for one-month (30 calendar days/21 weekdays) returns.

Skewness and kurtosis are the third and fourth central moments. Kurtosis is reported in excess of three, so a normal distribution has a kurtosis value of zero. We can also define *tail skewness* and *tail kurtosis* based on mean shortfalls and exceedances. Writing U_α for the mean exceedance of the $(1 - \alpha)$-quantile, and L_α as the mean shortfall of the α-quantile, Hogg (1972) proposed the following as a measure of kurtosis:

$$\frac{U_{0.05} - L_{0.05}}{U_{0.5} - L_{0.5}}$$

We define tail kurtosis to be the excess version of this statistic. That is, we subtract a constant so that normal random variables have zero kurtosis:

$$\text{Tail kurtosis} = \frac{U_{0.05} - L_{0.05}}{U_{0.5} - L_{0.5}} - 10 \exp\left\{ -\frac{1}{2}\Phi^{-1}(0.05)^2 \right\}$$

where $\Phi^{-1}(x)$ is the standard normal quantile function.

Along similar lines, we define tail skewness as the following measure of asymmetry between tails:

$$\text{Tail skewness} = \frac{U_{0.05} + L_{0.05} - 2M}{U_{0.5} - L_{0.5}}$$

where M is the median.

In Figure 3A.1, we show the kurtosis (top-right panel) and tail kurtosis (bottom-right panel) for Equities All U.S. over the full 1927–2017 sample period, for three subsamples, and for 10 industry portfolios for the 1927–2017 period also. Both kurtosis and tail kurtosis are much lower with volatility scaling, which is expected since we have already shown that both the left and right tails are thinned by volatility scaling.

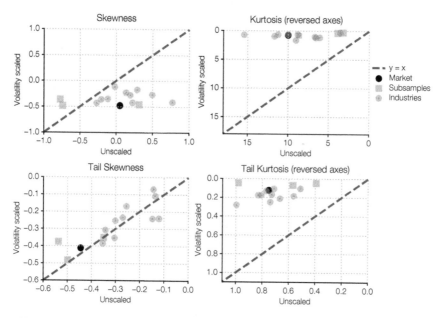

FIGURE 3A.1 Skewness and kurtosis for Equities All U.S. (1926–2017). This figure compares unscaled and volatility-scaled (exponentially weighted, 20-day half-life) excess returns for Equities All U.S. full sample (black dots), subsamples (grey squares), and 10 industries full sample (grey dots). For both skewness (left panel) and kurtosis (right panel), observations above the dashed diagonal line correspond to a situation where volatility scaling improves the statistic (using reversed axes for kurtosis). Both statistics are based on a rolling one-month (30 calendar days) evaluation frequency. To facilitate comparison, both the unscaled and volatility-scaled returns are shown at 10 percent full-sample volatility.

The results for skewness (top-left panel) are more mixed, with better (less negative) skewness in two of the three subsample periods, but worse skewness in the remaining subsample, the full sample, and the 10 industry portfolios. The tail skewness (bottom-left panel) is fairly similar for unscaled and volatility-scaled returns, in line with earlier findings that the left and right tail are reduced similarly when volatility scaling. As we argued before, we believe investors likely care about the left tail much more than the right tail (for a given Sharpe ratio), rendering skewness or tail skewness (which are impacted by both) less useful risk metrics.

In Figure 3A.2, we repeat the exercise for the 50 futures and forwards studied in this chapter. Kurtosis and tail kurtosis are much reduced with volatility scaling, while the results for skewness and tail skewness are mixed. This mirrors the results of the Equities All U.S. shown in Figure 3A.1.

Finally, in Figure 3A.3, we look at drawdown plots for Equities All U.S. (top panel), the balanced portfolio (middle panel), and the risk parity

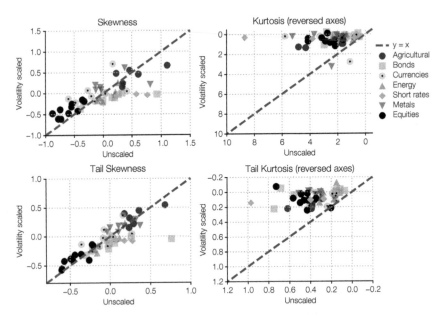

FIGURE 3A.2 Skewness and kurtosis for futures and forwards (1988–2017). This figure compares unscaled and volatility-scaled (exponentially weighted, 20-day half-life) returns for 50 global futures and forwards markets, where different sectors are represented by different shapes. For both skewness (left panel) and kurtosis (right panel), observations above the dashed diagonal line correspond to a situation where volatility scaling improves the statistic (using reversed axes for kurtosis). Both statistics are based on a rolling one-month (21 weekdays) evaluation frequency. To facilitate comparison, both the unscaled and volatility-scaled returns are shown at 10 percent full-sample volatility.

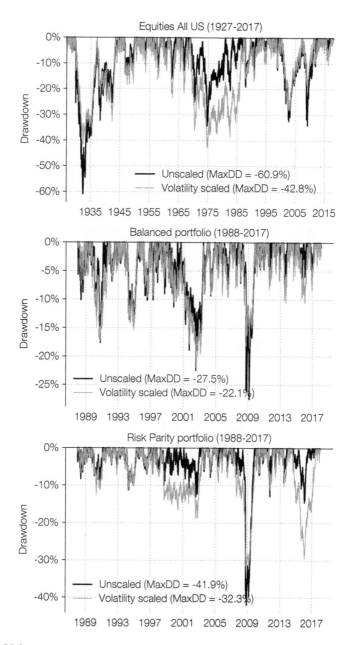

FIGURE 3A.3 Drawdown plot for Equities All U.S., Balanced portfolio, and Risk Parity portfolio. This figure compares the unscaled and volatility-scaled (exponentially weighted, 20-day half-life) drawdown plot for Equities All U.S. (1927–2017), the 60–40 equity-bond balanced portfolio (1988–2017), and the 25-25-25-25 equity-bond-credit-commodities risk parity portfolio (1988–2017).

portfolio (bottom panel). The drawdown level at a given point in time is determined by comparing the total return index level (cumulative return since the start) to the maximum level achieved up to that point in time (the high-water mark):

$$\text{Drawdown}_t = \frac{\text{Index}_t}{\max_{s \leq t} \text{Index}_s} - 1$$

In all three cases, the maximum drawdown (reported in the legend) is substantially reduced with volatility scaling: from to –60.9 percent to –42.8 percent for Equities All U.S. (top panel), from –28.1 percent to –22.2 percent for the balanced portfolio, and from –42.1 percent to –32.1 percent for the risk parity portfolio. Volatility scaling particularly reduced the drawdown during the Great Depression in the 1930s and during the 2007–2009 Global Financial Crisis. That said, (maximum) drawdown is not our preferred risk metric, because it is derived from a single realized return path and as such is not a robust metric.

APPENDIX 3B: AUTOCORRELATION OF VARIANCE

To further illustrate that equity volatility clusters, we show in Figure 3.B1 (left panel) the autocorrelation of the monthly squared volatility (i.e., variance) of daily returns.[26] The variance of adjacent months is around 0.6 correlated over the full (1926–2017) sample period. The correlation slowly decays for additional lags, and is around 0.2 for months a year apart. Of the three subsamples considered, the middle (1958–1987) stands out as having much less autocorrelation in the monthly variances. As was already visible in Figure 3.1, the middle subsample corresponds to a period with fewer extreme bursts in volatility in the first place. In Figure 3B.1 (right panel), we show the partial autocorrelation, measuring how predictive the lag k variance is for the current month, after taking into account the effect of lags 1 to $k-1$. Most of the predictive power is captured by lag 1.

In Figure 3B.2, we repeat the above exercise including bonds for the 1962–2017 period, for which we have (proxy) daily bond returns. Bond variance is much more persistent, and in fact the autocorrelation only slightly falls from lag 3 to 12. This is just another manifestation of the various prolonged volatility regimes the bond market has experienced, which we discussed earlier. In contrast, equity markets experience volatility clusters of, say, half a year, but do not exhibit the prolonged regimes the bond market experiences.

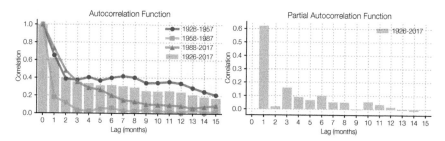

FIGURE 3B.1 Persistence of monthly variance for Equities All U.S. (1926–2017). The figure shows the autocorrelation (left panel) and partial autocorrelation (right panel) of the non-overlapping monthly variance of daily Equities All U.S. excess returns for the full sample period (1926–2017), and the autocorrelation also for the three 30-year subsample periods.

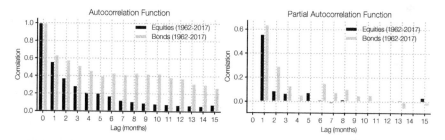

FIGURE 3B.2 Persistence of monthly U.S. equity and bond variance (1962–2017). The figure shows the autocorrelation (left panel) and partial autocorrelation (right panel) of the monthly variance of daily bond (U.S., proxied from yield data) and Equities All U.S. excess returns for the 1962–2017 period.

REFERENCES

Andersen, T., T. Bollerslev, F. Diebold, and P. Labys (2003). "Modeling and Forecasting Realized Volatility," *Econometrica*, 71(2), 579–625.

Asness, C., A. Frazzini, and L. Pedersen (2012). "Leverage Aversion and Risk Parity," *Financial Analysts Journal*, 68(1), 47–59.

Asvanunt, A., L. Nielsen, and D. Villalon (2015). "Working Your Tail Off: Active Strategies Versus Direct Hedging," *Journal of Investing*, 24(2), 134–145.

Barroso, P., and P. Santa-Clara (2015). "Momentum Has Its Moments," *Journal of Financial Economics*, 116(1), 111–120.

Bekaert, G., and G. Wu (2000). "Asymmetric Volatility and Risk in Equity Markets," *Review of Financial Studies*, 13(1), 1–42.

Black, F. (1976). "Studies of Stock Price Volatility Changes," *Proceedings from the American Statistical Association Business and Economic Statistics Section*, 177–181.

Bollerslev, T., B. Hood, J. Huss, and L. Pedersen (2018). "Risk Everywhere: Modeling and Managing Volatility," working paper.

Cook, M., E. Hoyle, M. Sargaison, D. Taylor, and O. Van Hemert (2017). "The Best Strategies for the Worst Crises," Man Group working paper.

Christie, A. (1982). "The Stochastic Behavior of Common Stock Variances: Value, Leverage and Interest Rate Effects," *Journal of Financial Economics*, 10(4), 407–432.

Dachraoui, K. (2018). "On the Optimality of Target Volatility Strategies," *Journal of Portfolio Management*, 44(5), 58–67.

Daniel, K., and T. Moskowitz (2016). "Momentum Crashes," *Journal of Financial Economics*, 122(2), 221–247.

Dopfel, F., and S. Ramkumar (2013). "Managed Volatility Strategies: Applications to Investment Policy," *Journal of Portfolio Management*, 40(1), 27–39.

Engle, R (1982). "Autoregressive Conditional Heteroskedasticity with Estimates of the Variance of UK Inflation," *Econometrica*, 50, 987–1008.

Fleming, J., C. Kirby, and B. Ostdiek (2001). "The Economic Value of Volatility Timing," *Journal of Finance*, 56(1), 329–352.

Fleming, J., C. Kirby, and B. Ostdiek (2003). "The Economic Value of Volatility Timing Using 'Realized' Volatility," *Journal of Financial Economics*, 67(3), 474–509.

Granger, N., D. Greenig, C. Harvey, S. Rattray, and D. Zou (2014). "Rebalancing Risk," AHL working paper. Available on SSRN at https://ssrn.com/abstract=2488552.

Harvey, Campbell R., Edward Hoyle, Russell Korgaonkar, Sandy Rattray, Matthew Sargaison, and Otto Van Hemert (2018, Fall). "The Impact of Volatility Targeting," *Journal of Portfolio Management*, 45(1), 14–33. DOI: https://doi.org/10.3905/jpm.2018.45.1.014.

Haydon, K. (2018). "Volatility Is Back: Better to Target Returns or Target Risk?," Man Group working paper.

Hocquard, A., S. Ng, and N. Papageorgiou (2013). "A Constant-Volatility Framework for Managing Tail Risk," *Journal of Portfolio Management*, 39(2), 28–40.

Hogg, R. (1972). "More Light on the Kurtosis and Related Statistics," *Journal of the American Statistical Association*, 67(338), 422–424.

Moreira, A., and T. Muir (2017). "Volatility Managed Portfolios," *Journal of Finance*, 72(4), 1611–1644.

Noureldin, D., N. Shephard, and K. Sheppard (2012). "Multivariate High-Frequency-Based Volatility (HEAVY) Models," *Journal of Applied Econometrics*, 27(6), 907–933.

CHAPTER 4

Strategic Rebalancing

INTRODUCTION

The previous chapter established that an active portfolio construction technique, volatility targeting, was particularly effective for risk assets in reducing downside exposure. There are two additional techniques that we will examine: rebalancing and drawdown control.[1]

We cover rebalancing in this chapter. Almost all investors rebalance their portfolios. Rebalancing is one of the most widely accepted portfolio management tools. However, we will argue that rebalancing is poorly understood. If implemented in a naïve, mechanical fashion, it can *increase* the risk of your portfolio. For example, if the equity market is in a prolonged selloff, rebalancing will be purchasing additional equity all the way down—increasing the size of the drawdown.

That said, a pure buy-and-hold portfolio has the drawback that the asset mix tends to drift over time, making it untenable for investors who seek diversification. As illustrated in Figure 4.1 for a U.S. stock-bond portfolio, an initial 60 percent of capital allocated to stocks in 1927 drifts to a 76 percent allocation by 1929, a 32 percent allocation by 1932, and a level close to 100 percent over time, as stocks tend to outperform bonds over the long run. So, obviously, an unrebalanced portfolio will eventually lead to the portfolio being undiversified by being concentrated in the high risk–high expected return asset.

However, a stock-bond portfolio that regularly rebalances tends to underperform a buy-and-hold portfolio at times of continued underperformance of one of the assets.

Using a simple two-period model, we explain the main intuition behind this effect: Under a mechanical rebalancing strategy, such as a monthly or quarterly reallocation toward fixed portfolio weights, winning asset

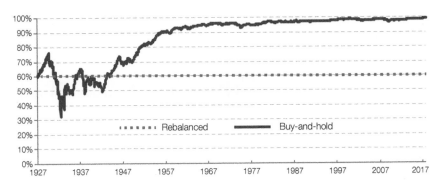

FIGURE 4.1 Allocation to stocks for a monthly-rebalanced and buy-and-hold portfolio. The figure shows the percent allocated to stocks for a monthly-rebalanced and a buy-and-hold portfolio. In both cases, at the start 60 percent of capital is allocated to stocks and 40 percent to bonds. We use monthly U.S. data from January 1927 to December 2017. The stock data are from Kenneth French's website. The bond data are from the Federal Reserve, prepended with Global Financial Data (GFD).

classes are sold and losers are bought. If winners continue to outperform, that detracts from the portfolio's overall performance. If losers continue to underperform, that also detracts from the portfolio's overall performance. As stocks typically have more volatile returns than bonds, relative returns tend to be driven by stocks. During crises, when markets are often trending, this can lead to substantially larger drawdowns than a buy-and-hold strategy. Hence, of particular interest are episodes with continued negative (absolute and relative) stock performance, such as the 2007–2009 Global Financial Crisis.

In Figure 4.2, we contrast monthly rebalanced and buy-and-hold cumulative performance over the financial crisis period. Both start with an initial 60–40 stock-bond capital allocation at the start of the evaluation period (at the end of December 2016). The maximum drawdown of the monthly rebalanced portfolio is 1.2 times (or 5 percentage points) worse than that of the buy-and-hold portfolio, right at the time when the financial markets' turmoil is greatest.

In earlier work, Granger et al. (2014) formally show that rebalancing is similar to starting with a buy-and-hold portfolio and adding a short straddle (selling both a call and a put option) on the relative value of the portfolio assets. The option-like payoff to rebalancing induces *negative* convexity by magnifying drawdowns when there are pronounced divergences in asset returns.[2]

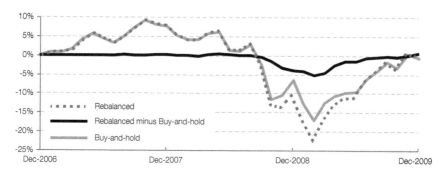

FIGURE 4.2 Performance of monthly-rebalanced and buy-and-hold portfolio (2007–2009). The figure shows the cumulative return for a monthly-rebalanced and buy-and-hold performance for the 2007–2009 financial crisis period, as well as the difference. Both portfolios start with an initial 60–40 stock-bond capital allocation in January 2007.

We show that time-series momentum (or trend) strategies, applied to futures on the same stock and bond markets, are natural complements to a rebalanced portfolio. This is because the trend payoff tends to mimic that of a long straddle option position, or exhibits *positive* convexity (see Chapter 1 and Martin and Zou 2012).[3]

In this chapter, our main analysis is for the 1960–2017 period, which includes the bond bear market of the 1960s and 1970s, but omits the different bond regime before 1960. As was mentioned in Chapter 3, the bond market was structurally different in the pre-1960 period and was characterized by unusually low volatility, reflecting the intervention of both the Treasury and the Federal Reserve. We evaluate how 1-, 3-, and 12-month trend strategies perform during the five worst drawdowns for the 60–40 stock-bond portfolio. Allocating 10 percent to a trend strategy and 90 percent to a 60–40 monthly-rebalanced portfolio improves the average drawdown by about 5 percentage points, compared to a 100 percent allocation to a 60–40 monthly-rebalanced portfolio. The trend allocation has no adverse impact on the average return over our sample period. That is, while one would normally expect a drag on the overall (long-term) performance when allocating to a defensive strategy, in our sample, the trend-following premium earned offsets the cost (or insurance premium) paid.[4]

An alternative to a trend allocation is actively timing and sizing rebalancing trades, which we label *strategic rebalancing*. We first consider a range of popular heuristic rules, varying the rebalancing frequency, using thresholds, and trading only partially back to the 60–40 asset mix. Such heuristic rules reduce the average maximum drawdown level for the five crises considered by up to 1 percentage point. However, using strategic rebalancing rules based on either the past stock or past stock-bond relative returns gives improvements of 2 to 3 percentage points.

The literature on rebalancing dates back to at least Perold and Sharpe (1988).[5] Our main contribution is that we show that the negative convexity induced by rebalancing is effectively countered with a trend exposure, which exhibits positive convexity and can be either implemented directly via an allocation to a trend product, or alternatively with a strategic trend-based rebalancing rule. The five worst drawdowns for a 60–40 portfolio over the 1960–2017 period considered are materially reduced.

To open this chapter, we show that the return difference between a rebalanced and a buy-and-hold portfolio is concave in the relative stock-bond performance, both analytically in a stylized two-period model and empirically for the 1960–2017 period. Then, we show that the return to a trend strategy applied to stocks and bonds is convex in the relative stock-bond performance. We illustrate that a modest allocation to a trend strategy can effectively counter the negative convexity induced by rebalancing and, as such, reduce drawdowns. We explore different heuristics as well as trend-based strategic rebalancing rules and show that the strategic rebalancing rules are particularly helpful for reducing drawdowns for a 60–40 stock-bond portfolio. Finally, we compare a direct allocation to trend and an indirect trend exposure obtained with a trend-based strategic rebalancing rule.

COMPARING REBALANCED AND BUY-AND-HOLD PORTFOLIO RETURNS

The notion that 60–40 equity/bond is a good asset mix has been around for decades (see e.g., Ambachtsheer [1987] for an early reference).[6] From a general equilibrium point of view this makes sense, as the ratio of equity and bond value in, for example, the United States has been around 60:40 over the past decades, even though this ratio is subject to considerable variability.[7] Large pension plans and sovereign wealth funds often explicitly target a fixed 60–40 asset mix. For example, the Norwegian Government Pension Fund Global in 2007 adopted a 60 percent target allocation to equities, with the remainder mostly invested in fixed income (see e.g., Chambers, Dimson, and Ilmanen 2012). In this section, we start by considering a two-period model to illustrate the difference between monthly rebalancing to a constant asset mix (*Rebal*) and buy-and-hold (*Hold*).

Writing the return for stocks and bonds in period $t = 1, 2$ as R_t^S and R_t^B respectively, the return of a portfolio that rebalances between period 1 and 2 to allocations w^S and w^B for stocks and bonds is:

$$1 + R^{REBAL} = \left(1 + w^S R_1^S + w^B R_1^B\right)\left(1 + w^S R_2^S + w^B R_2^B\right) \quad (4.1)$$

For a portfolio that starts with the same weights as above, but does not rebalance after period 1, we get:

$$1 + R^{HOLD} = w^S\left(1 + R_1^S\right)\left(1 + R_2^S\right) + w^B\left(1 + R_1^B\right)\left(1 + R_2^B\right) \quad (4.2)$$

We can rewrite the return for stocks and bonds in terms of the average returns $R_t^{Avg} = 0.5 R_t^S + 0.5 R_t^B$, and the stock-bond return difference, $\kappa_t = R_t^S - R_t^B$:

$$R_t^S = R_t^{Avg} + 0.5\kappa_t \quad (4.3)$$

$$R_t^B = R_t^{Avg} - 0.5\kappa_t \quad (4.4)$$

Substituting in these terms in above *Rebal* and *Hold* return expressions, taking the difference, using the fact that the allocations sum to one, and rearranging gives:

$$R^{REBAL} - R^{HOLD} = -w^S w^B \kappa_1 \kappa_2 \quad (4.5)$$

So, if the relative performance is trending (κ_1, κ_2 are either both positive or both negative), then the rebalanced portfolio underperforms. Intuitively, rebalancing means selling winners, and if winners continue to outperform, that detracts from performance. And vice versa, if there is reversal of relative performance, then the rebalanced portfolio outperforms.[8,9]

Notice some special cases. For an equally weighted portfolio (50 percent of capital allocated to stocks and 50 percent to bonds), the *Rebal-Hold* return difference is $-0.25\kappa_1\kappa_2$, while for the 60–40 stock-bond portfolio it is slightly less: $-0.24\kappa_1\kappa_2$. In case of a 100 percent allocation to either stocks or bonds, we have a zero return difference, which is intuitive, as there can be no drift in the relative allocation for a one-asset portfolio.

Also notice that the formula allows us to measure the order of magnitudes. If stocks underperform bonds by 40 percent in both periods 1 and 2 (i.e., $\kappa_1 = \kappa_2 = -40\%$), then a 60–40 rebalanced portfolio has a 3.84 percentage point more negative return than the buy-and-hold portfolio. These numbers roughly correspond to what happened between

October 2007 and February 2009, when stocks were down 50.3 percent (or two periods of –29.5 percent returns, taking into account compounding) and bonds were up 17.9 percent (or two periods of +8.6 percent returns). In Figure 4.1, the *Rebal-Hold* return difference is 5.3 percentage points per February 2009, which is slightly more, as compounding in a setting with more than two periods will exacerbate the rebalancing effect.

In a multi-period setting, the return difference between a monthly rebalanced and buy-and-hold portfolio is similar to that of a short straddle written on the relative performance of stocks and bonds.[10] Granger et al. (2014) make this point and provide both analytical expressions and simulation results.[11]

For our empirical analysis, we use we use monthly value-weighted returns of firms listed on the NYSE, AMEX, and NASDAQ from Kenneth French's website.[12] For bonds, we use U.S. Treasury bond data from the Federal Reserve.[13]

In Figure 4.3, we plot the *Rebal-Hold* return difference when both have a 60–40 stock-bond mix at the start of the period (vertical axis) versus the stock-bond relative return (horizontal axis). Each dot in the figure corresponds to a one-year (rolling 12-month) window, where data run

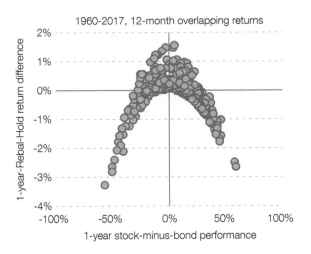

FIGURE 4.3 *Rebal*-minus-*Hold* versus stock-minus-bond one-year returns. The figure shows the return difference of a monthly-rebalanced versus a buy-and-hold portfolio, when both have a 60–40 stock-bond mix at the start of the one-year evaluation period (vertical axis) versus the stock-bond relative return over the same one-year period (horizontal axis). Each dot in the figure corresponds to a one-year (rolling 12-month) window, where data run from January 1960 to December 2017.

from January 1960 to December 2017.[14] Indeed, the *Rebal-Hold* return difference looks a lot like the payoff of a short straddle on the relative performance—this illustrates the negative convexity.

IMPACT OF A SIMPLE TREND STRATEGY ALLOCATION

We define a simple time-series momentum (trend) signal, similar to what we developed in Chapters 1 and 2, for asset k, as the return over the past N months, divided by a volatility estimate which we set equal to the standard deviation of the past 12 monthly returns and the square-root of N to make it approximately unit standard deviation:[15]

$$mom_{t-1}^k(N) = \frac{\sum_{i=1}^{N} \tilde{R}_{t-i}^k}{\sigma_{t-1}^k \sqrt{N}} \tag{4.6}$$

For the asset returns, we will use the stock and bond data used before, but in excess of one-month Treasury bill returns (denoted by a tilde), which is a proxy of the return on an unfunded futures contract on the stock or bond index. We cannot use stock and bond futures data directly, as they are not available as far back as 1960.

We consider a number of trend strategies, combining trend signals for stocks, bonds, and a long-stocks–short-bonds spread position. Equation 4.7 illustrates how we determine the strategy return for the case of putting equal risk on stocks and bonds trend (which we feature in Panel C of Figure 4.4). We set an ex ante reference volatility for monthly returns, σ^{Ref}, that leads to about 15–20 percent annualized realized volatility for the strategy returns.[16] We conservatively assume that 20 percent of capital needs to be posted for margin and earns no interest, while the remaining 80 percent earns the T-bill return, R_t^F. So we get the following expression for the strategy returns of an N-month trend strategy:

$$R_t^{mom(N)} = 0.5mom_{t-1}^S(N)\frac{\sigma^{Ref}}{\sigma_{t-1}^S}\tilde{R}_t^S + 0.5mom_{t-1}^B(N)\frac{\sigma^{Ref}}{\sigma_{t-1}^B}\tilde{R}_t^B + 0.8R_t^F \tag{4.7}$$

Other strategies that we feature, for example 100 percent equity, are defined analogously.

We introduce two more features so that the simple trend strategy has more bounded long and short positions in stock and bond futures. While the trend model is similar to the one introduced in Chapter 1, these

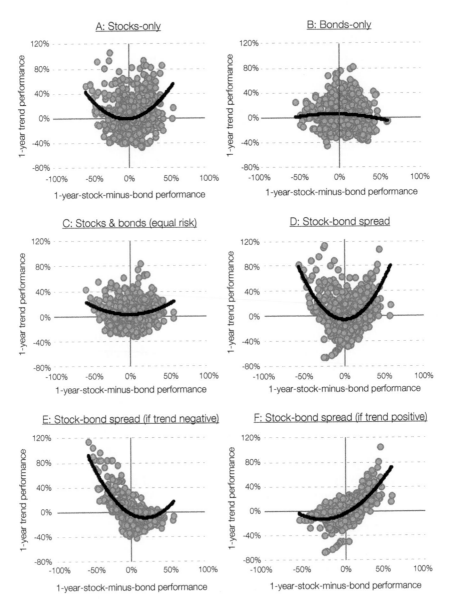

FIGURE 4.4 Three-month trend versus stock-minus-bond one-year return.
One-year (rolling 12-month) performance of various three-month trend strategies
(vertical axis) versus the one-year relative stock-bond performance (horizontal axis)
for the period 1960 to 2017. The solid line represents the best quadratic fit.

additional features are consistent with how practitioners implement trend strategies. First, we put a floor and cap on the signal value of −1 and +1 respectively. Second, for the annualized security volatility used in the second equation, we use a floor of 10 percent in case of stocks and the stock-bond spread asset, and 5 percent in case of bonds, which corresponds to about two-thirds of the full-sample realized value. This will limit the leverage at times of low realized asset volatilities. Neither of these additional features changes the return dynamics much, but they do achieve more bounded positions.[17]

For the trend strategy, implemented with futures, we assume a transaction cost of 1bp (0.01 percent) of the traded notional for equities and 0.5bp for bonds (an estimate for the current trading conditions; see Chapter 3). For rebalancing of the 60–40 target portfolio, implemented with cash equity and bond holdings, we follow a recent Norges Bank (2018) report and use 30bp for equities and 13bp for bonds (reflective of the 2015–2016 period).

In Figure 4.4, we plot the one-year return of various trend strategies (vertical axis) versus the one-year relative stock-bond return (horizontal axis), with the best quadratic fit added as a solid line. We use three-month trend signals, but we confirm results are similar for 1- and 12-month formulations. We consider six trend formulations in Panels A–F, varying the traded asset in the trend program: stocks only (A), bonds only (B), stocks and bonds with equal risk weight (C), a long-short stock-bond spread position (D), stock-bond spread, but only taking positions if the trend is negative (E), stock-bond spread, but only taking positions if the trend is positive (F).[18]

In case of a stock-bond spread trend strategy (Panel D), a very pronounced smile pattern is visible, which is expected given the known convexity property of trend strategy returns when evaluated against the returns of the traded asset (i.e., the horizontal axis in all panels is the stock-bond spread return). Also, for stock-only (Panel A) and stocks and bond, equal risk (Panel C), which follows Equation 4.7, the trend strategy returns are convex, which is unsurprising, given that the stock and stock-bond excess returns are 0.9 correlated over the 1960–2017 period (stock return variance dominates the stock-bond return spread). As such, a trend strategy with a stock weighting looks like a natural complement to a rebalancing strategy; as we have shown before, the *Rebal-Hold* return difference displays negative convexity. A bond-only trend strategy (Panel B) does not show a clear relation against the stock-bond relative return. Finally, we consider a stock-bond spread trend strategy that trades only in case of negative (Panel E) and positive (Panel F) trends. The payoff of these strategies mimics not so much a long straddle (put plus call), but rather that of just a put (in case of negative trend) and call (in case of positive trend).

Given their seemingly complementary return profile in most cases considered, we next combine a monthly rebalanced portfolio (90 percent) and the various trend strategies (10 percent). In Appendix 4B, we also consider combining a 100 percent allocation to the monthly rebalanced portfolio with a 10 percent trend strategy, financed by borrowing at the short rate. We are particularly interested in whether the addition of a trend reduces drawdowns. In Figure 4.5, we depict the drawdown level for the monthly-rebalanced 60–40 portfolio, computed as the return from the peak (highest cumulative return up to that point in time). On five occasions, the drawdown is worse than −15 percent, where the trough months are June 1970 ("Back to Earth day" for tech stocks), September 1974 (Oil crisis/Yom Kippur War, collapse of Bretton Woods, Watergate), November 1987 ("Black Monday," program trading), June 2002 (Tech bubble burst), and February 2009 (Global Financial Crisis).[19] In subsequent analyses, we will report the change in the drawdown level at these five worst moments for the 60–40 portfolio.

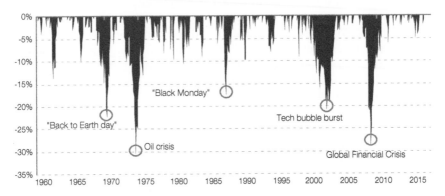

FIGURE 4.5 Drawdown level of a monthly rebalanced 60–40 portfolio. The figure shows the drawdown level for a monthly rebalanced 60–40 stock-bond allocation. Data are monthly from 1960 to 2017.

In Table 4.1, we report how a 90 percent monthly-rebalanced 60–40 portfolio (*Rebal*) plus 10 percent allocation to a trend strategy performs when compared with the benchmark of 100 percent *Rebal*. We cover the same six trend variations as before in Figure 4.4, and look at 1-, 3-, and 12-month trend windows. For trend systems applied to stocks-only (Panel A)

TABLE 4.1 *Rebal* plus trend performance statistics. We contrast a 100 percent allocation to a monthly-rebalanced portfolio with a 60–40 stock-bond capital allocation to one where 10 percent of the portfolio is replaced with an allocation to various 1-, 3-, and 12-month trend specifications. Performance statistics reported on are the average stock, bond, and total allocation (block 1), the annualized notional trading (as percentage of the total portfolio value) in the 60–40 rebalanced portfolio, stock and bond futures, as well as annualized trading costs (block 2), average return, standard deviation, the ratio of these two (not deducting the short rate), and the Sharpe ratio (which deducts the short rate) (block 3), and the change in the drawdown level for the five worst drawdowns (ΔDD) at the trough, compared to a 100 percent allocation to the monthly-rebalanced 60–40 portfolio. The data are from 1960 to 2017.

A: Trend applied to stocks-only

	Rebal (100%)	Rebal (90%) 1m trend (10%)	Rebal (90%) 3m trend (10%)	Rebal (90%) 12m trend (10%)
Stock allocation (avg)	60.0%	57.7%	60.1%	64.5%
Bond allocation (avg)	40.0%	36.0%	36.0%	36.0%
Total allocation (avg)	100.0%	93.7%	96.1%	100.5%
Rebal trade (ann)	10.2%	9.1%	9.1%	9.1%
Stock fut. trade (ann)	0.0%	207.3%	106.7%	45.1%
Bond fut. trade (ann)	0.0%	0.0%	0.0%	0.0%
Cost estimate (ann)	4.4 bps	6.0 bps	5.0 bps	4.4 bps
Return, (ann)	9.1%	9.0%	9.1%	9.6%
Volatility (ann)	9.8%	8.7%	9.1%	9.7%
Ret./Vol (ann)	0.92	1.03	1.00	0.99
Sharpe ratio (ann)	0.47	0.52	0.51	0.53
ΔDD Jun 1970	0.0%	3.6%	1.9%	5.4%
ΔDD Sep 1974	0.0%	9.7%	8.9%	9.8%
ΔDD Nov1987	0.0%	4.9%	–0.8%	–3.0%
ΔDD Sep 2002	0.0%	4.2%	4.2%	6.0%
ΔDD Feb 2009	0.0%	6.1%	7.9%	9.0%
ΔDD average	0.0%	5.7%	4.4%	5.4%

B: Trend applied to bonds-only

	Rebal (100%)	Rebal (90%) 1m trend (10%)	Rebal (90%) 3m trend (10%)	Rebal (90%) 12m trend (10%)
Stock allocation (avg)	60.0%	54.0%	54.0%	54.0%
Bond allocation (avg)	40.0%	39.9%	41.7%	45.3%
Total allocation (avg)	100.0%	93.9%	95.7%	99.3%
Rebal trade (ann)	10.2%	9.1%	9.1%	9.1%
Stock fut. trade (ann)	0.0%	0.0%	0.0%	0.0%
Bond fut. trade (ann)	0.0%	438.0%	245.4%	111.6%
Cost estimate (ann)	4.4 bps	6.1 bps	5.2 bps	4.5 bps
Return, (ann)	9.1%	9.4%	9.1%	9.3%
Volatility (ann)	9.8%	9.2%	9.2%	9.2%
Ret./Vol (ann)	0.92	1.02	0.99	1.01
Sharpe ratio (ann)	0.47	0.54	0.50	0.53
ΔDD Jun 1970	0.0%	5.1%	3.5%	5.6%
ΔDD Sep 1974	0.0%	6.0%	5.0%	6.2%
ΔDD Nov1987	0.0%	0.9%	0.8%	1.1%
ΔDD Sep 2002	0.0%	6.4%	5.2%	7.7%
ΔDD Feb 2009	0.0%	2.1%	3.8%	6.0%
ΔDD average	0.0%	4.1%	3.6%	5.3%

(Continued)

TABLE 4.1 (*Continued*)

C: Trend applied to stocks & bonds (equal risk)

	Rebal (100%)	Rebal (90%) 1m trend (10%)	Rebal (90%) 3m trend (10%)	Rebal (90%) 12m trend (10%)
Stock allocation (avg)	60.0%	55.8%	57.0%	59.3%
Bond allocation (avg)	40.0%	37.9%	38.8%	40.7%
Total allocation (avg)	100.0%	93.8%	95.9%	99.9%
Rebal trade (ann)	10.2%	9.1%	9.1%	9.1%
Stock fut. trade (ann)	0.0%	103.7%	53.4%	22.6%
Bond fut. trade (ann)	0.0%	219.0%	122.7%	55.8%
Cost estimate (ann)	4.4 bps	6.1 bps	5.1 bps	4.4 bps
Return, (ann)	9.1%	9.2%	9.1%	9.4%
Volatility (ann)	9.8%	8.8%	9.0%	9.3%
Ret./Vol (ann)	0.92	1.04	1.01	1.02
Sharpe ratio (ann)	0.47	0.54	0.51	0.54
ΔDD Jun 1970	0.0%	4.4%	2.7%	5.6%
ΔDD Sep 1974	0.0%	7.9%	7.0%	8.0%
ΔDD Nov1987	0.0%	2.9%	0.0%	-1.0%
ΔDD Sep 2002	0.0%	5.4%	4.7%	6.8%
ΔDD Feb 2009	0.0%	4.4%	6.5%	7.6%
ΔDD average	0.0%	5.0%	4.2%	5.4%

D: Trend applied to stock-bond spread

	Rebal (100%)	Rebal (90%) 1m trend (10%)	Rebal (90%) 3m trend (10%)	Rebal (90%) 12m trend (10%)
Stock allocation (avg)	60.0%	57.2%	59.1%	62.6%
Bond allocation (avg)	40.0%	32.8%	30.9%	27.4%
Total allocation (avg)	100.0%	90.0%	90.0%	90.0%
Rebal trade (ann)	10.2%	9.1%	9.1%	9.1%
Stock fut. trade (ann)	0.0%	200.1%	110.8%	49.7%
Bond fut. trade (ann)	0.0%	200.1%	110.8%	49.7%
Cost estimate (ann)	4.4 bps	6.9 bps	5.6 bps	4.7 bps
Return, (ann)	9.1%	9.0%	8.9%	9.1%
Volatility (ann)	9.8%	8.8%	9.0%	9.4%
Ret./Vol (ann)	0.92	1.02	0.99	0.97
Sharpe ratio (ann)	0.47	0.51	0.49	0.49
ΔDD Jun 1970	0.0%	3.9%	1.9%	4.9%
ΔDD Sep 1974	0.0%	7.9%	7.4%	6.9%
ΔDD Nov1987	0.0%	0.7%	-3.9%	-4.5%
ΔDD Sep 2002	0.0%	5.1%	6.2%	7.5%
ΔDD Feb 2009	0.0%	7.1%	8.2%	8.9%
ΔDD average	0.0%	4.9%	4.0%	4.7%

E: Trend applied to stock-bond, negative only

	Rebal (100%)	Rebal (90%) 1m trend (10%)	Rebal (90%) 3m trend (10%)	Rebal (90%) 12m trend (10%)
Stock allocation (avg)	60.0%	48.6%	49.2%	50.4%
Bond allocation (avg)	40.0%	41.4%	40.8%	39.6%
Total allocation (avg)	100.0%	90.0%	90.0%	90.0%
Rebal trade (ann)	10.2%	9.1%	9.1%	9.1%
Stock fut. trade (ann)	0.0%	89.6%	45.0%	18.0%
Bond fut. trade (ann)	0.0%	89.6%	45.0%	18.0%
Cost estimate (ann)	4.4 bps	5.3 bps	4.6 bps	4.2 bps
Return, (ann)	9.1%	8.4%	8.5%	8.6%
Volatility (ann)	9.8%	8.1%	8.0%	8.2%
Ret./Vol (ann)	0.92	1.04	1.06	1.04
Sharpe ratio (ann)	0.47	0.49	0.51	0.50
ΔDD Jun 1970	0.0%	5.2%	4.6%	6.2%
ΔDD Sep 1974	0.0%	9.3%	9.6%	8.5%
ΔDD Nov1987	0.0%	2.3%	2.3%	1.8%
ΔDD Sep 2002	0.0%	8.0%	7.9%	8.8%
ΔDD Feb 2009	0.0%	8.2%	10.7%	10.4%
ΔDD average	0.0%	6.6%	7.0%	7.1%

F: Trend applied to stock-bond, positive only

	Rebal (100%)	Rebal (90%) 1m trend (10%)	Rebal (90%) 3m trend (10%)	Rebal (90%) 12m trend (10%)
Stock allocation (avg)	60.0%	62.6%	63.9%	66.2%
Bond allocation (avg)	40.0%	27.4%	26.1%	23.8%
Total allocation (avg)	100.0%	90.0%	90.0%	90.0%
Rebal trade (ann)	10.2%	9.1%	9.1%	9.1%
Stock fut. trade (ann)	0.0%	110.5%	65.8%	31.7%
Bond fut. trade (ann)	0.0%	110.5%	65.8%	31.7%
Cost estimate (ann)	4.4 bps	5.6 bps	4.9 bps	4.4 bps
Return, (ann)	9.1%	9.1%	8.9%	9.1%
Volatility (ann)	9.8%	9.5%	9.8%	10.0%
Ret./Vol (ann)	0.92	0.95	0.91	0.91
Sharpe ratio (ann)	0.47	0.49	0.45	0.46
ΔDD Jun 1970	0.0%	1.5%	0.2%	1.5%
ΔDD Sep 1974	0.0%	2.0%	1.4%	1.8%
ΔDD Nov1987	0.0%	0.1%	-4.4%	-4.5%
ΔDD Sep 2002	0.0%	-0.3%	0.8%	1.3%
ΔDD Feb 2009	0.0%	1.7%	0.4%	1.3%
ΔDD average	0.0%	1.0%	-0.3%	0.3%

and bonds-only (Panel B), the average return is similar to the 9.1 percent of the 100 percent *Rebal* portfolio—but with lower volatility—even though the trend system is applied to just one asset.[20] The drawdowns tend to be less severe, with an average improvement (ΔDD average) ranging from 3.6 percent to 5.7 percent. In case of stocks (Panel A), the notable exception is the drawdown around Black Monday, when a slow, 12-month trend strategy actually exacerbates the drawdown. This drawdown is different than all the others because of its short length. A slower momentum strategy is not reactive enough and misses the turning point.

In case of bonds (Panel B), the average stock allocation is much reduced at 54 percent (versus 60 percent stocks for the 100 percent *Rebal* portfolio) and so the better performance during stock market drawdowns is intuitive, while it is noteworthy that the average return is not reduced with the lower stock allocation (the bond trend strategy payoff fully compensates for the reduced equity-premium capture).

In case of stocks and bonds trend, equal risk (Panel C), a 10 percent trend allocation again leads to average returns at least as good as the benchmark and an improved average drawdown level. Also, in particular for 12-month trend, the average allocation to stocks and bonds is close to that of the 60 percent stocks and 40 percent bonds of the benchmark.

In Panel D, we consider trend on the stock-bond spread asset. Note that this will lead to a 90 percent total stock and bond allocation by construction, as the total (stock and bond) allocation from the 10 percent trend strategy is zero. Here, the average return is slightly lower than that of the benchmark. In addition, the drawdown around Black Monday is more impacted in the case of 3- and 12-month trends compared to the specifications considered in Panel A, B, and C. In panels E and F, we consider a version where we only trade on the stock-bond signal if it is negative and positive, respectively. Just trading on negative signals helps for reducing drawdowns, but leads to a much lower stock allocation and also a lower average return compared to the benchmark.

The Sharpe ratios reported in Table 4.1 for strategies with a 10 percent trend allocation range from 0.45 to 0.54, which is similar to the 0.47 Sharpe ratio for the 100 percent *Rebal* baseline case. However, the benefit of the trend allocation is not so much a higher Sharpe ratio, but rather a more benign risk profile with more shallow drawdowns. To illustrate this further, we employ the Goetzmann et al. (2007) performance measure that controls for higher moments. This measure is the annualized certainty-equivalent return (CEQ) in a power utility framework and so penalizes negative skewness and excess kurtosis relative to the Sharpe ratio metric. Appendix 4A considers four different risk-aversion parameters applied to the results in Panel C of Table 4.1 (see Appendix Table 4A.1, Panels A and B). The results consistently show higher CEQs for the 10 percent to trend allocation. A similar insight can be gained by applying leverage to match the maximum drawdown size of the 100 percent rebalanced portfolio. Our results show that leveraged portfolios with 10 percent allocation to trend have significantly higher returns than the 100 percent rebalanced portfolio (Appendix 4A, Table 4A.1, Panel C).

We checked that allocating 5 percent (rather than the 10 percent considered in Table 4.1) to a trend strategy gives, not surprisingly, about half this reduction in the average drawdown. That is, the impact scales about proportionally with the trend allocation (for modest values).

One could argue that part of the improvement in the drawdown characteristics is partly due to the divestment of 10 percent of the rebalanced portfolio and partly due to the defensive nature of the 10 percent trend allocation. In Appendix 4B, we show that, when keeping the full 100 percent rebalanced portfolio, the addition of a 10 percent trend investment (in this case financed by borrowing at the short rate) generally improves the drawdowns of the overall portfolio.

In Appendix 4C, we show that the addition of trend has the same beneficial effect on drawdowns for the 30–70 stock-bond portfolio, which is much closer to equal risk to stocks and bonds than the 60–40 stock-bond portfolio.

Finally, in Figure 4.6, we contrast the allocation to stocks and bonds (index plus futures) for a monthly rebalanced portfolio with a 60–40 stock-bond capital allocation, a buy-and-hold portfolio that starts with the same allocation mix, and an allocation of 90 percent to the rebalanced portfolio and 10 percent allocation to a 12-month stocks and bonds (equal risk) trend strategy. Because of the signal caps and volatility floors used, the stock futures position is guaranteed to be between –15 percent and +15 percent and the bond futures position is between –30 percent and +30 percent. The *Rebal*-plus-trend combination has a fluctuating stock and bond allocation, but no long-term drift. It has a slight long bias with, on average, a 5.3 percent long stock and a 4.7 percent long bond futures position, coincidentally almost exactly replacing the 10 percent reduction in the 60–40 rebalanced portfolio (see Table 4.1, Panel C).

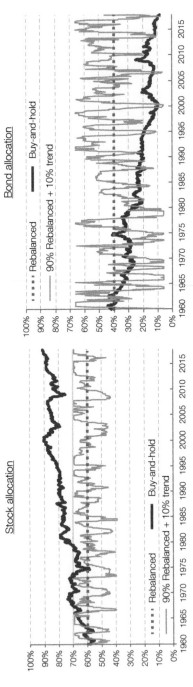

FIGURE 4.6 **Allocation to stocks and bonds for the various portfolios considered.** We show the (index plus futures) allocation to stocks (left panel) and bonds (right panel) for a monthly-rebalanced 60–40 stock-bond portfolio, a buy-and-hold portfolio that starts with the same allocation mix, and a 90 percent monthly-rebalanced and 10 percent 12-month (equity and bond, equal risk) trend strategy combination. Data run from 1960 to 2017.

STRATEGIC REBALANCING

We have discussed using an allocation trend strategy to counteract the tendency of rebalanced portfolios to underperform during equity market drawdowns. Now, we will study whether an investor can get similar benefits by smartly timing and sizing rebalancing trades, which we call *strategic rebalancing*. We consider both commonly used heuristics and trend-based rules.

There is a large literature on evaluating heuristic rebalancing rules. Typically, one varies the rebalancing frequency, takes a threshold-based method, or combines these two approaches. Also, rather than rebalancing fully toward the target asset mix, one can rebalance partially and so reduce turnover (and save on trading costs), providing yet another knob to turn. See, for example, Arnott and Lovell (1993) for early work on this topic.[21]

In Table 4.2, we produce statistics for combinations of these oft-used rules, again with our emphasis on whether drawdowns are less severe compared to rebalancing fully back to 60–40 every month (leftmost column). Rebalancing monthly, but only half or a quarter toward 60–40, mostly reduces drawdowns and moreover leads to lower turnover, with rebalancing trades per year of 6.2 percent[22] and 4.2 percent respectively, versus 10.2 percent with a full rebalance each month. The actual transaction cost savings will vary greatly across investors, but for the aforementioned transaction assumptions, the impact is arguably small at 0.4 to 4.4 basis points per annum. Quarterly and annual rebalancing further improves drawdowns, except with the 1987 drawdown (Black Monday), which quickly reversed.[23,24]

Threshold-based rules seem slightly less potent, where we consider rebalancing if the fraction of stocks is outside of the 60 ± 2 percent and 60 ± 4 percent range (but we also considered other ranges, which did not materially improve performance). In all cases, the correlation to the monthly, fully rebalanced strategy is near 1.0 (not reported in the table) and the average return is barely impacted.

Next, we turn our attention to trend-based strategic rebalancing rules. In Table 4.3, we show results when rebalancing is delayed if the stock-bond spread trend is negative, positive, or continues to be in the same direction (i.e., to rebalance only when the trend direction now is in the opposite direction of a month ago, which likely corresponds to a not-so-strong or inconsistent trending environment).[25] In months with no delay, there is a rebalancing halfway toward the 60–40 asset mix (mirroring the middle case considered Table 4.2). The trend direction is determined by comparing the return over the past 1-, 3-, and 12-months to the typical (average) return over 1-, 3-, and 12-month windows.[26]

TABLE 4.2 Rebalancing with frequency and threshold rules. We show results for frequency- (monthly, quarterly, annual) and threshold-based (60±2 percent and 60±4 percent) rebalancing rules. We consider a full, half, or quarter rebalancing toward the 60–40 capital allocation mix. We report in the different blocks: the average and standard deviation of the stock allocation, noting that the bond allocation is 100 percent minus the stock allocation (block 1); the fraction of months with rebal (block 2); the average and annualized amount of rebalancing, and annualized trading costs (block 3); the average and standard deviation of the return, as well as the ratio (block 3); and the change in the drawdown level for the five worst drawdowns (ΔDD) at the trough, compared to a 100 percent allocation to the monthly-rebalanced 60–40 portfolio (block 4). Data are from 1960 to 2017.

	Monthly			Quarterly			Annual			2% threshold			4% threshold		
	Full	Half	Quarter	Full	Half	Quarter	Full	Half	Quarter	Full	Half	Quarter	Full	Half	Quarter
Stock allocation (avg)	60.0%	60.1%	60.2%	60.1%	60.3%	60.6%	60.4%	61.1%	62.2%	60.2%	60.4%	60.5%	60.5%	61.1%	61.4%
Stock allocation (std)	0.0%	0.7%	1.4%	1.3%	1.7%	2.5%	2.9%	3.3%	4.1%	0.9%	1.2%	1.7%	1.7%	1.9%	2.3%
%months rebal	100.0%	100.0%	100.0%	33.3%	33.3%	33.3%	8.3%	8.3%	8.3%	15.8%	23.0%	34.5%	6.6%	9.3%	14.2%
Rebal trade (ann)	10.2%	6.2%	4.2%	6.6%	3.9%	2.5%	3.6%	1.8%	1.1%	5.2%	3.9%	3.1%	3.7%	2.6%	2.1%
Cost estimate (ann)	4.4 bps	2.7 bps	1.8 bps	2.9 bps	1.7 bps	1.1 bps	1.6 bps	0.8 bps	0.5 bps	2.3 bps	1.7 bps	1.4 bps	1.6 bps	1.1 bps	0.9 bps
Return (ann)	9.1%	9.2%	9.2%	9.2%	9.2%	9.2%	9.3%	9.2%	9.1%	9.1%	9.2%	9.2%	9.2%	9.2%	9.2%
Volatility (ann)	9.8%	9.8%	9.8%	9.8%	9.8%	9.8%	9.8%	9.8%	10.0%	9.9%	9.8%	9.8%	9.8%	9.9%	9.9%
Ret/Vol (ann)	0.93	0.94	0.94	0.94	0.95	0.94	0.95	0.94	0.92	0.93	0.94	0.94	0.93	0.94	0.94
ΔDD Jun 1970	0.0%	0.1%	0.1%	0.1%	0.3%	0.2%	0.5%	0.2%	-0.7%	-0.2%	0.0%	0.1%	-0.2%	0.2%	-0.2%
ΔDD Sep 1974	0.0%	0.2%	0.6%	0.5%	0.9%	1.3%	1.3%	1.7%	1.4%	0.0%	0.4%	0.7%	0.4%	0.4%	0.6%
ΔDD Nov1987	0.0%	0.1%	-0.3%	0.5%	-0.2%	-1.0%	-2.3%	-2.2%	-2.4%	-0.4%	-0.2%	-0.3%	-0.7%	-0.7%	-0.7%
ΔDD Sep 2002	0.0%	0.4%	0.9%	1.2%	1.5%	1.9%	1.7%	1.9%	-0.1%	-0.2%	0.5%	1.2%	0.0%	1.1%	1.3%
ΔDD Feb 2009	0.0%	0.8%	1.8%	0.9%	2.1%	3.0%	2.8%	3.2%	2.9%	0.2%	1.1%	2.0%	0.0%	1.1%	1.9%
ΔDD average	0.0%	0.3%	0.6%	0.6%	0.9%	1.1%	0.8%	0.9%	0.2%	-0.1%	0.4%	0.8%	-0.1%	0.4%	0.6%

TABLE 4.3 Strategic rebalancing with stock-bond trend rules. This shows the results for when rebalancing is delayed if the stock-bond trend is negative, positive, or continues to be of the same sign (in which case rebalancing only occurs if the trend just changed sign). In months with no delay, there is a rebalancing halfway toward the 60–40 asset mix. The trend direction is determined by comparing the return over the past 1-, 3-, and 12-months to the typical (average) return over 1-, 3-, and 12-month windows. We report in the different blocks: the average and standard deviation of the stock allocation, noting that the bond allocation is 100 percent minus the stock allocation (block 1); the fraction of months and annualized amount of rebalancing, and annualized trading costs (block 2); the average and standard deviation of the return, as well as the ratio (block 3); and the change in the drawdown level for the five worst drawdowns (ΔDD) at the trough, compared to a 100 percent allocation to the monthly-rebalanced 60–40 portfolio (block 4). Data are from 1960 to 2017.

	Delay if 1m trend			Delay if 3m trend			Delay if 12m trend		
	Negative	Positive	Continues	Negative	Positive	Continues	Negative	Positive	Continues
Stock allocation (avg)	59.3%	61.0%	60.0%	58.9%	61.5%	60.2%	58.1%	61.6%	59.9%
Stock allocation (std)	2.2%	1.6%	2.3%	2.6%	2.3%	2.8%	3.9%	2.5%	4.9%
%months rebal	49.3%	50.7%	48.3%	48.0%	52.0%	25.6%	42.2%	57.8%	12.6%
Rebal trade (ann)	4.0%	4.5%	3.8%	3.5%	4.4%	2.7%	4.5%	4.3%	1.7%
Cost estimate (ann)	1.7 bps	1.9 bps	1.7 bps	1.5 bps	1.9 bps	1.2 bps	1.9 bps	1.9 bps	0.7 bps
Return (ann)	9.1%	9.2%	9.1%	9.1%	9.2%	9.1%	9.0%	9.2%	9.1%
Volatility (ann)	9.6%	9.9%	9.7%	9.5%	10.0%	9.7%	9.4%	10.0%	9.7%
Ret/Vol (ann)	0.95	0.93	0.94	0.96	0.93	0.94	0.96	0.92	0.94
ΔDD Jun 1970	0.5%	-0.1%	0.3%	0.7%	-0.1%	0.4%	0.7%	0.0%	0.3%
ΔDD Sep 1974	1.6%	0.2%	1.2%	1.6%	0.1%	1.1%	3.0%	0.2%	2.5%
ΔDD Nov1987	0.3%	-2.2%	-1.8%	0.3%	-2.2%	-1.7%	0.5%	-1.9%	-1.7%
ΔDD Sep 2002	1.8%	0.2%	1.3%	2.0%	0.2%	1.4%	5.2%	0.2%	4.8%
ΔDD Feb 2009	4.2%	0.7%	3.5%	4.8%	0.7%	3.6%	5.6%	0.8%	5.6%
ΔDD average	1.7%	-0.2%	0.9%	1.9%	-0.2%	0.9%	3.0%	-0.1%	2.3%

For all three trend windows, delaying of the rebalancing when there is a negative trend in the stock-bond spread is most beneficial for reducing drawdowns. This is intuitive, as drawdowns typically occur when stock returns are negative and so a delay of rebalancing means not buying back stocks to bring the portfolio back in line with the 60–40 mix. This result is also consistent with Figure 4.4 (Panel E), which shows that the payoff of an explicit allocation to a stock-bond spread trend strategy that is constrained to be negative mimics that of a put option (on the stock-bond spread return), or with Table 4.1 (Panel E), which shows that the same explicit trend allocation much reduces drawdowns. Delaying of the rebalancing when the 12-month trend is negative leads to a reduction of more than 5 percentage points in case of the tech bubble burst (September 2002 trough) and financial crisis (February 2009 trough), which is comparable to that of the 10 percent trend allocations considered before in Table 4.1.

In Appendix 4C, we show that delaying rebalancing when there is a negative trend in the stock-bond spread similarly reduces drawdowns for the 30–70 stock-bond portfolio.

In Figure 4.7, we show the allocation to stocks for the strategic rebalancing rules where one delays rebalancing if the stock-bond return is in a negative trend, as considered before in Table 4.3. The strategic rebalancing rule using 12-month trends leads to holding only around 40 percent stocks (20 percentage points underweight) at the height of the two most severe stock market drawdowns, after the tech bubble burst and during the global financial crisis. Shorter-term trend models can pick up on temporary relief

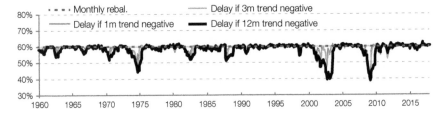

FIGURE 4.7 Stock allocation for different rebalancing rules. In this figure, we show the allocation to stocks for a monthly rebalanced 60–40 stock-bond portfolio as baseline case. Alongside that, we show the allocation to stocks when we apply a strategic rebalancing rule to delay the rebalancing if the stock-bond trend is negative. In months with no delay, there is a rebalancing halfway toward the 60–40 asset mix.[27] The trend direction is determined by comparing the return over the past 1-, 3-, and 12-months to the typical (average) return over 1-, 3-, and 12-month windows.

rallies that occur during a prolonged equity bear market, so they don't tend to deviate as much from the target mix.

The opposite case—delaying rebalancing when there is a positive trend in the stock-bond spread return—does not tend to reduce drawdowns. Between the negative and positive trend-based rules is the case of delaying if the trend continues to be of the same sign.

STRATEGIC REBALANCING VERSUS A DIRECT ALLOCATION TO TREND

In Figure 4.8, we show the impact of adding the two different types of trend exposures considered in this chapter to a monthly rebalanced 60–40 stock-bond portfolio, as a function of the one-year stock-minus-bond return. In the left panel, we show the change in the one-year return with a

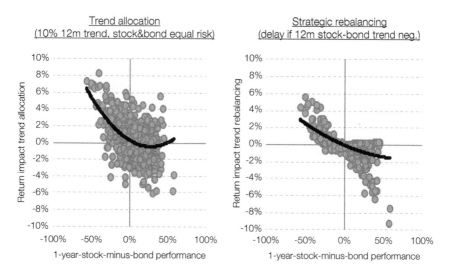

FIGURE 4.8 Impact of adding a trend exposure versus the stock-minus-bond one-year return. This figure plots the one-year (rolling 12-month) performance impact of adding a trend exposure to a monthly rebalanced 60–40 stock-bond strategy (vertical axis) versus the one-year relative stock-bond performance (horizontal axis) for the period 1960 to 2017. We consider a 10 percent allocation to a 12-month stocks and bonds (equal risk) trend strategy (left panel) and a strategic rebalancing rule to delay rebalancing when the 12-month stock-bond trend is negative (i.e., the return is below the average stock-bond 12-month return). Other statistics for these trend exposures can be found in Table 4.1, Panel C, for the trend allocation and Table 4.3 for the stock-bond trend rebalancing rule.

10 percent allocation to a 12-month stocks and bonds (equal risk) trend strategy (reported on in Table 4.1, Panel C). In the right panel, we show the same output for a strategic rebalancing rule to delay rebalancing if the 12-month stock-bond spread trend is negative (reported on in Table 4.3).

Note that in both cases the trend exposure tends to be particularly helpful when stocks underperform bonds. Given that stocks are much more volatile than bonds, this usually means the exposure helps when stock returns are negative. In case of a trend allocation (left panel), the asymmetry of the impact compares to a much more symmetric effect for the standalone trend performance as shown in Figure 4.4, Panel C. The reason is that in order to allocate to the trend strategy, we reduced the allocation to the 60–40 stock-bond portfolio from 100 percent to 90 percent, and this tends to help when the stock-bond performance is negative. In case of the strategic rebalancing rule (right panel), the asymmetric impact of the exposure comes directly from the rule itself, which is asymmetric (i.e., riding negative trends in the relative stock-bond return and not riding positive trends). The correlation between the two trend exposures in terms of their return difference with the 100 percent monthly rebalanced 60–40 stock-bond portfolio is 0.62, again suggesting they behave similarly.

In Figure 4.9, we show the impact on the drawdown level of the same two trend exposures that we considered before in Figure 4.8. Results at the

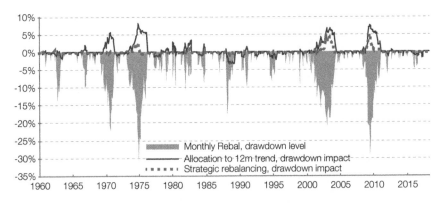

FIGURE 4.9 Impact of adding a trend exposure on the portfolio drawdown level. In this figure, we show the drawdown level of a monthly rebalanced 60–40 stock-bond portfolio (gray line) and the impact (change in drawdown level) when adding a trend exposure for the period 1960 to 2017. We consider a 10 percent allocation to a 12-month stocks and bonds (equal risk) trend strategy and a strategic rebalancing rule to delay rebalancing when the 12-month stock-bond trend is negative (i.e., the return is below the average stock-bond 12-month return). Other statistics for these trend exposures can be found in Table 4.1, Panel C, for the trend allocation and Table 4.3 for the stock-bond trend rebalancing rule.

trough of the five worst crises correspond to those reported in Table 4.1, Panel C, and Table 4.3. This figure compares the impact of the different trend exposures on the drawdown level alongside and over time. The main takeaway is that either a direct allocation to a trend strategy or using trend signals as a basis of a rebalancing rule tends to reduce the drawdown materially. The performance around Black Monday is the only exception here in case of an allocation to trend (less so for the strategic rebalancing rule).

CONCLUDING REMARKS

The second portfolio management tool that can impact the severity of portfolio drawdowns is strategic rebalancing. While most investors rebalance, many do not realize that mechanical rebalancing can exacerbate drawdowns in market selloffs.

On the other hand, a pure buy-and-hold portfolio is untenable for most investors as it leads to highly concentrated, undiversified portfolios. However, a 60–40 stock-bond portfolio (our use case) that rebalances every month to the 60:40 target ratio loses several percentage points more than a buy-and-hold portfolio during periods of continued stock market drawdowns. In essence, rebalancing to a constant asset mix means selling winners and buying losers, which is painful in trending markets. We show that the negative convexity induced by rebalancing is effectively countered with a trend exposure, which exhibits convexity and can be either implemented as a direct allocation to a trend strategy or with a strategic trend-based rebalancing rule.

While our focus is on countering the negative convexity induced by rebalancing, other considerations matter in practice as well. For example, investors can also use monthly in- and out-flows to move back toward the target asset mix. For example, Chambers, Dimson, and Ilmanen (2012) mention that the Norwegian Government Pension Fund Global directs monthly inflows into the asset class that is most underweight relative to the benchmark. For taxable investors, rebalancing using income has the added benefit that no assets need to be sold, which can be tax efficient; see Colleen, Kinniry, and Zilbering (2010).

We note that a stock-bond trend exposure is just one way to mitigate drawdowns at times of continued stock market losses. An investor has more arrows in her quiver. A good starting point is a more diversified portfolio that includes more asset classes and has an international exposure. An allocation to a broader trend strategy that benefits from trends in other macro assets at times of equity market distress may further dampen equity market losses (see Chapter 1). As shown in Chapter 3, volatility targeting can help manage the risk of a 60–40 stock-bond portfolio. We now turn to Chapter 5 where we show how the drawdown statistic can be used to make allocation and redemption decisions.

APPENDIX 4A: CERTAINTY EQUIVALENT PERFORMANCE GAIN

We employ the Goetzmann et al. (2007) manipulation-proof performance measure. This measure is the annualized certainty-equivalent return (CEQ) in a power utility framework and so penalizes negative skewness and excess kurtosis relative to the Sharpe ratio metric. For a given risk aversion parameter γ, it is defined as:

$$CEQ(\gamma) = \frac{1}{(1-\gamma)\Delta t} \ln\left[\frac{1}{T}\sum_{t=1}^{T}\left(\frac{1+R_t}{1+R_t^F}\right)^{1-\gamma}\right]$$

In Table 4A.1, we report the CEQ using monthly (Panel A) and annual (12-month overlapping) data (Panel B), for the case of trend applied to stocks and bonds (equal risk), which corresponds to Panel C in Table 4.1. The $\gamma = 0$ case corresponds to a risk-neutral setting, and the CEQ simply equals the annualized excess return. Using risk-aversion parameter values of 2, 5, and 10, we see the benefit from a 10 percent trend allocation. For $\gamma = 10$, the CEQ is around 1 percent higher using monthly returns and 2 percent in case of annual returns. The higher value in case of annual returns shows that the benefits of a trend allocation are more pronounced at lower frequencies, where the trend strategies require some time to start picking up on sustained market moves.

Note that the CEQ is still a measure that doesn't explicitly account for longer-term behavior, like the drawdown characteristic we have focused on. So in Panel C we also report returns unleveraged versus returns leveraged (taking into account the cost of borrowing) so that the average drawdown across the five episodes considered is equalized to that of the 100 percent *Rebal* benchmark. The leverage applied is around 1.2, as drawdowns are around a factor 1.2 lower without the leverage. A 10 percent trend allocation results in a 0.8 percent to 1.5 percent higher annualized return when leverage is applied to match the average drawdown depth. The t-stat on the return differential between the with-trend strategy and the 100 percent *Rebal* baseline case comes out as 2.7 to 4.2.

TABLE 4A.1 Alternative performance metrics (stocks and bonds trend, equal risk). The table reports the certainty-equity return (CEQ) using monthly (Panel A) and annual (12-month overlapping) returns (Panel B) for different levels of power-utility risk aversion, γ. In Panel C we also report returns unleveraged versus returns leveraged (taking into account the cost of borrowing) so that the average drawdown across the five episodes considered is equalized to that of the 100 percent *Rebal* benchmark. For all panels, the trend strategy is applied to stocks and bonds (equal risk), which is what the case covered in Table 4.1, Panel C. The data are from 1960 to 2017.

Panel A:	certainty-equivalent return (CEQ), using monthly returns		
	100% Rebal	90% Rebal 10% TsMom1m	90% Rebal 10% TsMom3m	90% Rebal 10% TsMom12m
	Certainty equivalent return (CEQ)			
$\gamma=0$ (risk neutral)	4.6%	4.7%	4.6%	4.9%
$\gamma=2$	3.7%	3.9%	3.8%	4.1%
$\gamma=5$	2.2%	2.8%	2.6%	2.8%
$\gamma=10$	−0.4%	0.8%	0.4%	0.5%
	CEQ vs. 100% Rebal			
$\gamma=0$ (risk neutral)	0.0%	0.1%	0.0%	0.3%
$\gamma=2$	0.0%	0.3%	0.1%	0.4%
$\gamma=5$	0.0%	0.6%	0.4%	0.6%
$\gamma=10$	0.0%	1.2%	0.8%	0.9%

Panel B:	certainty equivalent (CEQ), using annual returns		
	100% Rebal	90% Rebal 10% TsMom1m	90% Rebal 10% TsMom3m	90% Rebal 10% TsMom12m
	Certainty equivalent return (CEQ)			
$\gamma=0$ (risk neutral)	4.7%	4.8%	4.7%	5.0%
$\gamma=2$	3.6%	3.9%	3.7%	4.1%
$\gamma=5$	1.7%	2.4%	2.2%	2.6%
$\gamma=10$	−2.0%	−0.2%	−0.6%	0.0%
	CEQ vs. 100% Rebal			
$\gamma=0$ (risk neutral)	0.0%	0.1%	0.0%	0.3%
$\gamma=2$	0.0%	0.3%	0.1%	0.5%
$\gamma=5$	0.0%	0.8%	0.5%	0.9%
$\gamma=10$	0.0%	1.8%	1.4%	2.0%

(Continued)

TABLE 4A.1 (*Continued*)

Panel C: unleveraged versus leverage to match 100% *Rebal* average drawdown

	100% Rebal	90% Rebal 10% TsMom1m	90% Rebal 10% TsMom3m	90% Rebal 10% TsMom12m
	Return unleveraged and leveraged (matched DD)			
Unleveraged	4.6%	4.7%	4.6%	5.0%
Lev., matched DD	4.6%	5.8%	5.4%	6.2%
	Return vs 100% Rebal			
Unleveraged	0.0%	0.1%	0.0%	0.3%
Lev., matched DD	0.0%	1.1%	0.8%	1.5%
	T-stat return vs 100% Rebal			
Unleveraged	n.a.	0.3	−0.1	1.2
Lev., matched DD	n.a.	4.0	2.7	4.2

APPENDIX 4B: ADDING TREND TO A 100 PERCENT REBALANCED PORTFOLIO

In Table 4.1, we contrasted a 100 percent allocation to a monthly rebalanced portfolio with a 60–40 stock-bond capital allocation to one where the investor holds 90 percent of the rebalanced portfolio and 10 percent in a trend strategy. One could argue that part of the improvement in the drawdown characteristics is because of the divestment of 10 percent of the rebalanced portfolio and is due in part to the defensive nature of the 10 percent trend allocation. To isolate the latter effect, in Table 4B.1, we contrast a 100 percent rebalanced portfolio to a 100 percent rebalanced portfolio plus 10 percent trend investment. As trend specification we use 1-, 3-, and 12-month stocks and bonds (equal risk) trend, which we used before in Table 4.1, Panel C. We incorporate borrowing costs to allow for the effectively 110 percent investment. As can be seen in Table 4B.1, the addition of a trend strategy (without divestment of a portion of the rebalanced portfolio) still materially improves the average drawdown. Also notice that, as a consequence of holding onto all of the rebalanced portfolio when adding trend, the average return is increased versus the 90 percent rebalanced plus 10 percent trend case considered before in Table 4.1.

TABLE 4B.1 Performance for fully invested rebalanced portfolio with *stocks& bonds* trend. We contrast a 100 percent allocation to a monthly rebalanced portfolio with a 60–40 stock-bond capital allocation to one where, in addition to a 100 percent rebalanced portfolio, the investor borrows money to also allocate 10 percent to a 1-, 3-, and 12-month stocks and bonds (equal risk) trend strategy. Performance statistics reported on are the average stock, bond, and total allocation (block 1), the annualized notional trading (as percentage of the total portfolio value) in the 60–40 rebalanced portfolio, stock and bond futures, as well as annualized trading costs (block 2), average return, standard deviation, the ratio of these two, and the Sharpe ratio (block 3), and the change in the drawdown level for the five worst drawdowns (ΔDD) at the trough, compared to a 100 percent allocation to the monthly-rebalanced 60–40 portfolio. The data are from 1960 to 2017.

	Rebal (100%)	Rebal (100%) 1m trend (10%)	Rebal (100%) 3m trend (10%)	Rebal (100%) 12m trend (10%)
Stock allocation (avg)	60.0%	61.8%	63.0%	65.3%
Bond allocation (avg)	40.0%	41.9%	42.8%	44.7%
Total allocation (avg)	100.0%	103.8%	105.9%	109.9%
Rebal trade (ann)	10.2%	10.2%	10.2%	10.2%
Stock fut. trade (ann)	0.0%	103.7%	53.4%	22.6%
Bond fut. trade (ann)	0.0%	219.0%	122.7%	55.8%
Cost estimate (ann)	4.4 bps	6.5 bps	5.5 bps	4.9 bps
Return, (ann)	9.1%	9.6%	9.5%	9.9%
Volatility (ann)	9.8%	9.8%	10.0%	10.2%
Ret./Vol (ann)	0.92	0.99	0.96	0.97
Sharpe ratio (ann)	0.47	0.53	0.51	0.53
ΔDD Jun 1970	0.0%	1.5%	−0.1%	2.6%
ΔDD Sep 1974	0.0%	4.2%	3.3%	4.3%
ΔDD Nov1987	0.0%	1.1%	−1.8%	−2.7%
ΔDD Sep 2002	0.0%	2.8%	2.2%	4.2%
ΔDD Feb 2009	0.0%	1.6%	3.6%	4.7%
ΔDD average	0.0%	2.3%	1.4%	2.6%

TABLE 4C.1 *Rebal* plus *stocks&bonds* trend performance statistics for the 30–70 portfolio. We contrast a 100 percent allocation to a monthly rebalanced portfolio with a 30–70 stock-bond capital allocation to one where 10 percent of the portfolio is replaced with a 10 percent allocation to a 1-, 3-, and 12-month stocks and bonds (equal risk) trend strategy. Performance statistics reported on are the average stock, bond, and total allocation (block 1), the annualized notional trading (as percentage of the total portfolio value) in the 60–40 rebalanced portfolio, stock and bond futures, as well as annualized trading costs (block 2), average return, standard deviation, the ratio of these two, and the Sharpe ratio (block 3), and the change in the drawdown level for the five worst drawdowns (ΔDD) at the trough, compared to a 100 percent allocation to the monthly-rebalanced 60–40 portfolio. The data are from 1960 to 2017.

	Rebal (100%)	Rebal (90%) 1m trend (10%)	Rebal (90%) 3m trend (10%)	Rebal (90%) 12m trend (10%)
Stock allocation (avg)	30.0%	28.8%	30.0%	32.3%
Bond allocation (avg)	70.0%	64.9%	65.8%	67.7%
Total allocation (avg)	100.0%	93.8%	95.9%	99.9%
Rebal trade (ann)	10.2%	9.1%	9.1%	9.1%
Stock fut. trade (ann)	0.0%	103.7%	53.4%	22.6%
Bond fut. trade (ann)	0.0%	219.0%	122.7%	55.8%
Cost estimate (ann)	4.4 bps	6.1 bps	5.1 bps	4.4 bps
Return, (ann)	7.8%	8.0%	7.9%	8.3%
Volatility (ann)	7.4%	6.7%	6.9%	7.1%
Ret./Vol (ann)	1.06	1.19	1.15	1.16
Sharpe ratio (ann)	0.46	0.53	0.50	0.54
ΔDD May 1970	0.0%	3.4%	1.8%	4.8%
ΔDD Sep 1974	0.0%	6.3%	6.4%	7.7%
ΔDD Mar 1980	0.0%	4.7%	2.7%	3.5%
ΔDD Feb 2009	0.0%	1.6%	2.1%	2.1%
ΔDD average	0.0%	4.0%	3.2%	4.5%

TABLE 4C.2 Strategic rebalancing with stock-bond trend rules for the 30–70 portfolio. We show results when rebalancing is delayed if the stock-bond trend is negative, positive, or continues to be of the same sign (in which case rebalancing only occurs if the trend just changed sign). In months with no delay, there is a rebalancing halfway toward the 30–70 asset mix. The trend direction is determined by comparing the return over the past 1-, 3-, and 12-months to the typical (average) return over 1-, 3-, and 12-month windows. We report in the different blocks: the average and standard deviation of the stock allocation (block 1); the fraction of months and annualized amount of rebalancing, and annualized trading costs (block 2); the average and standard deviation of the return, as well as the ratio (block 3); and the change in the drawdown level for the five worst drawdowns (ΔDD) at the trough, compared to a 100 percent allocation to the monthly rebalanced 60–40 portfolio (block 4). Data are from 1960 to 2017.

	Delay if 1m trend			Delay if 3m trend			Delay if 12m trend		
	Negative	Positive	Continues	Negative	Positive	Continues	Negative	Positive	Continues
Stock allocation (avg)	29.4%	31.0%	30.1%	29.1%	31.5%	30.3%	28.6%	31.7%	30.4%
Stock allocation (std)	1.7%	1.5%	1.9%	1.9%	2.1%	2.4%	2.9%	2.7%	4.2%
%months rebal	50.1%	49.9%	48.0%	50.0%	50.0%	27.0%	46.4%	53.6%	13.8%
Rebal trade (ann)	3.5%	4.0%	3.3%	3.1%	3.8%	2.4%	4.1%	3.7%	1.6%
Cost estimate (ann)	1.5bp	1.7bp	1.4bp	1.3bp	1.6bp	1.1bp	1.8bp	1.6bp	0.7bp
Return (ann)	7.9%	7.9%	7.9%	7.9%	8.0%	7.9%	7.8%	7.9%	7.9%
Volatility (ann)	7.3%	7.4%	7.3%	7.3%	7.4%	7.3%	7.3%	7.4%	7.4%
Ret/Vol (ann)	1.08	1.07	1.08	1.08	1.07	1.07	1.07	1.07	1.07
ΔDD May 1970	0.2%	0.1%	0.4%	0.8%	0.1%	0.5%	0.8%	0.1%	0.4%
ΔDD Sep 1974	1.5%	0.1%	1.1%	1.5%	0.1%	1.0%	2.7%	0.2%	2.3%
ΔDD Mar 1980	0.0%	0.2%	0.3%	1.7%	0.2%	0.4%	1.8%	0.3%	0.5%
ΔDD Feb 2009	2.0%	0.6%	1.9%	1.9%	0.7%	1.9%	2.2%	0.7%	2.1%
ΔDD average	0.9%	0.3%	0.9%	1.5%	0.3%	0.9%	1.9%	0.3%	1.3%

APPENDIX 4C: THE 30–70 PORTFOLIO

Here we consider a 30–70 stock-bond portfolio instead of the 60–40 stock-bond portfolio considered before. The 30–70 stock-bond portfolio is closer to equal risk to stocks and bonds and may be held by more conservative investors. The 30–70 stock-bond portfolio experiences some of its worst drawdowns on different dates. Focusing on the four drawdowns that exceeded 10 percent, we get: May 1970 (–13.2 percent), September 1974 (–15.7 percent), March 1980 (–10.7 percent), and February 2009 (–10.3 percent). The March 1980 drawdown for the 30–70 portfolio did not show up in the 60–40 analysis before because bonds in particular were getting hit when inflation spiked in 1980. Vice versa, the November 1987 and September 2002 drawdowns for the 60–40 portfolio don't show up here.

In Table 4C.1, one can see that investing 10 percent in trend applied to stocks and bonds (equal risk), drawdowns are reduced for all four worst drawdowns for the 30–70 portfolio, and for all three trend speeds.

We also repeat the analysis of the strategic rebalancing rules for the 30–70 stock-bond portfolio; see Table 4C.2. A rule to hold off rebalancing when the stock-bond trend is negative tends to improve drawdowns, as it did for the 60–40 stock-bond portfolio considered before in Table 4.3.

REFERENCES

Ambachtsheer, K.P. (1987). "Pension Fund Asset Allocation: In Defense of a 60/40 Equity/Debt Asset Mix," *Financial Analysts Journal*, 43(5), 14–24.

Arnott, Robert D., and Robert M. Lovell (1993). "Rebalancing: Why? When? How often?," *Journal of Investing*, 2(1), 5–10.

Asvanunt, A., L. Nielsen, and D. Villalon (2015). "Working Your Tail Off: Active Strategies versus Direct Hedging," *Journal of Investing*, 24(2), 134–145.

Booth, D., and E. Fama (1992). "Diversification Returns and Asset Contributions," *Financial Analyst Journal*, 48(3), 26–32.

Brown, S. (2015). "Historical Context of Smart Beta," INQUIRE UK presentation.

Chambers, D., E. Dimson, and A. Ilmanen (2012). "The Norway Model," *Journal of Portfolio Management*, 38(2), 67–81.

Colleen, J., F. Kinniry, and Y. Zilbering (2010). "Best Practices for Portfolio Rebalancing," Vanguard working paper.

Daniel, K., and T. Moskowitz (2016). "Momentum crashes," *Journal of Financial Economics*, 122(2), 221–247.

Donohue, C., and K. Yip (2003). "Optimal Portfolio Rebalancing with Transaction Costs," *Journal of Portfolio Management*, 29(4), 49–63.

Driessen, J., and I. Kuiper (2017). "Rebalancing for Long-Term Investors," working paper.

Erb, C.B., and C.R. Harvey (2006). "The Strategic and Tactical Value of Commodity Futures," *Financial Analyst Journal*, 62(2), 69–79.

Fernholz, R., and B. Shay (1982). "Stochastic Portfolio Theory and Stock Market Equilibrium," *Journal of Finance*, 37(2), 615–624.

Fung, W., and D. Hsieh (2001). "The Risk in Hedge Fund Strategies: Theory and Evidence from Trend Followers," *Review of Financial Studies*, 14(2), 313–341.

Goetzmann, W., J. Ingersoll, M. Spiegel, I. Welch (2007). "Portfolio Performance Manipulation and Manipulation-Proof Performance Measures," *Review of Financial Studies*, 20(5), 1503–1546.

Granger, N., D. Greenig, C.R. Harvey, S. Rattray, D. Zou (2014). "Rebalancing Risk," SSRN working paper: https://ssrn.com/abstract=2488552.

Harvey, Campbell R., Edward Hoyle, Russell Korgaonkar, Sandy Rattray, Matthew Sargaison, and Otto Van Hemert (2018, Fall). "The Impact of Volatility Targeting," *Journal of Portfolio Management*, 45(1), 14–33. DOI: https://doi.org/10.3905/jpm.2018.45.1.014.

Huss, J., and T. Maloney (2017). "Portfolio Rebalancing: Common Misconceptions," working paper.

Ilmanen, A., and T. Maloney (2015). "Portfolio Rebalancing—Part 1 of 2: Strategic Asset Allocation," working paper.

Israelov, R., and H. Tummala (2017). "An Alternative Option to Portfolio Rebalancing," working paper.

Levine, A., and L. Pedersen (2016). "Which Trend Is Your Friend?," *Financial Analyst Journal*, 72(3), 51–66.

Martin, R., and D. Zou (2012). "Momentum Trading: Skews Me," *Risk*, 25(8), 52–57.

Masters, S. (2003). "Rebalancing," *Journal of Portfolio Management*, 29(3), 52–57.

Moskowitz, T., Y. Ooi, and L. Pedersen (2012). "Time Series Momentum," *Journal of Financial Economics*, 104(2), 228–250.

Norges Bank (2018). "No-Trade Band Rebalancing Rules: Expected Returns and Transaction Costs," 2018-01 Norges Bank Investment Management report.

Perold, A., and W. Sharpe (1988). "Dynamic Strategies for Asset Allocation," *Financial Analysts Journal*, 44(1), 16–27.

Rattray, S., N. Granger, C. Harvey, and O. Van Hemert (2020). "Strategic Rebalancing," *Journal of Portfolio Management Multi-Asset*, Special Issue, 46(6) 10–31. DOI: https://doi.org/10.3905/jpm.2020.1.150.

CHAPTER 5

Drawdown Control

INTRODUCTION

Chapters 3 and 4 focused on two portfolio mechanisms that serve to reduce the severity of portfolio drawdowns: strategic rebalancing and volatility targeting. We now explore the information in the drawdown risk metric. That is, conditional on a drawdown, is there information in drawdowns that could be useful for strategic portfolio management? In addition, how does the application of drawdown control impact portfolio expected returns?[1]

Common risk metrics reported in academia include volatility, skewness, and factor exposures, but the maximum drawdown statistic is rarely calculated, perhaps because it is path dependent and estimated with greater uncertainty. In practice, however, asset managers and fiduciaries routinely use the drawdown statistic for fund allocation and redemption decisions. When evaluating managers or strategies, investors pay close attention to the maximum drawdown, which is the largest peak-to-trough return over the life of an investment. For example, for hedge fund investments, money is often pulled out when a threshold for the maximum drawdown is crossed. The maximum drawdown statistic is appealing because it is unambiguous in its calculation and captures the most unfavorable investment outcome: buying at the peak and selling at the bottom.

Unlike other metrics, such as volatility, and downside measures, like skewness or semi-variance, the maximum drawdown statistic crucially depends on the *order* in which the returns occur. Closed-form solutions are hard to obtain, except under very restrictive assumptions.[2] In the first part of this chapter, we conduct a simulation study to determine what drives the probability of reaching a given maximum drawdown threshold. The size of the drawdown is impacted by key parameters (or assumptions). We use the term "drawdown Greeks" to refer to the sensitivities of the probability of hitting a given drawdown. These are the key drivers of the maximum drawdown, and we identify the following: the evaluation horizon (time to dig a hole), Sharpe ratio (ability to climb out of a hole), and the persistence in risk (chance of having a losing streak). The latter may motivate a manager to actively target a more stable risk profile over time when facing strict drawdown limits. We find that non-normal, but still time-independent, returns—for example the occasional gap move down—only matter much when they are large compared to what we generally observe for a range of financial markets. The reason is that with independent returns, the central limit theorem kicks in: Multi-period returns start to look more normal as one increases the number of periods.

Next, we compare the ability of different manager replacement rules to improve investment performance over time. Drawdown-based rules can be particularly useful for improving investment performance over time by detecting managers who lose their ability to outperform. Using this approach, we introduce a framework to decide whether to replace a manager (or strategy). This decision will be subject to two types of errors: a Type I error of replacing a *Good* manager and a Type II error of mistakenly not firing a *Bad* manager.[3] We also recognize that the timing of these replacements matters as a *Bad* manager can do more harm the longer they are managing assets.

When managers are of constant (but unknown) quality, a replacement rule based on the total return is typically preferred because that makes full use of all historical return data available. However, drawdown-based rules are more suitable when there is a meaningful chance that managers lose their skill over time. In practice, this can happen as a result of structural market changes, staff turnover, increased competition for the type of strategy employed (crowding), or a fund accumulating too much assets.

Drawdown-based rules can be used as a risk reduction technique, but doing so impacts both expected returns and risk. Reducing the allocation to an underperforming manager using drawdown-based rules can be seen as a halfway point between no action and immediate replacement of the manager. However, it's necessary to compensate for such risk reductions by increasing risk elsewhere in the portfolio; otherwise, they will generally lead to lower expected returns. There could be exceptions if a manager's conditional expected returns (in excess of the cash rate) turn negative. This requires one of two beliefs: first, that a manager is actually destroying value (in which case, immediate replacement seems more appropriate than reducing his or her allocation), or, second, that there is a very high degree of persistence in returns and previous returns were negative.

Finally, we summarize the main results and discuss five key takeaways for allocators choosing among managers, or for managers choosing between different investments strategies.

We have not tried to identify the impact of drawdown rules on manager behavior, but we are very aware that the presence of such rules will cause managers to act differently; after all, nobody likes getting fired. In light of this, a drawdown rule might be considered to have some similarities to volatility scaling; managers who show behavioral aversion to being fired will reduce risk when they are near the drawdown limit. From this perspective, drawdown rules might serve a similar role as volatility scaling. (See Chapter 3 for a discussion on the impact of volatility scaling on risk-and-return characteristics.)

DRAWDOWN GREEKS

In this section, we explore how sensitive the likelihood of hitting a certain drawdown level is to key drivers like the Sharpe ratio, evaluation time window, and autocorrelation of returns. Borrowing terminology from option pricing theory, we call these sensitivities the "drawdown Greeks."[4]

Probability Distribution for Maximum Drawdown Level

We start with a simple setting of normal, independent, and identically distributed (IID) monthly returns.[5] In Figure 5.1, we show the probability distribution of the maximum drawdown statistic for our baseline case: 10-year time window, 10 percent annualized volatility, 0.5 annualized Sharpe ratio. Throughout, we rely on simulations, where each parameterization is evaluated with 100,000 simulations of monthly returns for the evaluation window.

Vertical lines in Figure 5.1 highlight maximum drawdown levels of 1, 2, 3, and 4 annual standard deviation (or sigma) moves, corresponding to −10 percent, −20 percent, −30 percent, and −40 percent drawdown levels. The associated probability of reaching a maximum drawdown of that level or worse is given by the area under the curve to the left of the associated vertical line. It is 97.1 percent, 43.0 percent, 9.9 percent, and 1.5 percent for 1, 2, 3, and 4 sigma levels, respectively. This means that in almost half of the cases, one reaches a drawdown of two full annual standard deviations (or −20 percent) over the 10-year period, even though the annual Sharpe ratio is a respectable 0.5. In one-in-ten cases, one even reaches a drawdown of three full annual standard deviations (or −30 percent).

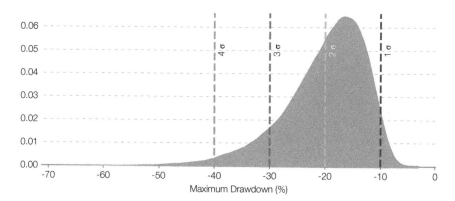

FIGURE 5.1 Probability distribution for the maximum drawdown statistic. The figure shows probability distribution for the maximum drawdown statistic using normal, IID monthly returns over a 10-year window with a 10 percent annualized volatility and 0.5 annualized Sharpe ratio (the baseline case). The vertical, dashed lines correspond to drawdowns of size 1, 2, 3, and 4 annual standard deviations.

Drawdown Greeks without Higher-Order Effects

Next, we consider how deviations from the baseline assumptions impact the probability of hitting a drawdown level. In Figure 5.2, we illustrate how the probability of a given level of maximum drawdown changes if we modify one of the following assumptions at a time: (A) annualized volatility, 10 percent baseline; (B) time window, 10 years baseline; (C) annualized Sharpe ratio, 0.5 baseline; and (D) autocorrelation, 0.0 baseline.[6]

In Panel A, we show how the probability of a given maximum drawdown changes when we vary the standard deviation of the return process while holding constant the Sharpe ratio. The lightest gray line represents the probability of a maximum drawdown that is –2 sigma (annual return standard deviations), or worse.[7] This value is 43 percent for the baseline case (see also the discussion of Figure 5.1), indicated by the vertical dashed line. The lightest gray line is nearly horizontal, which means that varying the standard deviation of returns hardly changes the probability of reaching a certain maximum drawdown level, as long as you assume the Sharpe ratio stays constant and the threshold is expressed in terms of sigmas. That is, the probability of a 20 percent maximum drawdown when returns have a 10 percent standard deviation is similar to the probability of 10 percent maximum drawdown when returns have a 5 percent standard deviation (assuming the Sharpe ratio is 0.5 in both cases; i.e., the expected returns increase as volatility increases). As mentioned, the lightest gray line is nearly

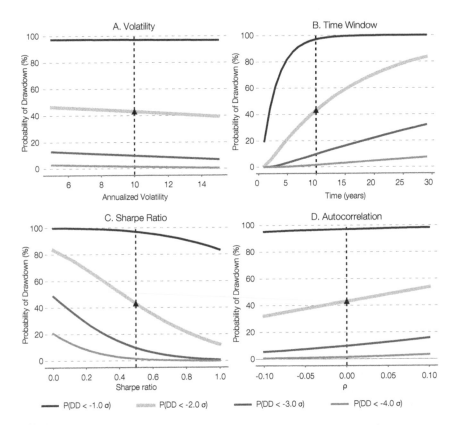

FIGURE 5.2 Sensitivity of the probability of a maximum drawdown to key parameters. The figure shows probability of reaching a maximum drawdown of 1, 2, 3, and 4 sigma (annual standard deviations). In all cases returns are normal and identically distributed. In the different panels, we vary the (A) volatility holding constant the Sharpe ratio, (B) time window, (C) Sharpe ratio, and (D) autocorrelation. The vertical dashed line corresponds to the baseline case of 10 percent annualized volatility, 10-year window, 0.5 annualized Sharpe ratio, and 0.0 autocorrelation.

horizontal, but not exactly. In fact, it is gently sloping downwards, reflecting the influence of compounding of returns.

In Panel B, we examine the impact of changing the evaluation time horizon. The baseline case is 10 years. As a return stream is evaluated over a longer window, the probability of hitting a certain drawdown level naturally increases.

In Panel C, we vary the Sharpe ratio while holding the constant standard deviation of returns. In the default case, we have an annualized Sharpe ratio of 0.5. The impact of Sharpe ratio on the probability of reaching a certain maximum drawdown level is large, which is intuitive because the Sharpe ratio captures the ability to lift yourself out of a hole. It is exactly this effect that investors using drawdown rules are hoping to isolate; managers with low Sharpe ratios will be removed by the presence of the rule.

In Panel D, we vary the correlation, ρ, between time t and time $t - 1$ monthly returns. In the formula below, the $\tilde{\mu}$ and $\tilde{\sigma}$ terms capture the unconditional mean and standard deviation, respectively, where we use a tilde to make clear it concerns monthly returns (in contrast to, e.g., Figure 5.2, where we used σ, without a tilde, for the annualized standard deviation). The mean and standard deviations are pre-multiplied with a term featuring ρ to offset the effect of non-zero autocorrelation on the mean and standard deviation:

$$R_{t+1} = (1 - \rho)\tilde{\mu} + \rho R_t + \sqrt{(1 - \rho^2)}\tilde{\sigma}\varepsilon_{t+1} \qquad (5.1)$$

where ε is standard normal and independent and identically distributed (IID).

We illustrate the impact of autocorrelation in monthly returns for values ranging from –0.1 to +0.1. We consider an autocorrelation of 0.1 (or similarly –0.1) a large value, as it implies a large degree of predictability.[8] The impact of a 0.1 autocorrelation in monthly returns on the expected maximum drawdown (versus a baseline value of 0) is comparable to that of reducing the Sharpe ratio from 0.5 to 0.4.

Bootstrapped U.S. Equity Returns

Next, we bootstrap two-year blocks from U.S. equity returns since 1926 with monthly returns scaled to have 10 percent unconditional volatility.[9] Using actual return realizations allows us to determine if the inference is different from our simulated, normally distributed returns. Selecting blocks, rather than individual months, is to preserve the original time-series structure within a block.

In the left panel of Figure 5.3, we present the sensitivity to the time window, holding the Sharpe ratio constant at 0.5 (by adjusting the mean returns appropriately). In the right panel of Figure 5.3, we present the sensitivity to the Sharpe ratio while holding the time window constant at 10 years. As such, these figures can be directly compared to Panels B and C in Figure 5.2, where we simulated from a normal, independent, and identical distribution.

For the case of a 10-year window and Sharpe ratio of 0.5, we had a 43 percent probability of hitting a two-sigma drawdown (see Figure 5.2, baseline case for our simulated returns). This probability increases to

55 percent for the bootstrapped actual returns in Figure 5.3 (see dashed line crossing thickest gray line). This increased probability of hitting a drawdown level is a result of both non-normality of monthly returns and heteroskedasticity (clustering of volatility). This is illustrated in Appendix 5A for U.S. equity returns since 1926, with volatility persistently high around, for example, 1929 (the Great Depression) and 2008 (the Global Financial Crisis).

While non-normality and volatility clustering tends to increase the probability of hitting a certain drawdown level, the sensitivity to the time window and Sharpe ratio looks very similar between the normal (Figure 5.2) and non-normal, bootstrapped case (Figure 5.3).

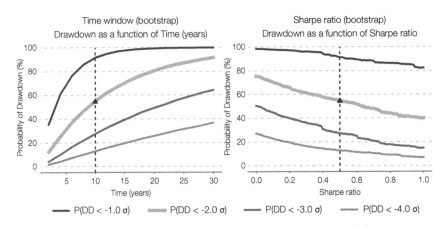

FIGURE 5.3 Drawdown probability with bootstrapped U.S. equity returns. The figure shows probability of reaching a maximum drawdown of 1, 2, 3, and 4 sigma (annual standard deviations), as a function of the time window (left panel) and Sharpe ratio (right panel). We bootstrap 2-year blocks from U.S. equity returns since 1926. We hold constant the unconditional volatility at 10 percent. In the left panel we hold constant the Sharpe ratio at 0.5. In the right panel we hold constant the time window at 10 years.

The Impact of Gap Risk

Financial markets can experience sudden, negative returns of a magnitude that is implausible under the assumption of normally distributed returns. For example, we are writing this during the "COVID-19 Crash" of March 2020 (also see Chapter 7). That is, markets can experience a gap move down. To illustrate this point, in Appendix 5B, Table 5B.1, we list, for a range of securities, the worst negative monthly return, expressed as a number of (annualized) standard deviations. We see that for the 25 to

50 years of available history, the worst monthly returns are −1 to −1.5 annual standard deviations (which corresponds to 3.5 to 5.2 monthly standard deviations).[10]

We will explore the impact on the expected maximum drawdown of having a monthly move equal to −k annual standard deviations with a 1 percent probability (once every 8.3 years on average). We adjust the mean of the returns in the other 99 percent cases, so that the average return is held constant while we vary the size of the gap move. In other words, we have the following distribution, where we continue to assume returns are IID:

$$R = baseline\ case + \begin{cases} -k\sigma & with\ 1\%\ probability \\ +\frac{1}{99}k\sigma & with\ 99\%\ probability \end{cases} \qquad (5.2)$$

In Figure 5.4, we vary the size of the gap move (k in the formula above). The baseline corresponds to $k = 0$. Note that $k = 1$ is already a large value. Appendix Table 5B.1 shows that the largest monthly return is just greater than 1, but this is over typically a 25- to 50-year window, rather than a 10-year period. While the probability of a large drawdown indeed increases with an increased probability of a gap move, the impact is

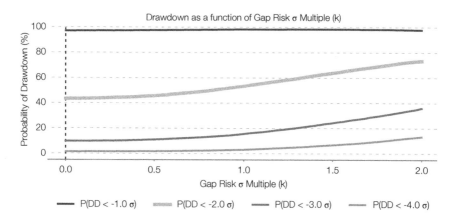

FIGURE 5.4 Impact of gap risk. The figure shows probability of reaching a maximum drawdown of 1, 2, 3, and 4 sigma (annual standard deviations). In the baseline case (indicated by the vertical dashed line), we have normal, independent and identically distributed (IID) monthly returns, with an annualized mean, standard deviation, and Sharpe ratio of 5 percent, 10 percent, and 0.5, respectively, and an evaluation window of 10 years. We vary the size of the gap move (occurring in 1 percent of the months, or once every 8.3 years on average), with a zero gap size corresponding to the baseline case.

somewhat limited for a $k = 1$ (monthly move equal to 1 annual standard deviation, or 3.5 monthly standard deviations). We think this is intuitive, as such a move doesn't immediately take you through a, say, –2 sigma, drawdown limit. Additionally, the drivers of returns in the medium to long term, like the Sharpe ratio, remain the key drivers of the probability to hit a drawdown.

MANAGER REPLACEMENT RULES

Investors face considerable uncertainty around the quality of the managers (or strategies) when selecting them. Moreover, after investment, a manager's quality may deteriorate for a variety of reasons, including crowding of the investment style, excessive asset gathering by the manager, or a less favorable macroeconomic backdrop. This raises the question how to deal with a situation like the one illustrated in Figure 5.5, where the total return for a manager still looks quite healthy, but the recent drawdown looks worrisome. Did something change? Was the manager never of the Good type in the first place?

To navigate the uncertainty around the quality of managers, investors need a framework for deciding whether to replace a manager. Otherwise, behavioral biases can lead to suboptimal decisions, as illustrated by Goyal and Wahal (2008), for example, who show that investors are too quick to hire and to fire managers.[11]

To illustrate the key considerations involved, we use a stylized setting in this section with only two types of managers:[12]

1. *Good*: producing returns with an (expected) annualized Sharpe ratio of 0.5
2. *Bad*: producing returns with an (expected) zero Sharpe ratio

The central question we seek to answer is: What performance statistics are the most informative for deciding whether to replace a manager? We will first discuss a setting with a single decision moment, which reduces the analysis to a question of how well we can disentangle *Good* and *Bad* managers, based on different statistics. Next, we explore a richer setting, with a monthly decision to replace a manager or not. In this case, it also matters how quickly one is able to detect (and replace) *Bad* managers. In the final part of this section, we look at time-varying drawdown thresholds, which are more complex (perhaps explaining why they are not commonplace), yet more appropriate for the case.

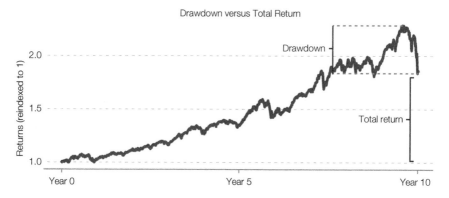

FIGURE 5.5 Illustrative manager performance. Illustrative example of a manager's cumulative return with the maximum drawdown and total return since inception highlighted.

Classification at the End of a 10-Year Observation Period

We need to recognize that the decision to replace a manager will be subject to two types of errors:

Type I error: replacing a *Good* manager (false positive)

Type II error: not replacing a *Bad* manager (false negative)

In Figure 5.6, we show the tradeoff between these two error types for three rules applied after a 10-year observation window:

1. Total return over the 10 years
2. Drawdown level at the 10-year point
3. Maximum drawdown during the 10-year period

Each dot in Figure 5.6 corresponds to a different cutoff value for the respective statistic. A larger diamond highlights the case where we use −10 percent (−1 annual standard deviation) as the cutoff value for each statistic.

In the left panel of Figure 5.6, we assume we have a pool consisting of 50 percent *Good* (Sharpe ratio 0.5) and 50 percent *Bad* (Sharpe ratio 0.0) managers with returns that are normal, IID, and with an annualized standard deviation of 10 percent. This means the annualized mean return is 5 percent or 0 percent, depending on whether the manager is *Good* or *Bad*. Crucially, we assume managers are of constant type. Here, it is clear that classification based on the total return leads to a better Type I/Type II tradeoff than using a drawdown-based rule, as the curve is closer to the origin (low Type I and Type II errors). This should come as no surprise, as the only unknown of the manager return distribution is the mean return. The realized mean (or total) return is a sufficient statistic, using all historical returns with equal weight. In contrast, the statistics based on peak and/or trough returns are a complicated, path-dependent function of historical returns.

In the right panel of Figure 5.6, we assume all managers start off as *Good*, but that they migrate to *Bad* at a constant monthly rate over time. The assumed monthly migration rate is 0.5 percent, which means that after 10 years, around 45 percent of managers have migrated from *Good* to *Bad*. These assumptions are motivated by the fact that in practice, managers or strategies can migrate from *Good* to *Bad* because of structural market changes, increased competition for the strategy style employed, staff turnover, or a fund accumulating too many assets. Now, the rules based on drawdown and total return are similarly effective. This is a big change from the case of constant manager types (left panel), where the total return–based rule was superior. The pickup in the appeal of drawdown-based rules here is intuitive, as they put more emphasis on recent history and so are more tailored to the possibility of a migration from *Good* to *Bad*.

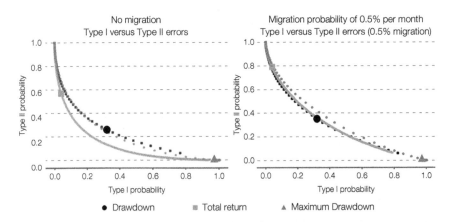

FIGURE 5.6 Efficacy classification rules with a 10-year horizon. We show the Type I error (mistakenly replacing a *Good* manager) and Type II error (mistakenly keeping a *Bad* manager) for three replacement rules. Evaluation takes place after observing 10 years of monthly data. In the left panel, the pool of managers consists of 50 percent *Good* and 50 percent *Bad* managers. In the right panel, all managers start off as *Good*, but each month there is a 0.5 percent chance of migrating to a *Bad* manager type. *Good* and *Bad* managers have a Sharpe ratio of 0.5 and 0.0, respectively. Returns are normal, IID, with 10 percent annualized volatility for both manager types. Different observations correspond to different cutoff values for the replacement rule, with a diamond corresponding to a −1 sigma cutoff.

As can be seen in Figure 5.6, a –10 percent cutoff value (represented by the big diamonds in the plot) leads to very different Type I error values. It is, for example, much more common for the drawdown level to hit –10 percent than it is for the total return to reach –10 percent. In fact, every time the total return hits –10 percent, the drawdown must also be at least as *Bad* as –10 percent. The reverse does not hold.

In order to do a sensible comparison, in Table 5.1, we report the Type I and II error rates across the three rules for a given implied probability of replacement (reported in the first column). The rules require different cutoff values in order to have the same probability of hitting the cutoff after the 10-year window (with no type migration). Consistent with the left panel of Figure 5.6, we see that the total return-based rule is preferred. The total-return rule is superior in terms of its lower Type 1 error (fewer *Good* managers are incorrectly identified as *Bad*).

TABLE 5.1 Cutoff values associated with a given probability of replacement after 10 years. For different probabilities of replacement, we tabulate the associated cutoff value for the three replacement rules considered, as well as the Type I and Type II error rate.

Proba-bility of replace-ment (%)	Total Return			Drawdown			Maximum Drawdown		
	Threshold (%)	Type I	Type II	Threshold (%)	Type I	Type II	Threshold (%)	Type I	Type II
10	–27	0.01	0.80	–35	0.01	0.81	–41	0.01	0.82
20	–15	0.03	0.64	–26	0.05	0.63	–34	0.05	0.64
30	–3	0.07	0.47	–20	0.10	0.49	–30	0.10	0.51
40	9	0.13	0.33	–15	0.18	0.37	–26	0.19	0.37
50	22	0.22	0.21	–11	0.29	0.28	–23	0.29	0.26

Monthly Evaluation

In reality, the decision to replace a manager is not done once, at the end of a long observation window, but intermittently. For example, some multi-manager hedge funds state very clearly at what drawdown level a portfolio manager is fired. Interestingly, typically a constant cutoff value is used, rather than allowing for larger drawdowns when a manager has been running for a longer time. The reasons for this may be behavioral; in other words, the rule is intended to alter manager behavior whether the manager has long tenure or not. It is also possible that the fund is acknowledging the difficulty of determining which managers are *Good* at any point and allowing the drawdown rule to do the work for them, recognizing that some *Good* managers become *Bad*. In this subsection, we follow this practice and assume constant cutoff values. In the next subsection, we will contrast a constant with a time-varying drawdown rule.

Concretely, we now consider an investor who evaluates managers monthly for a 10-year period. In Figure 5.7, we compare the efficacy of a total return and maximum drawdown rule to replace managers, where we make the same assumptions on manager types as in Figure 5.6.[13] That is, in the left panel, managers are of constant type (50 percent *Good*, 50 percent *Bad*), while in the right panel, all managers start off as *Good*, but migrate to *Bad* at a constant rate. Replacement means drawing a new manager from the same pool (i.e., 50–50 odds of *Good–Bad* in the case of the left panel), and a *Good* manager (that can deteriorate subsequently) in the case of the right panel.

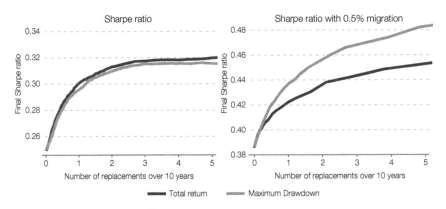

FIGURE 5.7 Efficacy of replacement rules with monthly evaluation. We show the average Sharpe ratio over a 10-year window, with a monthly decision to replace managers based on either a total return- or drawdown-based rule. In the left panel, the pool of managers consists of 50 percent *Good* and 50 percent *Bad* managers. In the right panel, all managers start off as *Good*, but each month there is a 0.5 percent chance of migrating to a *Bad* manager type. *Good* and *Bad* managers have a Sharpe ratio of 0.5 and 0.0 respectively. The average Sharpe ratios in the right panel are higher because of a greater proportion of *Good* managers. Monthly returns are normal, IID, with 10 percent annualized volatility for both manager types. We vary the cutoff value used in the replacement rule and plot the average Sharpe ratio against the average number of replacements.

In the case of monthly evaluation, it is not just about ultimately making the right call (Type I and II error rates), but also how quickly one detects and replaces a *Bad* manager. So instead, Figure 5.7 shows the Sharpe ratio over a 10-year window, with managers being replaced when they hit the threshold value.

Replacing a manager can be costly because it requires due diligence into new managers, involves legal costs, and resets the high-water mark in case of performance-fee charges for hedge funds. For this reason, in Figure 5.7, we plot the resulting Sharpe ratio when using the two replacement rules as a function of the average number of replacements during the 10-year window. To this end, we vary the cutoff value and, for each value, plot the average Sharpe ratio as a function of the total number of replacements over the 10-year period.

In the left panel of Figure 5.7, we see that in case of constant manager types, the total return is better than the drawdown-based rule. This is consistent with the left panel of Figure 5.6. Again, the intuition is that the total return is an efficient statistic for estimating a manager's average return, while the drawdown statistic is path-dependent and so more wasteful in its use of historical return observations.

In the right panel of Figure 5.7, we see that in case of a manager migrating from *Good* to *Bad*, a drawdown-based replacement rule is more effective in that it results in a higher Sharpe ratio for a given number of replacements over 10 years. The superior performance of the drawdown-based rule is intuitive, as it more naturally picks up on recent, sudden drop-offs in performance.

Monthly Evaluation with a Changing Drawdown Threshold

In practice, investors often employ fixed drawdown thresholds, even though the probability of hitting said value increases through time, as previously illustrated in Figure 5.2 (Panel B). In order to have a more consistent rate of replacement through time, we now also consider a drawdown cutoff value that increases with time. Specifically, the cutoff is:

$$cutoff(t) = k \times max(1, \sqrt{t/12}) \qquad (5.3)$$

for different threshold values, k, and number of months, t. The square-root term is motivated by the fact that the volatility of cumulative returns tends to grow approximately with the square root of time. We take the maximum of 1 and the square-root of time/12, so that in the first year, we are not working with a very low threshold.

In Figure 5.8, we show the Sharpe ratio over a 10-year window for the time-varying drawdown rule versus the constant rule considered before. As before, in Figures 5.6 and 5.7 (left panels), replacement means drawing a new manager from a constant pool of 50 percent *Good* and *Bad* managers. The time-dependent rule leads to better performance for a given number of replacements over the 10-year window. The effect seems to flatten off, though, with more frequent replacements as the time effect is less relevant then.

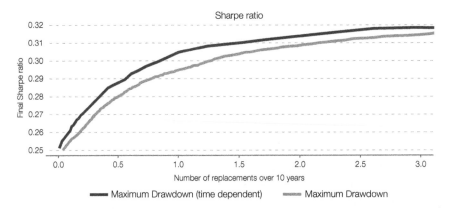

FIGURE 5.8 Efficacy of the drawdown replacement rules with monthly evaluation and a static or time-dependent threshold. We show the average Sharpe ratio over a 10-year window, with a monthly decision to replace managers based on a drawdown rule with either a stationary or time-dependent threshold. The pool of managers consists of 50 percent *Good* (Sharpe ratio 0.5) and 50 percent *Bad* (Sharpe ratio 0.0) managers. Monthly returns are normal, IID, with 10 percent annualized volatility for both manager types. We vary the cutoff value used in the replacement rule and plot the average Sharpe ratio against the average number of replacements.

In Figure 5.9, we show the static and time-varying drawdown thresholds in case of 1 and 2 replacements per 10 years on average in the left and right panel, respectively. The time-varying rule starts off with a significantly lower drawdown threshold, but is less stringent at longer horizons. This lines up better with the probability of drawdowns of a given level increasing with time (see Figure 5.2, Panel B).

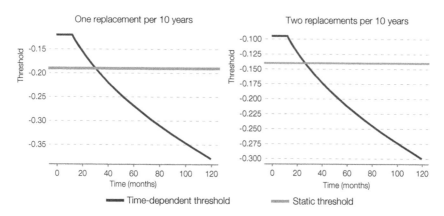

FIGURE 5.9 Equivalent thresholds through time for the different drawdown replacement rules. We show the equivalent threshold through time used for each drawdown rule for one and two replacements over two years.

DRAWDOWN-BASED RISK REDUCTION RULES

In the previous section, we considered rules for replacing managers. Another common application of drawdown rules is to use them to first lower the risk of a manager while continuing to evaluate subsequent performance.

In Figure 5.10, we illustrate the effect of a drawdown-based rule, where a risk reduction of 50 percent is triggered if the drawdown dips below a cutoff value. Full risk taking is restored if the manager recoups half of the losses. That is, they would have recovered the peak-to-trough loss if their risk had not been reduced by half. We vary the cutoff used and plot the Sharpe ratio, annualized return, and annualized volatility against the probability of having at least one risk reduction over the 10-year evaluation window. While the Sharpe ratio can improve slightly from such a risk reduction rule, the annualized return is lower. This is perhaps an obvious result, as there is always still a chance the manager is *Good* (0.5 Sharpe ratio). In the worst case that they are *Bad*, it has a zero (and not negative) Sharpe ratio.

While this illustration may be obvious, it shows that risk reductions may only serve to reduce risk, and not improve the annualized return, unless one takes up risk elsewhere in the portfolio. Of course, if the pool of managers is finite or there are costs to taking on new managers, then a rule like this might serve a practical purpose.

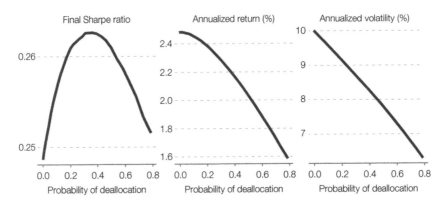

FIGURE 5.10 Efficacy of risk reduction rule, monthly evaluation, no type migration. We show the average Sharpe ratio over a 10-year window, with a monthly decision to reduce risk based on a drawdown rule. We simulate a pool of managers with a 50 percent chance of being *Good* (Sharpe ratio 0.5) or *Bad* (Sharpe 0.0).

For a risk reduction method to improve average returns, the conditional expected returns need to be negative. This can happen if there is a large chance of having a manager with a negative Sharpe ratio, but this seems a stretch because it requires negative skill or very high transaction costs. An alternative is a setting with a very high degree of autocorrelation, where one may have a negative expected return following a negative realized return.[14]

CONCLUDING REMARKS

What type and size of drawdown should cause you to change an investment manager? We offer five main conclusions, presented here in the order in which they are discussed in this chapter.

First, know your stats. Drawdowns are easy to compute. However, it is challenging to estimate the probability of hitting a certain drawdown level. As such, we help you set sensible drawdown limits for given (or stated) parameters of the return distribution.

Second, a preset drawdown rule may prevent peak risk taking. Taking risk in bursts (leading to heteroskedastic or kurtotic returns) will increase the probability of hitting a certain drawdown level relative to more constant risk taking (holding constant the long-term volatility). Hence, clearly communicated drawdown limits can motivate a manager to take more even risk over time. Also, automatic deallocation at a given drawdown level may prevent a manager from adverse behavior to exploit the "trader put." This occurs when a trader takes on extra risk when returns drop sharply, maximizing the chances of getting out of the hole. In such a position, the trader recognizes that even if this does not work, and there are additional losses, the trader has limited liability, so there is no extra pain. Similarly, a deep out-of-the money put is only very valuable with a high degree of volatility.

Third, think in terms of the relative cost of Type I and Type II errors; (see also Harvey and Liu (2020)). If hiring a manager is a costly endeavor, Type I errors (booting *Good* managers) are costly. If a *Bad* manager just adds noise (has a Sharpe ratio of zero) in an otherwise diversified portfolio, and if ample cash is available, some Type II errors (keeping a *Bad* manager) may not be that *Bad*. However, if *Bad* managers have a negative Sharpe ratio (e.g., because of transaction costs, or because they unwittingly take the other side of the trade of some shrewd investors), Type II errors become much more of a concern. Thinking in terms of the costs of Type I and Type II errors is crucial for the hiring and firing process.

Fourth, look at both total return and drawdown statistics. Total-return (or Sharpe-ratio) rules are best at measuring the constant ability of a manager to create positive returns. Drawdown-based rules, on the other hand, are better suited to deal with a situation where a manager abruptly loses their skill. In reality, the two are complementary, where the relative weights on total returns versus drawdown depend crucially on the assessment of how likely it is that a *Good* manager can transition into a *Bad* one. Obviously, alternative criteria that may hint at a possible deterioration of a manager's quality (such as turnover, fast asset growth, publication of their secret sauce) may provide a warning that an investor should start to place more weight on the drawdown statistic.

Fifth, consider a time-varying drawdown rule. The probability of hitting a certain drawdown level naturally increases over time, even if a manager continues to be of the same type, generating returns from a constant distribution. Somewhat puzzlingly, drawdown limits in practice are typically set at a constant (time-invariant) level. Even though it adds some complexity, a time-varying drawdown rule is advisable.

We have set out here the foundations of strategic risk management. We began by detailing how allocation to particular strategies improved the risk characteristics of portfolios. Next, we detailed three portfolio management mechanisms, volatility targeting, strategic rebalancing, and drawdown control, which also serve to improve the risk characteristics of portfolios. There is one commonality to all of these ideas: they are all quantitative. Next, we will explore the interplay between discretionary and systematic asset management. Given the importance of using quantitative information in both asset selection as well as risk management, it is important to compare these two approaches. We will show that even discretionary managers are much more quantitatively oriented than most believe.

APPENDIX 5A: HETEROSKEDASTICITY FOR U.S. STOCKS

Panel A: monthly returns

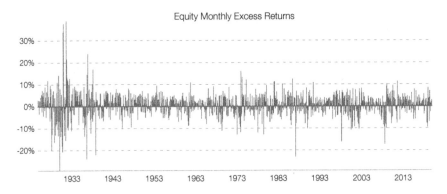

Panel B: rolling 12-month realized volatility

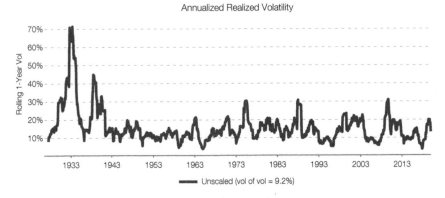

FIGURE 5A.1   Monthly U.S. equity returns and rolling 12-month volatility.
In Figure 5A.1 we show monthly U.S. equity returns (panel A) and the rolling
12-month realized volatility (panel B) for U.S. equity returns from June 1926 to
December 2019. Volatility is persistently high around, for example, 1929 (Great
Depression) and 2008 (Global Financial Crisis).[15]

TABLE 5B.1 Historical biggest negative (gap) moves. The table shows for a number of liquid securities the sample period (start date, end date, total number of years) and the worst monthly return (which month, percent return, number of annual standard deviations).

Description	Sample period		Most negative return			Vol of Vol (re-scaled to 10%)	Auto correlation
	Start	End	Month	Value	#STDs (ann)		
			EQUITY INDICES				
CAC 40 Index	Nov 1988	Feb 2020	Aug 1990	-16.6%	-1.27	5.6%	0.09
DAX Index	Nov 1990	Feb 2020	Sep 2002	-23.0%	-1.64	6.2%	0.05
NASDAQ 100 Index	Apr 1996	Feb 2020	Feb 2001	-28.8%	-1.85	7.2%	0.05
Russell 2000 Index	Sep 2000	Feb 2020	Oct 2008	-20.5%	-1.88	6.5%	0.05
S+P 500 Index	Apr 1982	Feb 2020	Oct 1987	-20.4%	-1.77	3.5%	0.04
Euro-STOXX	Jun 2000	Feb 2020	Sep 2002	-18.0%	-1.76	6.8%	0.10
FTSE	May 1984	Feb 2020	Oct 1987	-27.6%	-2.30	4.3%	-0.01
Hang Seng	Jan 1987	Feb 2020	Oct 1987	-40.7%	-2.21	5.2%	0.02
Korean Kospi	Sep 2000	Feb 2020	Sep 2001	-23.3%	-1.85	7.3%	0.02
Nikkei	Mar 1987	Feb 2020	Oct 1987	-32.8%	-2.15	5.1%	-0.01
Average				-25.2%	-1.87	5.8%	0.04

(*Continued*)

Description	Sample period		Most negative return				Vol of Vol (re-scaled to 10%)	Auto correlation
	Start	End	Month	Value	#STDs (ann)			
			GOVERNMENT BONDS					
German Bonds	Mar 1997	Feb 2020	Jan 2011	−0.9%	−1.31		7.0%	0.20
German Bonds	Jun 1983	Feb 2020	Feb 1990	−6.1%	−1.53		4.1%	0.05
Gilts	Nov 1982	Feb 2020	Sep 1986	−9.4%	−1.60		3.7%	0.05
Japanese Bonds	Mar 1983	Feb 2020	Sep 1987	−7.2%	−1.84		4.7%	0.01
German Bonds	Oct 1991	Feb 2020	Feb 1994	−1.9%	−0.96		6.0%	0.14
US Treasuries	Sep 1977	Feb 2020	Jul 2003	−9.4%	−1.06		1.7%	0.05
US Treasuries	Jul 2005	Feb 2020	Apr 2008	−1.1%	−1.95		6.8%	0.22
US Treasuries	Oct 1991	Feb 2020	Apr 2004	−3.1%	−1.15		6.1%	0.12
US Treasuries	May 1982	Feb 2020	Jul 2003	−5.6%	−1.08		3.2%	0.05
Average				−5.0%	−1.39		4.8%	0.10

OIL

Crude Oil	Jun 1988	Feb 2020	Oct 2008	−37.3%	−1.51	5.4%	0.26
Crude Oil	Oct 1983	Feb 2020	Oct 2008	−35.9%	−1.47	4.5%	0.17
Heating Oil	Mar 1979	Feb 2020	Oct 2008	−32.7%	−1.29	2.7%	0.09
Gas Oil	Apr 1981	Feb 2020	Oct 2008	−30.7%	−1.21	4.0%	0.21
RBOB Gasoline	Dec 1984	Feb 2020	Oct 2008	−41.1%	−1.55	4.6%	0.07
Average				−35.5%	−1.41	4.2%	0.16

METALS

Aluminium	Jan 1980	Feb 2020	Sep 1988	−20.0%	−1.17	3.2%	0.02
Copper	Jul 1959	Feb 2020	Oct 2008	−36.3%	−1.37	0.4%	0.11
Gold	Jan 1975	Feb 2020	Mar 1980	−25.4%	−1.60	1.6%	−0.05
Lead	Jun 1989	Feb 2020	May 2008	−29.9%	−1.59	5.7%	0.04
Nickel	Jul 1979	Feb 2020	Oct 2008	−27.3%	−0.98	3.6%	0.13
Silver	Jun 1963	Feb 2020	Mar 1980	−45.6%	−1.62	1.3%	0.01
Zinc	Jan 1975	Feb 2020	Oct 2008	−34.0%	−1.67	2.0%	0.01
Average				−31.2%	−1.43	2.5%	0.04

REFERENCES

Bailey, D., and M. López de Prado (2015). "Stop-Outs Under Serial Correlation and the Triple Penance Rule," *Journal of Risk*, 18(2), 61–93.

Bordalo, P., N. Gennaioli, and A. Shleifer (2012). "Salience Theory of Choice Under Risk," *Quarterly Journal of Economics*, 127(3), 1243–1285.

Busseti, E., E. Ryu, and S. Boyd (2016). "Risk-Constrained Kelly Gambling," *Journal of Investing*, 25(3), 118–134.

Carr, P., H. Zhang, and O. Hadjiliadis (2011). "Maximum Drawdown Insurance," *International Journal in Theoretical and Applied Finance*, 8(14), 1195–1230.

Casati, A., and S. Tabachnik (2012). "The Statistical Properties of the Maximum Drawdown in Financial Time Series," working paper.

Chekhlov, A., S. P. Uryasev, and M. Zabarankin (2005). "Drawdown Measure in Portfolio Optimization," *International Journal of Theoretical and Applied Finance*, 8(1), 13–58.

Cvitanic, J., S. Kou, X. Wan, and K. Williams (2019). "Pi Portfolio Management: Reaching Goals While Avoiding Drawdowns," working paper.

Douady, R., A. Shiryaev, and M. Yor (2000). "On Probability Characteristics of Downfalls in a Standard Brownian Motion," *Theory of Probability and its Applications*, 44, 29–38.

Efron, B., and R. Tibshirani (1986). "Bootstrap Methods for Standard Errors, Confidence Intervals, and Other Measures of Statistical Accuracy," *Statistical Science*, 1(1), 54–75.

Goyal, A., and S. Wahal (2008). "The Selection and Termination of Investment Management Firms by Plan Sponsors," *Journal of Finance*, 63(4), 1805–1847.

Grossman, S. J., and Z. Zhou (1993). "Optimal Investment Strategies for Controlling Drawdowns," *Mathematical Finance*, 3(3), 241–276.

Hadjiliadis, O., and J. Vecer (2006). "Drawdowns Preceding Rallies in a Brownian Motion Model," *Quantitative Finance*, 5(6), 403–409.

Harvey, C. R., and Y. Liu (2020). "False (and Missed) Discoveries in Financial Economics," *Journal of Finance*, 75(5), 2503–2553.

Kaminski, K.M., and A.W. Lo (2014). "When Do Stop-Loss Rules Stop Losses?," *Journal of Financial Markets*, 18, 234–254.

Korn, O., P.M. Möller, and C. Schwehm (2020). "Drawdown Measures: Are They All the Same?," working paper.

Leal, R.P.C., and B. de M. Mendes (2015). "Maximum Drawdown: Models and Applications," *Journal of Alternative Investments*, 7(4), 83–91.

Magdon-Ismail, M., A. Atiya, A. Pratap, and Y. Abu-Mostafa (2004). "On the Maximum Drawdown of a Brownian Motion," *Journal of Applied Probability*, 41(1), 147–161.

Molyboga, M., and C. L'Ahelec (2017). "Portfolio Management with Drawdown-Based Measures," *Journal of Alternative Investments*, 19(3),75–89.

Sornette, D. (2003). *Why Stock Markets Crash: Critical Events in Complex Financial Systems* (Princeton: Princeton University Press).

Thaler, R., and E. Johnson (1990). "Gambling with the House Money and Trying to Break Even: The Effects of Prior Outcomes on Risky Choice," *Management Science*, 36(6), 643–660.

Van Hemert, O., M. Ganz, C. R. Harvey, S. Rattray, E. Sanchez Martin, and D. Yawitch (2020). "Drawdowns," *Journal of Portfolio Management*, 46(8), 34–50.

Vecer, J. (2006). "Maximum Drawdown and Directional Trading," *Risk*, 19(12), 88–92.

CHAPTER 6

Man versus Machine

INTRODUCTION

In the first five chapters, we detailed the tools necessary to implement a holistic approach to risk management. All of the tools are quantitative. It is reasonable at this point to push the analysis further. Is it more likely that managers who use systematic or algorithm-driven investment strategies have different return-risk profiles than managers that rely on discretionary techniques? How widespread is the use of quantitative techniques in discretionary asset management? Is there a difference in risk exposures to well-known factors across discretionary and systematic funds by category?[1]

In addition, so far we have taken a broad view of risk—mainly from a portfolio point of view (i.e., portfolio volatility and portfolio downside risk). However, what are the drivers of these risk exposures? We explore a number of systematic risk factors and compare the exposures of systematic and discretionary managers. Discretionary managers rely on human skills to interpret new information and make day-to-day investment decisions. Systematic managers, on the other hand, use strategies that are rules-based and implemented by a computer, with little or no daily human intervention. How does this difference play out on the risk dimension?

In our experience, some allocators to hedge funds, including some of the largest in the world, either partially or entirely avoid allocating to systematic funds. The reasons we have heard for this include: systematic funds are homogeneous; systematic funds are hard to understand; the investing experience in systematic has been worse than discretionary; systematic funds are less transparent than discretionary; and systematic funds are bound to perform worse than discretionary because they use only data from the past. These reasons seem to be consistent with a distrust of systems, or "algorithm aversion," as illustrated by a series of experiments in Dietvorst, Simmons, and Massey (2015). In line with our experience and algorithm aversion, only 31 percent of hedge funds are systematic and they manage just 26 percent of the total of assets under management (AUM), as at the end of 2014.

Despite the literature on the topic, we find no empirical basis for such an aversion. In this chapter, we show that the lack of confidence in systematic funds is not justified by comparing their performance to that of their discretionary counterparts after adjusting for volatility and factor exposures. Our analysis covers over 9,000 funds from the Hedge Fund Research (HFR) database over the period 1996–2014. We classify funds as either systematic or discretionary based on algorithmic text analysis of the fund descriptions, as the categories used by HFR do not provide an exact match for our research question. We consider both macro and equity funds.

We find that systematic and discretionary manager performance is similar, after adjusting for volatility and factor exposures (i.e., in terms of their appraisal ratio). It is sometimes claimed that systematic funds have a greater exposure to well-known risk factors. We find, however, that for discretionary funds (in aggregate) more of the average return and the volatility of returns can be explained by risk factors.

Our main results are summarized in Table 6.1. In the first row, we report the average (unadjusted) return for the different styles considered. All returns are in excess of the local short-term interest rate. Hedge fund returns are averaged across funds of a particular style (i.e., we form an equally weighted index) and are after transaction costs and fees. Based on unadjusted returns, systematic macro funds outperform discretionary macro funds, while the reverse is true for equity funds.

In the second row, we report the amount of the return that can be attributed to well-known and easy-to-implement risk factors, based on a regression analysis. For discretionary funds, more of the return can be attributed to factors than for their systematic counterparts. We consider three sets of risk factors: traditional factors (equity, bond, credit), dynamic factors (stock value, stock size, stock momentum, FX carry), and a volatility factor. The latter is defined as a strategy of buying one-month, at-the-money S&P 500 calls and puts (i.e., straddles) at month-end and letting them expire at the next month's end. In rows three to five of Table 6.1, we show the attribution to the three underlying sets of factors. For all four styles, the return attributed to traditional factors is meaningful, as it ranges from 1.5 percent to 2.2 percent. The return attributed to dynamic factors is also positive in all cases, ranging from 0.2 percent to 1.3 percent. The return attributed to the volatility factor is negative for systematic and discretionary macro funds, at –3.2 percent and –1.3 percent respectively, and close to zero for equity funds. Macro funds on average have a long exposure to the volatility factor, which leads to negative returns over time. The negative risk

TABLE 6.1 **Performance of different hedge fund styles.** Reported statistics are for the returns of four hedge fund styles, averaged across funds of a particular style, in excess of the short-term interest rate, and annualized. The first row reports unadjusted average returns while subsequent rows report the output based on a regression of hedge fund returns on returns of risk factors. We consider well-known and easy-to-implement risk factors: traditional (equity, bonds, credit), dynamic (size, value, momentum, FX carry), and volatility (buying one-month, at-the-money S&P 500 calls and puts at month-end). Only aggregate factor attributions are reported here. Figures 6.3 and 6.4 show full regression results, as well as the attribution to individual factors. We use monthly data from HFR for the June 1996 to December 2014 period.

	Systematic Macro	Discretionary Macro	Systematic Equity	Discretionary Equity
Return average	5.01%	2.86%	2.88%	4.09%
Return attributed to factors	0.15%	1.28%	1.77%	2.86%
Traditional	2.08%	1.58%	1.47%	2.19%
Dynamic	1.28%	0.98%	0.23%	1.08%
Volatility	−3.21%	−1.28%	0.07%	−0.41%
Adjusted return average (alpha)	4.85%	1.57%	1.11%	1.22%
Adjusted return volatility	10.93%	5.10%	3.18%	4.79%
Adjusted return appraisal ratio	0.44	0.31	0.35	0.25

premium for the long volatility factor makes sense, given that being long volatility can act as a hedge for holding risky assets in general. Correcting macro funds' returns for their long volatility exposure essentially gives them credit for this hedging characteristic.

In the sixth row of Table 6.1, we report the average risk-adjusted return, which is simply the difference between the average unadjusted return and the return attributed to risk factors. Systematic macro stands out with an average risk-adjusted return of 4.9 percent. Discretionary macro has an average risk-adjusted return of 1.6 percent, while systematic and discretionary equity funds have similar values at 1.1 percent and 1.2 percent, respectively. However, the risk-adjusted returns of systematic macro also have the highest volatility, as shown in the seventh row. In the eighth row of Table 6.1, we report the ratio of the average risk-adjusted return to its volatility, called the appraisal ratio, and see that systematic macro still outperforms, but by less.[2]

All in all, the above results show that the hedge fund styles we consider have historically realized small positive alphas, which are determined: (1) in excess of the short-term interest rate, (2) after transaction costs and fees, and (3) corrected for any return attributed to risk factors. We note that the factors themselves (especially the dynamic factors) cannot be produced for zero cost, and so a manager simply implementing these factor exposures would undoubtedly show a negative alpha.

The empirical analysis conducted in this chapter allows us to comment not only on performance statistics, like the alpha and appraisal ratio, but also on the return variation explained by the risk factors. We find that for systematic funds a slightly smaller proportion of variance is explained by the factors (both for macro and equity funds). A much larger proportion of variance is explained by factors for equity funds than for macro funds. This is mostly driven by a long equity market exposure in equity funds. For investors who already have a meaningful investment in equities outside of their hedge fund portfolio, it seems important to take this into account.

Finally, we look at the dispersion of manager returns (results discussed above were based on an index for each category). We establish that the dispersion in Sharpe and appraisal ratios across funds within a hedge fund style is similar (and large) for systematic and discretionary funds. This means that the concern that systematic funds are more homogeneous does not appear to stand up to scrutiny. So, in addition to style selection, fund selection seems to be just as important in each category. Particular attention should be paid to this when holding a concentrated portfolio of hedge funds.

This chapter begins with a description of the hedge fund data and textual analysis used to classify funds as either systematic or discretionary. Then, we discuss the risk factors and analyze the alpha and exposure to risk factors for systematic and discretionary macro funds. Next, we repeat our empirical analysis for equity funds. After that, we discuss the diversification potential of different hedge fund styles and some fund-level results. Finally, we offer some concluding remarks.

CLASSIFICATION OF HEDGE FUNDS

The research presented in this chapter uses hedge fund data from the HFR database. We exclude backfilled returns from before the moment a fund was added, and include the graveyard database to mitigate selection and survivorship bias concerns respectively. We start our analysis in 1996 due to the widely held view that hedge fund databases suffer from measurement biases prior to the mid-1990s.[3] We exclude a limited number of funds that report less frequently than monthly, or for which the reported performance is not classified as "Net of All Fees." See Appendix 6A for more details on the fund selection filters and the fund classification method, which we discuss next.

We use the two largest strategy types covered in the HFR database: Equity Hedge (6,955 funds) and Macro (2,182 funds). Within the HFR Macro category, the two main sub-strategies conveniently cover:

1. Systematic Diversified: " ... with little or no influence of individuals over the portfolio positioning."
2. Discretionary Thematic: " ... interpreted by an individual or group of individuals who make decisions on portfolio positions."

For Equity Hedge, the HFR-provided categorization is less tailored to our research question, though. None of the sub-strategy names contain the words "systematic" or "discretionary" and none of the HFR descriptions clearly specify whether the decision making is done by algorithms or by humans. Some Equity Hedge sub-strategy names and descriptions contain the word "quantitative," but most hedge funds will employ some form of quantitative analysis, which does not mean they take trading decisions without human overlay. To illustrate this, we find that the word "quantitative" occurs in the description of Systematic Diversified macro funds only 1.7 times more often than it does for Discretionary Thematic.

Given that the HFR categorization does not bifurcate equity funds into systematic and discretionary categories, we chose to rely on text analysis of the fund descriptions. Our method utilizes the HFR-provided split into systematic and discretionary macro funds (see Appendix 6A). Following a formal natural language processing method for picking the words used, we arrive at the following classification rule:

- Systematic if the fund description contains any of the following words or word parts: "algorithm," "approx," "computer," "model," "statistical," "system"
- Discretionary if the fund description contains none of the system-related words described above

For consistency, and because funds may be misclassified by HFR, we also use our classification for macro funds (instead of the HFR classification). Sampling the Macro Systematic Diversified funds that we classify as discretionary, there does not generally seem to be a clear indication that the fund is in fact systematic. So we deem it probable that the fund is not purely systematic but rather partially systematic or quantitative, but not rules-based.[4]

RISK FACTORS

We want to evaluate whether hedge funds add value over and above any performance that can be attributed to factors that: (1) were well known by 1996, when our sample period starts and (2) are easy to implement. In this section, we discuss three types of factors: traditional, dynamic, and a volatility factor. See Figure 6.1 (Panel A) for the full list of factors included.

As traditional factors, we include the main large and easily investable asset classes: equities (S&P 500 index), bonds (Barclays US Treasury Index), and credit (Citigroup US Big High-Grade Credit Index minus the Barclays US Treasury Index). The data are from Bloomberg.[5]

The dynamic factors we include are the three Fama-French U.S. stock factors and an FX carry factor. The Fama-French factors are size (small-minus-big U.S. stocks), value (high-minus-low book value U.S. stocks), and momentum (winner-minus-loser U.S. stocks). These factors were well known by the mid-1990s, following papers by Fama and French (1993) on size and value and Jegadeesh and Titman (1993) on the cross-sectional momentum factor.[6] The returns for these three factors can be obtained from Kenneth French's website.[7] The FX carry factor is applied to the most liquid G10 currency pairs.[8] The existence of an FX carry factor is a direct implication of the failing of the "uncovered interest rate parity," which has been extensively discussed in the academic finance literature, going back to Meese and Rogoff (1983) and Fama (1984). The data for the FX carry factor are from Deutsche Bank.[9]

We do not include dynamic factors that only recently became better known and documented, typically after hedge funds had profitably exploited them, and they had thus garnered widespread attention (macro trend-following, for example). As Frazzini, Kabiller, and Pedersen (2013) show, with the benefit of hindsight even

> ... Buffett's performance can be largely explained by "exposures to value, low-risk, and quality factors" together with "a leverage of about 1.6-to-1."

While cross-sectional momentum strategies applied to U.S. stocks were well known before 1996, time-series momentum applied to futures has been documented only much more recently, and is therefore not included. See Appendix 6B for a further discussion on this.

Finally, we note that our research is focused on past performance, rather than advocating a strategy for the future. While we are aware that an analysis starting at the time of writing would most likely use a simple macro time-series momentum factor as well as fixed income and commodity carry,

Panel A: Description risk factors

Category	Name	Instruments
Traditional	Equity market	S&P 500 index
	Bond market	Barclays US Treasury Index
	Credit market	Citigroup US BIG High-Grade Credit Index minus the Barclays US Treasury Index
Dynamic	Size (stocks)	Small-minus-big U.S. stocks
	Value (stocks)	High-minus-low book value U.S. stocks
	Momentum (stocks)	Winner-minus-loser U.S. stocks
	FX carry	Deutsche Bank G10 currency carry index
Volatility	Vol S&P 500	Straddles for S&P500

Panel B: Cumulative excess returns of the risk factors, scaled to 10 percent volatility (Sharpe ratios reported in the legend)

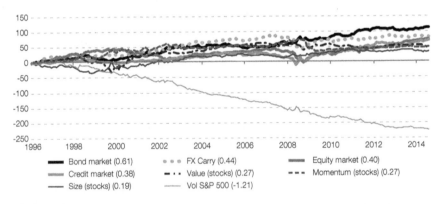

FIGURE 6.1 Risk factors. In Panel A, we list the risk factors considered in this chapter. Panel B shows the cumulative excess returns over the June 1996 to December 2014 sample period, where we scale the annualized volatility (ex-post) to 10 percent to facilitate comparison. The realized Sharpe ratio for each factor is reported in parentheses in the legend. In Panel C we report the correlation between the monthly factor returns.

Panel C: Correlation risk factor returns

	Equity market	Bond market	Credit market	Size (stocks)	Value (stocks)	Momentum (stocks)	FX Carry	Vol S&P 500
Equity market		−0.23	−0.25	−0.11	−0.16	−0.33	−0.49	−0.13
Bond market	−0.23		−0.40	−0.16	−0.04	−0.15	−0.12	−0.00
Credit market	−0.25	−0.40		−0.03	−0.02	−0.13	−0.27	−0.27
Size (stocks)	−0.11	−0.16	−0.03		−0.35	−0.09	−0.11	−0.18
Value (stocks)	−0.16	−0.04	−0.02	−0.35		−0.15	−0.11	−0.08
Momentum (stocks)	−0.33	−0.15	−0.13	−0.09	−0.15		−0.11	−0.06
FX Carry	−0.49	−0.12	−0.27	−0.11	−0.11	−0.11		−0.14
Vol S&P 500	−0.13	−0.00	−0.27	−0.18	−0.08	−0.06	−0.14	

FIGURE 6.1 *(Continued)*

for example, our objective here is to explain returns using factors known at the inception of the strategies, rather than on an ex-post basis. If these funds are to remain successful, they will need to innovate beyond currently known factors, as they have done before (see also Appendix 6B).

The volatility factor that we include is a long, one-month, at-the-money S&P 500 straddle (call and put option) position, bought at month-end and held to expiry. The data are from Goldman Sachs, who provided us with mid-prices for OTC options.[10] Hedge funds may have an exposure to the volatility factor due to positions in nonlinear instruments, like options. Hedge funds may also end up with an exposure to volatility due to the nature of their dynamic trading strategies. For example, in Chapter 1, we draw a parallel between a trend-following strategy and the dynamic replication of a straddle position. Finally, hedge funds may be exposed to the volatility factor if they trade in securities that are disproportionately hit at times of crisis, like collateralized debt obligations (CDOs).

Comparing the risk factors discussed above to what Balia, Brown, and Caglayan (2014) refer to as a set of "standard risk factors," we notice three main differences. First, instead of using the change in yield for the bond and credit factor, it is important to express all factor returns as investment returns. Second, we augment the list of dynamic factors with an FX carry factor, as described above. Third, we don't use the Fung and Hsieh (2001) volatility factors. The main reason for this is that these would, in our opinion, not be straightforward (or cheap) to implement.[11]

All factor returns are determined on an unfunded basis, which is done by using futures, a dollar-neutral long-short portfolio, or returns in excess of the three-month money-market rate. For reporting purposes, we scale all factors to have 10 percent volatility (ex post). The alphas and risk-adjusted returns are not affected by this scaling. The scaling allows for an easy comparison of betas to different factors: the larger the beta, the more variance is explained by the factor (in a multivariate sense). Figure 6.1 (Panel B) shows the cumulative factor returns, where we do not compound returns, so a straight line would correspond to a constant performance over time. The Sharpe ratios of each factor are presented in parentheses in the legend and are calculated as the ratio of the mean to the standard deviation of the monthly excess returns, annualized by multiplying by the square root of 12. The traditional and dynamic factors have a positive risk premium while the S&P 500 volatility factor carries a negative premium (i.e., a long volatility strategy has a negative return on average) with a Sharpe ratio of –1.21. This is mostly driven by the put leg of the straddle, for which the price is bid up by the large demand to hedge against sudden equity market drawdowns.

In Figure 6.1 (Panel C) we report the correlation between the different risk factors. The highest correlation (0.49) is between the equity and FX carry returns.

EMPIRICAL ANALYSIS: MACRO FUNDS

We select the subset of funds that we deem institutional-sized by applying an AUM cutoff of $100 million in December 2014, and before that a value in proportion to the size of the overall hedge fund industry relative to December 2014 (i.e., $10m in December 1996). This size filter is implemented at the start of each calendar year, based on the median of the prior year's monthly AUMs.[12]

Also, we endeavor to remove funds which are repeats of each other. We identify repeats based on the similarity in fund name, taking into account that strings like "class A" and "LLP" tend to be uninformative about the underlying strategy and are more reflective of particular structures. Having identified a group of repeated funds, we use the fund with the longest history as the representative of that group. Lastly, we sum AUMs across these groups of repeated funds, assigning the total AUM to the selected representative before applying the size screen mentioned above.

We conduct our performance analysis on hedge fund excess returns, so we deduct the short-term interest rate of the currency the returns are denominated in. In 74 percent of cases, the funds are U.S. dollar denominated and we deduct the three-month money-market rate. Most of our empirical analysis performed for the average returns of funds in a particular category, like systematic macro. The average is taken at each point in time using the then-available funds, hence forming an index return series. Later, we will also provide some results based on individual funds' returns.

In Figure 6.2, we report the results for the following regression:

$$R_t = \alpha + \sum_i \beta^i F_t^i + \varepsilon_t \qquad (6.1)$$

where R is the excess return, F are factor excess returns, α and β are the regression coefficients, and ε is the error term.

In Panel A, we report the regression coefficients for systematic (left side) and discretionary (right side) macro funds. We indicate whether a coefficient is significant at the 10 percent, 5 percent, and 1 percent significance level with *, **, and *** respectively (using a Newey-West adjustment with one lag).[13] In the left column, we only include a constant, in which case the alpha (which we annualize) simply equals the average unadjusted (annual) return.

In the second column, we include traditional factors. For systematic macro managers, the long bond exposure (significant at the 1 percent significance level) stands out, which is intuitive given that many systematic macro managers employ trend signals, and bond prices trended upwards over the 1996–2014 sample period. Discretionary macro managers have a meaningful long exposure to both equites and bonds.

In this third column, we also add dynamic factors. For systematic macro managers, there is a large exposure to U.S. stock momentum, which again can be understood from the prevalence of trend following in this category. Discretionary macro managers have a modest positive exposure to U.S. stock momentum, and also to FX carry.

In the fourth column, we add the long S&P options straddle (volatility) factor, which systematic macro managers have a (highly significant) positive exposure to. In Chapter 1, we show this is almost by design for a trend-following manager by showing it would hold positions that are similar to what a straddle delta-replication strategy would imply. For discretionary macro funds the coefficient on volatility is positive also, but less large and less significant.

Finally, Panel A of Figure 6.2 also reports the R^2 statistic (i.e., the proportion of the return variance explained by the factors). For our baseline case (including traditional, dynamic, and vol S&P 500 factors), this is 16 percent

Panel A: Risk factor exposures and excess performance

	Systematic Macro					Discretionary Macro			
	None	Traditional	Traditional +Dynamic	Traditional +Dynamic +Vol S&P500		None	Traditional	Traditional +Dynamic	Traditional +Dynamic +Vol S&P500
Alpha (annualized)	5.01%*	3.08%	1.85%	4.85%*	Alpha (annualized)	2.86%**	1.24%	0.38%	1.57%
Equity		0.01	0.03	0.03	Equity		0.21***	0.19***	0.19***
Bond		0.36***	0.36***	0.33***	Bond		0.12**	0.13***	0.12**
Credit		−0.08	−0.09	−0.01	Credit		0.01	−0.01	0.02
Size (stocks)			0.02	0.06	Size (stocks)			0.06	0.07*
Value (stocks)			0.09	0.08	Value (stocks)			0.03	0.03
Momentum (stocks)			0.18**	0.18**	Momentum (stocks)			0.09*	0.09*
FX Carry			0.10	0.11	FX Carry			0.11**	0.12***
Vol S&P 500				0.26***	Vol S&P 500				0.11**
R-squared	0%	8%	11%	16%	R-squared	0%	15%	22%	25%

FIGURE 6.2 Regression analysis for macro funds. We run regressions of systematic macro (left panels) and discretionary macro (right panels) returns on different subsets of the risk factor returns. The factors are (ex-post) scaled to 10 percent volatility to facilitate interpretation of the reported coefficients in Panel A, where significance is indicated by *, **, *** for the 10 percent, 5 percent, and 1 percent significance levels, respectively (under the assumption of a single hypothesis test). Panel B reports annualized performance statistics for the different subsets of risk factors considered, including the return attributed to factors, which is computed as the coefficient times the average factor return. Panel C shows the unadjusted and risk-adjusted cumulative excess returns, as well as the correction. The risk-adjusted return is corrected for any variation explained by the exposure to traditional, dynamic, and vol S&P 500 factors (the fourth specification in Panels A and B). The classification of funds into systematic and discretionary is done using text analysis. We use monthly data from HFR for the June 1996 to December 2014 period.

Panel B: Factor performance attribution (annualized)

Systematic Macro

	None	Traditional	Traditional +Dynamic	Traditional +Dynamic +Vol S&P500
Return average	5.01%	5.01%	5.01%	5.01%
Attributed to factors	0.00%	1.94%	3.17%	0.15%
Equity		0.04%	0.14%	0.11%
Bond		2.21%	2.16%	2.01%
Credit		-0.31%	-0.34%	-0.04%
Size (stocks)			0.04%	0.11%
Value (stocks)			0.25%	0.22%
Momentum (stocks)			0.49%	0.47%
FX Carry			0.43%	0.48%
Vol S&P 500				-3.21%
Adj. return avg. (alpha)	5.01%	3.08%	1.85%	4.85%
Adj. return volatility	11.71%	11.29%	11.19%	10.93%
Appraisal ratio	0.43	0.27	0.17	0.44

Discretionary Macro

	None	Traditional	Traditional +Dynamic	Traditional +Dynamic +Vol S&P500
Return average	2.86%	2.86%	2.86%	2.86%
Attributed to factors	0.00%	1.62%	2.48%	1.28%
Equity		0.83%	0.75%	0.74%
Bond		0.73%	0.80%	0.74%
Credit		0.06%	-0.02%	0.10%
Size (stocks)			0.11%	0.14%
Value (stocks)			0.09%	0.08%
Momentum (stocks)			0.25%	0.24%
FX Carry			0.50%	0.52%
Vol S&P 500				-1.28%
Adj. return avg. (alpha)	2.86%	1.24%	0.38%	1.57%
Adj. return volatility	5.77%	5.37%	5.19%	5.10%
Appraisal ratio	0.50	0.23	0.07	0.31

FIGURE 6.2 (Continued)

Panel C: Risk-adjusted returns (correcting for traditional, dynamic, and vol S&P 500 factor exposures)

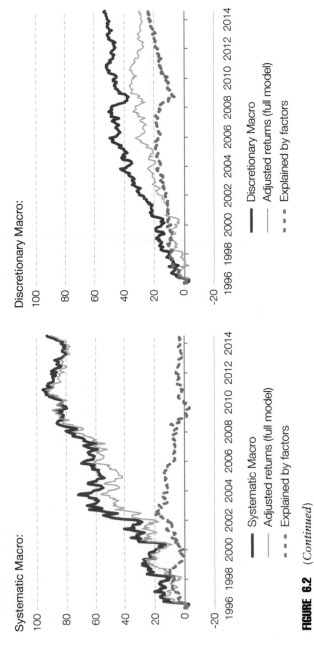

FIGURE 6.2 (*Continued*)

for systematic macro managers and 25 percent for discretionary macro managers. So the majority of the return variation is in fact not explained by the well-known factors.

Panel B of Figure 6.2 reports annualized performance statistics, including the return attributed to factor exposures. The latter can be extracted from the regression analysis by taking the average over time of the left- and right-hand sides of Equation 6.1 and recognizing that the average error is zero by construction:

$$Avg\{R\} = \alpha + \sum_i \beta^i Avg\{F^i\} \qquad (6.2)$$

Concretely, in Panel B we report the average annual return, $12 * Avg\{R\}$, in the first row. The return attributed to factors, that is, $12 * \beta * Avg\{F\}$, aggregated over all factors is reported in the second row, and the attribution to individual factors is reported below that. Next we report the annualized alpha, $12 * \alpha$, the annualized volatility of adjusted returns, $\sigma(\varepsilon)$ times square-root 12, and the ratio of the two, which is known as the appraisal ratio and given by:

$$AppraisalRatio = \frac{\alpha}{\sigma(\varepsilon)} * \sqrt{12} \qquad (6.3)$$

For systematic macro funds, the average unadjusted excess return is 5.01 percent (first row). Based on the baseline case specification (i.e., including traditional, dynamic, and the vol S&P 500 factors), 2.01 percent of that is attributed to the bond factor and –3.21 percent to the vol S&P 500 factor, leaving an alpha of 4.85 percent after taking into account the smaller effects of other factors as well. In regard to the risk-adjustment for the vol S&P 500 exposure, notice that systematic macro funds have a long exposure to the volatility factor, which has negative returns over time. The negative risk premium for the volatility factor is intuitive given that being long volatility can act as a hedge. Correcting systematic macro funds' returns for the long volatility exposure essentially gives them credit for this hedging feature.

For discretionary macro funds, the average unadjusted return is 2.86 percent. Based on the baseline case specification, 0.74 percent of that is attributed to the equity factor, and also 0.74 percent to the bond exposure. The attribution to the vol S&P 500 factor is –1.28 percent, leaving an alpha of 1.57 percent after taking into account the smaller effects of other factors as well.

Looking at the appraisal ratio rather than the alpha, the performance difference between systematic and discretionary macro funds is smaller;

for example, for the baseline case we observe 0.44 and 0.31, respectively. The reason is that systematic macro returns are more volatile, both in terms of unadjusted returns and the unexplained returns (regression error term).

Finally, in Panel C of Figure 6.2, we plot the risk-adjusted returns, which are obtained by rearranging Equation 6.1:

$$R_t^{Adj} = R_t - \sum_i \beta^i F_t^i = \alpha + \varepsilon_t \qquad (6.4)$$

For this figure, we use the baseline case specification with traditional, dynamic, and the vol S&P 500 factors. We show the history of the unadjusted (dark gray line) and risk-adjusted (light gray line) cumulative returns, where, as before in Figure 6.1, we do not compound returns. We also show the difference, specifically, what is explained by the factors (dashed line). For systematic macro managers the unadjusted and risk-adjusted cumulative returns are fairly close; adjustments for the various risk factors, notably the bond and volatility factors, are mostly offsetting. For discretionary macro managers, the risk-adjusted returns are well below unadjusted returns and the dip in unadjusted returns at the end of 2008 can be largely explained by factor exposures (particularly the long equity exposure).

We ran an additional regression with the difference between the systematic and discretionary macro returns as the dependent variable, and all factor returns as explanatory variables. The alpha difference (captured by the constant) for the baseline case is 3.28 percent (annualized), which (of course) is identical to the difference of the alphas reported in Figure 6.2. More informative is the fact that the t-stat on the alpha difference is only 1.66, failing to exceed two standard errors from zero.

At minimum, our results suggest that systematic macro funds have performed at least as well as discretionary macro funds—a conclusion that is robust to using a number of performance metrics (average unadjusted return, average risk-adjusted return, and appraisal ratio).

EMPIRICAL ANALYSIS: EQUITY FUNDS

In Figure 6.3, we repeat our analysis for systematic equity (left panel) and discretionary equity (right panel) funds.

In Panel A, the large (and significant) positive exposure to the equity market factor stands out, for both systematic (left table) and discretionary (right table) equity managers. While many equity managers may advertise their funds as being market-neutral, these results show that this does not hold up for the group in aggregate. The bond and credit factors are significant but

Panel A: Risk factor exposures and excess performance

Systematic Equity

	None	Traditional	Traditional +Dynamic	Traditional +Dynamic +Vol S&P500
Alpha (annualized)	2.88%*	1.36%	1.17%	1.11%
Equity		0.45***	0.42***	0.42***
Bond		-0.08***	-0.07***	-0.07***
Credit		0.05	0.05	0.05
Size (stocks)			0.09***	0.09***
Value (stocks)			-0.09**	-0.09**
Momentum (stocks)			0.05*	0.05*
FX Carry			0.04	0.04
Vol S&P 500				-0.01
R-squared	0%	66%	73%	73%

Discretionary Equity

	None	Traditional	Traditional +Dynamic	Traditional +Dynamic +Vol S&P500
Alpha (annualized)	4.09%	1.80%	0.83%	1.22%
Equity		0.69***	0.62***	0.62***
Bond		-0.16***	-0.11***	-0.12***
Credit		0.13***	0.10**	0.11**
Size (stocks)			0.27***	0.28***
Value (stocks)			-0.10**	-0.10**
Momentum (stocks)			0.08*	0.08*
FX Carry			0.14***	0.14***
Vol S&P 500				0.03
R-squared	0%	63%	77%	77%

FIGURE 6.3 Regression analysis for equity funds. We run regressions of systematic equity (left panels) and discretionary equity (right panels) returns on different subsets of the risk factor returns. The factors are (ex-post) scaled to 10 percent volatility to facilitate interpretation of the reported coefficients in Panel A, where significance is indicated by *, **, *** for the 10 percent, 5 percent, and 1 percent significance level respectively under the assumption of a single hypothesis test. Panel B reports annualized performance statistics for the different subsets of risk factors considered, including the return attributed to factors, which is computed as the coefficient times the average factor return. Panel C shows the adjusted, and risk-adjusted cumulative excess returns, as well as the correction. The risk-adjusted return is corrected for any variation explained by the exposure to traditional, dynamic, and vol S&P 500 factors (the fourth specification in Panels A and B). The classification of funds into systematic and discretionary is done using text analysis. We use monthly data from HFR for the June 1996 to December 2014 period.

Panel B: Factor performance attribution (annualized)

Systematic Equity

	None	Traditional	Traditional +Dynamic	Traditional +Dynamic +Vol S&P500
Return average	2.88%	2.88%	2.88%	2.88%
Attributed to factors	0.00%	1.51%	1.71%	1.77%
Equity		1.79%	1.70%	1.70%
Bond		-0.48%	-0.41%	-0.41%
Credit		0.20%	0.19%	0.18%
Size (stocks)			0.17%	0.17%
Value (stocks)			-0.23%	-0.23%
Momentum (stocks)			0.13%	0.13%
FX Carry			0.16%	0.16%
Vol S&P 500				0.07%
Adj. return avg. (alpha)	2.88%	1.36%	1.17%	1.11%
Adj. return volatility	5.97%	3.53%	3.17%	3.18%
Appraisal ratio	0.48	0.39	0.37	0.35

Discretionary Equity

	None	Traditional	Traditional +Dynamic	Traditional +Dynamic +Vol S&P500
Return average	4.09%	4.09%	4.09%	4.09%
Attributed to factors	0.00%	2.29%	3.25%	2.86%
Equity		2.78%	2.51%	2.51%
Bond		-1.00%	-0.70%	-0.72%
Credit		0.51%	0.36%	0.40%
Size (stocks)			0.51%	0.52%
Value (stocks)			-0.26%	-0.27%
Momentum (stocks)			0.22%	0.21%
FX Carry			0.61%	0.62%
Vol S&P 500				-0.41%
Adj. return avg. (alpha)	4.09%	1.80%	0.83%	1.22%
Adj. return volatility	9.78%	5.96%	4.79%	4.79%
Appraisal ratio	0.42	0.30	0.17	0.25

FIGURE 6.3 (*Continued*)

Panel C: Risk-adjusted returns (correcting for traditional, dynamic, and vol S&P 500 factor exposures)

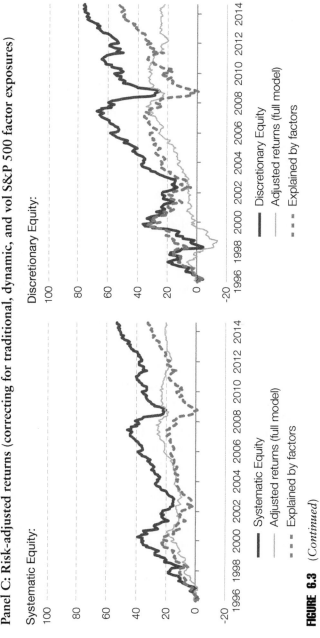

FIGURE 6.3 (*Continued*)

have small coefficient values, which implies less economic meaning because the factors were scaled to equal volatility (as previously described).

Looking at the third column, where we also add dynamic factors, we note that both systematic and discretionary equity managers have a sizable exposure to the stock size factor, suggesting that there is a tendency to be long small-cap/short large-cap stocks on average. One possible explanation for this is that, for the short side, it may be more feasible (and cheaper) to use the futures contract on a large-cap index, like the S&P 500 index. Alternatively, it may just be easier for managers to find opportunities in small caps. For discretionary equity funds, there is also an important long exposure to the FX carry factor. A possible explanation is that discretionary equity funds find (long) investment opportunities in less liquid stocks, which (just like FX carry) may suffer when liquidity suddenly dries up.

The reported R^2 statistic in Panel A of Figure 6.3 is 73 percent for systematic equity managers and 77 percent for discretionary equity managers in the baseline case (i.e., including traditional, dynamic, and the vol S&P 500 factor). This is much higher than the 16 percent and 25 percent that we reported before for systematic and discretionary macro funds, respectively. The equity factor is the dominant driver of the R^2 statistic.

In Panel B of Figure 6.3, we report different performance statistics (for the method, see the discussion and formulas in the previous section). For systematic equity funds, the average unadjusted return is 2.88 percent (see first row). Based on the baseline case specification, 1.70 percent of that is attributed to the equity factor, leaving an alpha of 1.11 percent after taking into account the smaller effects of other factors as well.

For discretionary equity funds, the average unadjusted return is 4.09 percent. Based on the baseline case specification, 2.51 percent of that is attributed to the equity factor, leaving an alpha of 1.22 percent after taking into account the smaller effects of other factors as well. Hence for the baseline case specification, the alpha for discretionary equity funds is slightly higher than it is for systematic equity funds. However, the appraisal ratio is slightly lower with a value of 0.25 for discretionary equity funds, versus 0.35 for systematic equity funds.

As we did for macro funds in the previous section, we plot in Panel C of Figure 6.3 the history of the unadjusted and risk-adjusted cumulative returns. Given the dominance of the equity risk factor, for both systematic and discretionary equity funds, the difference between the unadjusted and risk-adjusted returns follows closely the returns of the S&P 500 index, with drawdowns when the tech bubble burst in 2000 and during the financial crisis in 2008.

We also ran an additional regression with the difference between the systematic and discretionary equity return as the dependent variable, and all factor returns as explanatory variables. The alpha difference for the baseline case is an insignificant –0.11 percent (annualized) with a t-statistic of –0.11.

In sum, while the average unadjusted return is higher for discretionary equity than it is for systematic equity, when we control for risk factors the performance is similar (both the alpha and appraisal ratios are similar).

DIVERSIFICATION POTENTIAL OF DIFFERENT HEDGE FUND STYLES

In Figure 6.4, we report the correlations between the different hedge fund styles using unadjusted returns (left panel) and risk-adjusted returns (right panel). Macro and equity funds returns historically have a low correlation with each other (in the 0.0 to 0.5 range), allowing for potentially substantial diversification benefits when combining both asset classes. However, discretionary and systematic funds within macro or within equity are historically more highly correlated (in the 0.6–0.9 range). This suggests to us that discretionary and systematic managers' investment strategies are more similar than one might think.

Unadjusted returns

| | | Macro | | Equity | |
		systematic	discretionary	systematic	discretionary
Macro	systematic		0.72	0.02	0.00
Macro	discretionary	0.72		0.47	0.47
Equity	systematic	0.02	0.47		0.89
Equity	discretionary	0.00	0.47	0.89	

Risk-adjusted returns

| | | Macro | | Equity | |
		systematic	discretionary	systematic	discretionary
Macro	systematic		0.77	0.22	0.16
Macro	discretionary	0.77		0.44	0.41
Equity	systematic	0.22	0.44		0.63
Equity	discretionary	0.16	0.41	0.63	

FIGURE 6.4 Correlation between different hedge fund style returns. Correlations are between the unadjusted excess returns (left panel) and risk-adjusted returns (right panel) of different categories using monthly data from HFR for the June 1996 to December 2014 period. The risk-adjusted return is corrected for any variation explained by the exposure to traditional, dynamic, and vol S&P 500 factors.

Panel A: No factors (unadjusted returns)
Average return (annualized)

	Macro		Equity	
	Systematic	Discretionary	Systematic	Discretionary
25th percentile	0.79%	0.82%	0.40%	1.42%
50th percentile	3.78%	3.27%	4.47%	5.40%
75th percentile	6.96%	6.36%	8.05%	9.02%
Spread 75th–25th	6.17%	5.54%	7.65%	7.60%

Panel B: Baseline case factors (risk-adjusted returns)
Alpha (annualized)

	Macro		Equity	
	Systematic	Discretionary	Systematic	Discretionary
25th percentile	−4.35%	−2.02%	−0.55%	−0.97%
50th percentile	1.67%	1.78%	2.03%	2.76%
75th percentile	6.10%	5.98%	5.31%	6.19%
Spread 75th–25th	10.45%	8.00%	5.86%	7.16%

FIGURE 6.5 Fund-level statistics. In this figure we report the 25th, 50th, and 75th percentile of the average return and Sharpe ratio distribution for unadjusted fund returns (Panel A) and similarly the alpha and appraisal ratio for risk-adjusted fund returns based on the baseline case with eight risk factors (Panel B). For the risk-adjusted returns we also report the R^2 statistic. We only include funds with at least 36 months of return data. The sample period is June 1996 to December 2014.

Sharpe ratio (annualized)

	Macro		Equity	
	Systematic	Discretionary	Systematic	Discretionary
25th percentile	0.06	0.10	0.05	0.13
50th percentile	0.28	0.33	0.46	0.43
75th percentile	0.48	0.63	0.83	0.78
Spread 75th–25th	0.42	0.53	0.78	0.65

Appraisal ratio (annualized)

	Macro		Equity	
	Systematic	Discretionary	Systematic	Discretionary
25th percentile	−0.36	−0.19	−0.07	−0.12
50th percentile	0.13	0.20	0.29	0.33
75th percentile	0.47	0.72	0.75	0.70
Spread 75th–25th	0.83	0.91	0.82	0.82

R^2 statistic

	Macro		Equity	
	Systematic	Discretionary	Systematic	Discretionary
25th percentile	15%	21%	24%	30%
50th percentile	24%	34%	39%	46%
75th percentile	34%	50%	57%	63%
Spread 75th–25th	19%	29%	33%	33%

FIGURE 6.5 (Continued)

So far we have evaluated index returns by means of looking at returns averaged over all the funds in a particular category.[14] Next we turn our attention to fund-level returns. In order to conduct a meaningful statistical analysis, we require that funds have a minimum of 36 months of data. This may create a survivorship bias, affecting the overall performance level. However, our main goal is to get a sense for the dispersion in performance, which is likely less affected by the selection method. It should also be noted that one cannot directly compare the fund-level results with the previous index-level results. For example, the index-level results funds with a longer history implicitly get more weight because they are constituents for longer.

In Figure 6.5, we show the 25th, 50th, and 75th percentile of the average return and Sharpe ratio distribution for unadjusted fund returns (Panel A) and similarly the alpha and appraisal ratio for risk-adjusted returns (Panel B). The risk-adjusted returns are for the baseline case, which uses traditional, dynamic, and the vol S&P 500 factor. The analysis is performed on individual fund returns for each of the four different hedge fund styles. The spread between the 75th and 25th percentile average return ranges from 5.5 percent to 7.7 percent and the spread in alpha values is even larger, ranging from 5.9 percent to 10.5 percent. Dispersion between best and worst managers therefore is large for each of the hedge fund styles. Again, discretionary and systematic managers are historically more similar than some observers might think.

In Panel B of Figure 6.5, we also report the 25th, 50th, and 75th percentile of the R^2 statistic of the regression underpinning the risk-adjustment. Risk factors explain a slightly larger proportion of the return variance for equity funds than they do for macro funds. At the index level (Figures 6.3 and 6.4), where idiosyncratic risk is diversified, we found that the contrast is much bigger, with R^2 statistics of 16 percent and 25 percent for systematic and discretionary macro funds, and 73 percent and 77 percent for systematic and discretionary equity funds.

CONCLUDING REMARKS

There are many dimensions to risk management. In this chapter, we have explored two key issues. First, we take a broader view of "risk" by decomposing returns into the individual risk drivers. Second, we explore the risk exposures (as well as the performance attribution) of systematic versus discretionary managers.

We used text analysis to categorize hedge funds as systematic (employing rules-based or algorithmic strategies) or discretionary (relying on human decision making). Our main focus is on risk-adjusted returns.

These are corrected for any variation in returns that is simply due to an exposure to risk factors that were well known already in 1996, when our empirical analysis starts. We found that for equity and macro strategies, systematic and discretionary funds have historically had similar average risk-adjusted returns.

Our results show that an aversion to systematic managers, as displayed by some investors, and in line with a more general "algorithm aversion" phenomenon, may be unjustified.

Our results should not be misconstrued to imply that systematic funds are intrinsically superior to discretionary. We believe it is likely that some market inefficiencies are more suitable for a systematic approach while others are better exploited by a discretionary approach. Also, most of our analysis was for hedge fund–style index returns. The outlook for an investor who is skilled at selecting the best managers within a style may be quite different.

One could argue that the term "hedge fund" suggests hedged (or zero net) exposure to well-known risk factors. As a byproduct of our risk-adjustment methodology, we mapped out the dominant risk factors for the different hedge fund styles. We find that in many cases the exposure is statistically significant and economically meaningful. It is important for investors who allocate to hedge funds as part of a larger portfolio to be aware of the specific risk exposures of the different styles, as the non–hedge fund investments may have a meaningful exposure to the same risk factors.

The research that we consider the core of strategic risk management (positive convexity strategies, strategic rebalancing, volatility scaling, and drawdown control) was all conducted before the COVID-19 market drawdown. The extraordinary market episode in 2020 provides an opportunity to conduct an "out-of-sample" test of some of the concepts detailed in earlier chapters. This is what we do next.

APPENDIX 6A: FUND CLASSIFICATION METHOD

We use the HFR database on hedge funds, which classifies all hedge funds into four broad strategies: Equity Hedge, Event Driven, Macro, and Relative Value.[15] We focus on the Equity Hedge and Macro strategies, which are the largest and second-largest in terms of number of funds, respectively, and which naturally allow for both a discretionary and a systematic approach. For both strategies, we omit sub-strategies referred to as "multi-strategy," as it is likely hard to pinpoint the trading style, and sector-specific sub-strategies like "Equity Technology/Healthcare" or "Macro Commodity-Agriculture." Doing so, we are left with the top-four Equity Hedge and top-two Macro sub-strategies in terms of fund count (see Table 6A.1).

TABLE 6A.1 HFR category names, fund count, systematic words used. We present for our six chosen HFR sub-strategies the name, fund count, and the percentage of fund descriptions containing a given word. In the last three columns, we also present the three criteria that all need to be met for a word to be deemed a "systematic word." We will classify funds with at least one systematic word in their description as systematic and other funds as discretionary (see the "ANY" row in the shaded block, labeled "This chapter"). For contrast, we also show the statistics for the words used in Chincarini (2014).

		EQUITY Equity Market Neutral	EQUITY Quantitative Directional	EQUITY Fundamental Growth	EQUITY Fundamental Value	MACRO Systematic Diversified	MACRO Discretionary Thematic	%Systematic - %Discretionary (Cutoff: > 6.0%)	%Systematic / %Discretionary (Cutoff: > 4.0)	%EQUITY / %MACRO (Cutoff: > 0.21)
	Total fund count	1152	689	2084	3030	1440	742			
	Word							Material	Polarizing	Universal
		Descriptions containing word (% of total)								
This Chapter	algorithm	4.2%	8.3%	0.2%	0.3%	6.7%	0.3%	6.4%	24.7	0.37
	approx	9.6%	6.2%	3.3%	4.0%	9.1%	1.8%	7.3%	5.2	0.75
	computer	2.8%	5.4%	0.3%	0.5%	8.8%	0.5%	8.2%	16.2	0.22
	model	28.5%	24.1%	7.2%	10.3%	30.8%	7.3%	23.5%	4.2	0.60
	statistical	12.2%	5.8%	0.3%	1.1%	11.3%	1.9%	9.4%	6.0	0.39
	system	18.8%	23.8%	4.8%	5.5%	54.0%	11.5%	42.6%	4.7	0.24
	ANY	48.8%	40.9%	14.0%	17.8%	68.4%	18.1%	50.3%	3.8	0.47
Chincarini (2014)	algorithm	4.2%	8.3%	0.2%	0.3%	6.7%	0.3%	6.4%	24.7	0.37
	automate	2.1%	3.2%	0.0%	0.2%	3.9%	0.1%	3.8%	28.9	0.28
	econometric	0.8%	0.7%	0.0%	0.0%	0.6%	1.1%	-0.5%	0.5	0.29
	mathematical	2.0%	0.7%	0.2%	0.3%	4.9%	0.7%	4.3%	7.3	0.17
	model	28.5%	24.1%	7.2%	10.3%	30.8%	7.3%	23.5%	4.2	0.60
	quantitative	26.8%	21.2%	4.8%	8.2%	22.6%	13.2%	9.4%	1.7	0.59
	statistic	12.3%	6.0%	0.5%	1.2%	11.6%	2.3%	9.3%	5.1	0.39
	ANY	45.9%	42.4%	11.3%	16.5%	47.7%	18.5%	29.2%	2.6	0.59

Using Macro funds as a learning set, we search for "systematic words" defined as words that are more likely to occur in Macro Systematic Diversified than in Macro Discretionary Thematic fund descriptions. More precisely, we considered all strings of consecutive letters with a length of four or more and with the first letter coinciding with the start of a word. So the string "system" is counted not only if it occurs as a standalone word, but also if "systems" or "systematic" occur. We use three formal criteria that all need to be met:

1. *Material.* The difference between the percentage of systematic funds with the specified word and the percentage of discretionary funds with that word needs to be at least 6 percentage points.
2. *Polarizing.* The ratio of the percentage of systematic funds with the specified word and the percentage of discretionary funds with that word needs to be at least 4 times.
3. *Universal.* The ratio of the percentage of equity funds with the word and the percentage of macro funds with the word needs to be 0.21 times.[16]

The three criteria serve to select only the words that are material, polarizing, and universal in the sense that they are also relevant in an equity context. In Table 6A.1, we present the words that satisfy the three criteria (rows labeled as "This chapter"). The statistics associated with the three criteria are shown in the final three columns. Often several similar words satisfy the criteria (e.g., "compute" and "computer"), in which case we typically went for the longer word, unless it had a noticeably lower score on any of the three criteria used. The default choice for the longer word is to reduce the chance of the word being used in an unexpected way in a different context (notably the equity fund context).

A related paper by Chincarini (2014) compares performance and fees of quantitative and qualitative (as he calls it) funds. This is quite different from our study as quantitative techniques are widely used (to a greater or lesser degree) by both systematic and discretionary funds. Also, Chincarini classifies Equity Market Neutral funds as quantitative by default. This is particularly problematic for comparing the equity market exposure (i.e., beta) of quantitative and qualitative funds. In fact, Chincarini's finding that quantitative funds are more market neutral may be a direct result of the chosen categorization method. The differences between our words and Chincarini's is apparent in Table 6A.1. A comparison of our words with those used by Chincarini (2014), who partially relies on sub-strategy classifications as well, reveals many differences. On the one hand, we pick up on "approx," "computer," and "system," which are highlighted gray for contrast. On the other hand, we don't use words like "econometric" (which actually occurs more often in Discretionary Thematic descriptions) and "quantitative" (which is quite common in Discretionary Thematic descriptions also).[17]

Putting it all together, we classify funds for which the description contains at least one systematic word as systematic and all other funds are classified as discretionary. We considered using a list of discretionary words also, but we found that it is harder to identify many words that are specific to discretionary managers and thus discretionary funds are best identified as not having any systematic words in their fund description. The fraction of funds classified as systematic for each HFR category is therefore given by the ANY row of the section labeled "This chapter" in Table 6A.1. For consistency, and because funds may be misclassified, we also use our classification for macro funds, rather than using the HFR classification. From Table 6A.1, Macro Systematic Diversified funds are classified as systematic in 68 percent of the cases, while for Macro Discretionary Thematic this is only 18 percent. Looking through the Macro Systematic Diversified funds that we don't classify as systematic, there typically doesn't seem to be a clear indication that the fund is in fact systematic, and we deem it probable that the fund is rather partially systematic or quantitative, but not rules based. For equity funds, 49 percent of Equity Market Neutral, 41 percent of Quantitative Directional, 14 percent of Fundamental Growth, and 18 percent of Fundamental Value funds are classified as systematic.

In addition, we browsed through a number of descriptions for Equity Quantitative Directional funds not classified as systematic (so classified as discretionary) and typically found no suggestions that the fund is actually systematic and in fact often found language suggestive of a discretionary approach, such as "also opportunistically trades dislocations" or "identify investment opportunities through extensive meetings with company managements."

APPENDIX 6B: THE RECENT RISE OF LIQUID ALTERNATIVE CTA MUTUAL FUNDS

Following the academic publications on cross-sectional stock momentum in the 1990s, Kenneth French started reporting monthly updates on his website for what subsequently became a standard set of cross-sectional equity risk factors: size, value, and momentum. It is likely that active (and fixed-fee) mutual funds started making use of this very public set of risk factors soon afterwards, and so we include these factors in the empirical analysis in this chapter.[18]

In contrast, the mainstream academic literature on momentum applied to other securities is more recent. As a recent paper by Goyal and Wahal

(2015) provides a detailed account of the timeline in their opening paragraph (underlining added):

> *Momentum, the notion that winners continue to win and losers continue to lose, is robust and pervasive. It exists cross sectionally in individual stocks (Jegadeesh and Titman (1993), (2001)), in portfolios (Lewellen (2002)), outside the United States (Rouwenhorst (1998), Griffin, Ji, and Martin (2003), and Chui, Titman, and Wei (2010)), in various asset classes (Asness, Moskowitz, and Pedersen (2013)), and apparently in the time series (Moskowitz, Ooi, and Pedersen (2012)).*

On January 1, 2016, the bank Société Générale (SG) introduced the SG CTA Mutual Fund Index to track the live performance of CTA mutual funds, which predominantly employ trend-following strategies. These funds started getting traction around 2013, as can be seen in Figure 6B.1, which plots the AUM reported on Bloomberg for the current constituents of the SG CTA Mutual Fund Index. AQR, to which the authors of the Moskowitz, Ooi, and Pedersen (2012) paper are affiliated, managed to turn their timely research into a market-leading position for their CTA mutual fund.

Contemporaneously with early drafts of Moskowitz, Ooi, and Pedersen (2012), the now well-known and widely followed SG Trend Indicator (formerly Newedge Trend Indicator) was introduced on August 26, 2010, by Newedge (2010).[19] Given the timing of these papers, and given the timing of asset accumulation in CTA mutual funds, we argue that 2011 is the earliest date one could consider time-series futures trend following as a well-known risk factor. We confirmed that our baseline case empirical results are robust to ending our study in 2011.

Finally, in Table 6B.1 we report the return attribution for macro funds when we add the SG Trend Indicator as a risk factor. In order to interpret the results, however, we should note two differences with the factors included in the baseline case: (1) we use backfill data from 2000 onwards (the earliest available date), but the indicator was published only in 2010 and was further updated in 2012 (at which point returns were backfilled for the full history), and (2) returns are reported net of estimated cost and fees. As such, this exercise sheds light on the question of the positive performance for macro funds reported earlier as mainly driven by these funds trading trend-following strategies well before it became a well-known and widely accepted trading style. We note in Table 6B.1 that for both systematic and discretionary macro funds some of the returns are attributed to the trend indicator exposure and, unsurprisingly, the attribution is larger for systematic macro funds. Adding the trend indicator reduces the alpha, but it

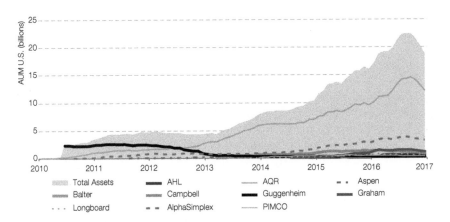

FIGURE 6B.1 AUM for the constituents of the SG CTA Mutual Fund Index (2010–2016). We present the assets under management (AUM) for the constituents (per 2016) of the SG CTA Mutual Fund Index. This index comprises the largest 10 single-manager CTA mutual funds that are priced daily and open for investment. We also show the sum of these constituent AUMs as "Total Assets." Data are from Bloomberg. Full manager names can be found at: https://cib.societegenerale.com/fileadmin/indices_feeds/SG_CTAM_Index_Constituents.pdf.

TABLE 6B.1 Return attribution for macro funds when including the SG Trend Indicator (2000–2014). We run regressions of systematic macro (left side) and discretionary macro (right side) returns on the baseline set of risk factor returns, and also with the SG Trend Indicator (SGTI) added as an additional risk factor. We report annualized performance statistics, including the return attributed to factors, which is computed as the coefficient times the average factor return. Funds are classified into the same systematic and discretionary categories as in the body of the chapter, using text analysis. We use monthly data from HFR for the January 2000 to December 2014 period. The later start date, compared to the 1996 start used elsewhere, is because the (backfilled) returns for the SG Trend Indicator only start in 2000.

Factor performance attribution (annualized)					
Systematic Macro			**Discretionary Macro**		
	Baseline	Baseline + SGTI		Baseline	Baseline + SGTI
Return average	−4.66%	4.66%	Return average	2.28%	2.28%
Return attributed to factors	−0.11%	3.23%	Return attributed to factors	0.91%	1.97%
Equity	−0.06%	−0.25%	Equity	−0.26%	−0.32%
Bond	−1.91%	−1.32%	Bond	−0.48%	−0.29%

TABLE 6B.1 *(Continued)*

	Baseline	Baseline + SGTI		Baseline	Baseline + SGTI
Credit	−0.09%	−0.04%	Credit	−0.19%	−0.17%
Size (U.S. stocks)	−0.21%	−0.37%	Size (U.S. stocks)	−0.27%	−0.32%
Value (U.S. stocks)	−0.22%	−0.09%	Value (U.S. stocks)	−0.10%	−0.06%
Momentum (U.S. stocks)	−0.20%	−0.12%	Momentum (U.S. stocks)	−0.07%	−0.04%
FX Carry	−0.36%	−0.35%	FX Carry	−0.50%	−0.49%
Vol S&P 500	−3.16%	−1.81%	Vol S&P 500	−0.95%	−0.52%
SG Trend Indicator		−2.50%	SG Trend Indicator		−0.79%
Adj. return average (alpha)	1 4.77%	1.43%	**Adj. return average (alpha)**	1.37%	0.31%
Adj. return volatility	10.91%	7.86%	**Adj. return volatility**	4.74%	4.09%
Appraisal ratio	00.44%	0.18%	**Appraisal ratio**	0.29%	0.08%

remains positive, suggesting that the returns of macro funds cannot just be explained by a simple trend system, not even when using the trend indicator prior to it becoming a better-known factor.

REFERENCES

Abis, Simona (2016). "Man vs. Machine: Quantitative and Discretionary Equity Management," working paper.

Asness, C., T. Moskowitz, and L. Pedersen (2013). "Value and Momentum Everywhere," *Journal of Finance*, 68 (3), 929–985.

Balia, T., S. Brown, and M. Caglayan (2014). "Macroeconomic Risk and Hedge Fund Returns," *Journal of Financial Economics*, 114(1), 1–19.

Carhart, Mark. (1997). "On Persistence in Mutual Fund Performance," *Journal of Finance*, 52(1), 57-82.

Chincarini, L. (2014). "A Comparison of Quantitative and Qualitative Hedge Funds," *European Financial Management*, 20(5), 857–890.

Chui, A., S. Titman, and K. Wei (2010). "Individualism and Momentum Around the World," *Journal of Finance*, 65(1), 361–392.

Dietvorst, B., J. Simmons, and C. Massey (2015). "Algorithm Aversion: People Erroneously Avoid Algorithms After Seeing Them Err," *Journal of Experimental Psychology: General,* 144(1), 114–126.

Fama, E. (1984). "Forward and Spot Exchange Rates," *Journal of Monetary Economics,* 14(3), 319–338.

Fama, E., and K. French (1993). "Common Risk Factors in the Returns of Stocks and Bonds," *Journal of Financial Economics,* 33(1), 3–56.

Frazzini, A., D. Kabiller, and L. Pedersen (2013). "Buffett's Alpha," working paper.

Fung, W., and D. Hsieh (2001). "The Risk in Hedge Fund Strategies: Theory and Evidence from Trend Followers," *Review of Financial Studies,* 14(2), 313–341.

Fung, W., and D. Hsieh (2002). "Benchmarks of Hedge Fund Performance: Information Content and Measurement Biases," *Financial Analyst Journal,* 58(1), 22–34.

Goyal, A., and S. Wahal (2015). "Is Momentum an Echo?," *Journal of Financial and Quantitative Analysis,* 50(6), 1237–1267.

Granger, N., D. Greenig, C. Harvey, S. Rattray, and D. Zou (2014). "Rebalancing Risk," working paper.

Griffin, J., S. Ji, and S. Martin (2003). "Momentum Investing and Business Cycle Risk: Evidence from Pole to Pole," *Journal of Finance,* 58(6), 2515–2547.

Hamill, C., S. Rattray, and O. Van Hemert (2016). "Trend Following: Equity and Bond Crisis Alpha," working Paper.

Harvey, C., Y. Liu, and H. Zhu (2016). "…and the Cross-Section of Expected Returns," *Review of Financial Studies,* 29(1), 5–68.

Harvey, C.R., S. Rattray, A. Sinclair, and O. Van Hemert (2017, Summer). "Man versus Machine: Comparing Discretionary and Systematic Hedge Fund Performance," *Journal of Portfolio Management,* 55–69.

Jegadeesh, N., and S. Titman (1993). "Returns to Buying Winners and Selling Losers: Implications for Stock Market Efficiency," *Journal of Finance,* 48(1), 65–91.

Jegadeesh, N., and S. Titman (2001). "Profitability of Momentum Strategies: An Evaluation of Alternative Explanations," *Journal of Finance,* 56(2), 699–720.

Lewellen, J. (2002). "Momentum and Autocorrelation in Stock Returns," *Review of Financial Studies,* 15(2), 533–563.

Meese, R., and K. Rogoff (1983). "Empirical Exchange Rate Models of the Seventies: Do They Fit Out of Sample?" *Journal of International Economics,* 14, 3–24.

Moskowitz, T., Y. Ooi, and L. Pedersen (2012). "Time Series Momentum," *Journal of Financial Economics,* 104(2), 228–250.

Newedge (2010). "Two Benchmarks for Momentum Trading." *AlternativeEdge Note.*

Rouwenhorst, G. (1998). "International Momentum Strategies," *Journal of Finance,* 53(1), 267–284.

CHAPTER 7

Out-of-Sample Evidence from the COVID-19 Equity Selloff

INTRODUCTION

We have advocated a quantitative approach to strategic risk management that involves the addition of positive convexity strategies, as well as three portfolio management tools: strategic rebalancing, volatility targeting, and drawdown control. Much of this research was conducted in the late 2010s, when equity and bond markets were booming and the U.S. economy was in a historically long period of uninterrupted growth. Volatility was low and confidence high.[1]

We believed the time was right to undertake a research program on the topic of strategic risk management, which involves the integration of risk management and the investment function. Given that many markets were at all-time highs, it seemed prudent to develop investment programs that sought crisis alpha (i.e., outperformance during the inevitable drawdown).

But was the success of our methods due to the particular sample period that we examined? The best way to test is with an out-of-sample exercise. The COVID-19 pandemic produced an equity drawdown that offered an ideal test of our defensive strategies and portfolio management tools.

Chapters 1 through 6 of this book were written over the 2016–2019 period and focus on the topic of strategic risk management, which is the embedding of risk management into investment strategy design. In Chapters 1 and 2, we studied time-series momentum (or trend-following) strategies and noted that faster formulations tend to be more defensive in nature. In this chapter, we update the main analysis presented in Chapter 1 and confirm that the same result was seen during the February–March 2020 equity market selloff, which was triggered by the COVID-19 pandemic. Consistent with Chapter 1, the good performance of strategic risk management during the COVID-19 equity market selloff does not just come from following trends in only equity markets; other asset classes contribute materially as well.[2]

Among the long-short quality stock strategies considered in Chapter 2, profitability in particular continued to show defensive characteristics during the February–March 2020 equity market drawdown. Low-risk (or safety) long-short stock strategies are vulnerable to tightening credit conditions, something we had documented in relation to the 2007–2009 Financial Crisis (Chapter 2). Credit concerns also surfaced during the recent COVID-19 equity selloff, and low-risk strategies performed less well.

In the volatility targeting analysis in Chapter 3, we argued that sizing positions in proportion to volatility, rather than holding a constant notional exposure, creates a more balanced return stream. Empirically, in case of risk assets like equities, volatility targeting resulted in a higher Sharpe ratio of returns, correlating to a lower impact of volatility. In this chapter, we show that volatility targeting led to a reduced drawdown and higher cumulative returns for equities over the first quarter of 2020 as well.[3]

Finally, in Chapter 4, we proposed a rule to postpone the rebalancing of a 60–40 equity-bond portfolio after equity market selloffs. The "strategic rebalancing" rule tends to reduce drawdowns of 60–40 portfolios during extended equity market selloffs. In this paper, we extend the sample period to include the first quarter of 2020, and find that the strategic rebalancing rule would have called for postponing rebalance trades during the COVID-19 equity market selloff, and so helped reduce the drawdown of a 60–40 equity-bond portfolio.

THE BEST STRATEGIES DURING THE COVID-19 EQUITY SELLOFF

In Figure 7.1 and Table 7.1, we extend the analysis in Chapter 2 ("The Best Strategies for the Worst of Times") to the end of March 2020. Importantly, this gives us a ninth drawdown of –15 percent or worse for the S&P 500, which we refer to as "COVID-19," and runs from the close of February 19 to the close of March 23, 2020.

We note that the COVID-19 selloff in the S&P 500 was much faster than most other selloffs. Buying puts provided a good offset, but short credit risk was more potent with a +102 percent return (in excess of T-bills) over this period. As in Chapter 2, the credit portfolio employs leverage to obtain a 10 percent long-term volatility, and this amplifies the good performance over the COVID-19 equity selloff period. Over the same period, Treasury bonds provided only a modest payoff, and gold was slightly down.

TABLE 7.1 Performance over drawdown periods. We report the total return of the S&P 500 and various strategies during the nine worst drawdowns for the S&P 500, the annualized (geometric) return during drawdown, normal, all periods, and the hit rate (percentage of drawdowns periods with positive return). The annualized standard deviation ranges between 6.4 percent for bonds to 16.5 percent for the S&P 500, with dynamic strategies all scaled to 10 percent. The row "Peak = HWM?" indicates whether the index was at a high-water mark (HWM) before the drawdown began. The data are from January 1985 to March 2020.

	Black Monday	Gulf War	Asian crisis	Tech burst	Financial crisis	Euro crisis I	Euro crisis II	2018Q4	COVID-19	Draw-down (14%)	Normal (86%)	All (100%)	Hit rate
Peak day	25-Aug-87	16-Jul-90	17-Jul-98	1-Sep-00	9-Oct-07	23-Apr-10	29-Apr-11	20-Sep-18	19-Feb-20				
Trough day	19-Oct-87	11-Oct-90	31-Aug-98	9-Oct-02	9-Mar-09	2-Jul-10	3-Oct-11	24-Dec-18	23-Mar-20				
Weekdays count	39	63	31	548	369	50	111	67	23				
Peak = HWM?	Yes	Yes	Yes	Yes	Yes	No	No	Yes	Yes				
Strategy	Total return												
										Drawdown (14%)	Normal (86%)	All (100%)	%
										Annualized return			
S&P 500 (funded)	−32.9%	−19.2%	−19.2%	−47.4%	−55.2%	−15.6%	−18.6%	−19.4%	−33.8%	−48.2%	25.3%	10.6%	n.a.
S&P 500 (excess)	−33.5%	−20.7%	−19.7%	−51.0%	−56.3%	−15.7%	−18.6%	−19.8%	−33.9%	−49.6%	21.3%	7.1%	n.a.
Long puts (excess)	38.0%	12.4%	15.5%	44.7%	40.5%	15.8%	13.4%	18.0%	32.8%	49.8%	−14.3%	−6.9%	100%
Shortcreditrisk (excess)	7.6%	3.3%	12.1%	17.0%	127.7%	11.7%	26.1%	9.5%	101.6%	59.8%	−10.8%	−2.7%	100%
Long bonds (excess)	−8.3%	−2.7%	3.0%	24.2%	20.4%	5.7%	10.1%	2.5%	5.5%	11.6%	3.2%	4.3%	78%
Long gold (excess)	4.4%	5.5%	−6.9%	7.5%	18.9%	4.6%	6.3%	4.5%	−2.7%	8.2%	0.1%	1.2%	78%

(*Continued*)

TABLE 7.1 (Continued)

Strategy	Black Monday	Gulf War	Asian crisis	Tech burst	Financial crisis	Euro crisis I	Euro crisis II	2018Q4	COVID-19	Draw-down (14%)	Normal (86%)	All (100%)	Hit rate %
	Total return										Annualized return		
1m MOM unconstrained	5.6%	19.3%	9.0%	31.3%	28.6%	2.7%	4.9%	8.1%	40.8%	30.8%	5.7%	8.9%	100%
1m MOM EQ position cap	9.5%	22.8%	12.5%	37.4%	34.3%	4.8%	8.4%	9.7%	45.3%	38.4%	2.6%	7.0%	100%
3m MOM unconstrained	10.3%	10.5%	9.3%	50.7%	32.6%	0.5%	10.9%	0.8%	24.1%	30.1%	5.8%	8.9%	100%
3m MOM EQ position cap	15.4%	18.7%	14.4%	61.3%	41.4%	4.7%	13.7%	2.7%	32.2%	42.2%	3.0%	7.8%	100%
12m MOM unconstrained	0.4%	12.2%	7.7%	52.3%	17.3%	-4.0%	-4.1%	-2.8%	9.2%	16.3%	11.0%	11.8%	67%
12m MOM EQ position cap	8.3%	18.7%	16.2%	71.7%	23.7%	2.1%	0.2%	-0.9%	18.2%	30.8%	8.1%	11.0%	89%
Profitability, dollar-neutral	-1.6%	-2.1%	3.0%	161.9%	33.9%	10.5%	10.9%	4.5%	9.5%	37.5%	0.9%	5.4%	78%
Profitability, beta-neutral	2.3%	2.9%	9.1%	160.7%	21.2%	2.4%	3.3%	1.7%	3.7%	32.4%	1.6%	5.4%	100%
Payout, dollar-neutral	0.1%	6.3%	9.1%	178.6%	20.5%	7.0%	5.0%	7.6%	-1.3%	36.2%	0.0%	4.5%	89%
Payout, beta-neutral	-2.8%	8.0%	11.9%	196.1%	13.1%	1.2%	1.2%	5.1%	-2.6%	32.9%	3.0%	6.7%	78%

Growth, dollar-neutral		−6.6%	−9.6%	−8.6%	9.0%	10.8%	9.8%	−1.3%	12.3%	2.6%	1.8%	1.9%	50%
Growth, beta-neutral		−3.0%	−5.7%	−16.2%	12.4%	3.1%	2.8%	1.4%	10.7%	0.5%	0.3%	0.4%	63%
Safety, dollar-neutral	5.0%	9.5%	9.1%	90.7%	12.2%	7.9%	13.6%	9.9%	0.9%	29.7%	−4.1%	0.1%	100%
Safety, beta-neutral	−3.5%	4.8%	0.8%	96.9%	−9.1%	1.8%	4.2%	1.9%	−13.9%	11.2%	4.9%	5.8%	67%
Quality All, dollar-neutral	4.3%	7.3%	8.2%	142.9%	26.3%	10.2%	15.2%	4.5%	5.6%	39.2%	−1.4%	3.6%	100%
Quality All, beta-neutral	−3.3%	7.0%	6.6%	164.9%	9.6%	2.4%	4.6%	1.7%	−4.1%	27.4%	5.2%	8.1%	78%

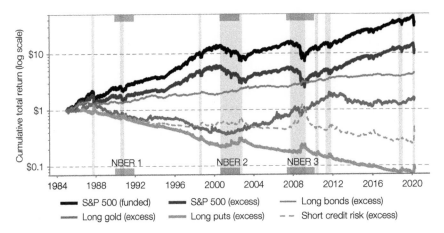

FIGURE 7.1 Passive investment total return over time. We show the cumulative return of the S&P 500 (funded and in excess of cash), as well as the excess return of long puts (one-month, at-the-money S&P 500 puts), short credit risk (duration-matched U.S. Treasuries over U.S. investment-grade corporate bonds), long bonds (U.S. 10-year Treasuries), and long gold (futures). We highlight the nine worst drawdowns for the S&P 500. NBER recessions are indicated on both the top and bottom of the figure. The data are from January 1985 to March 2020.

Moving on to the dynamic strategies in Table 7.1, we note that all time-series momentum (*mom*) strategies did well over the COVID-19 equity selloff period. As could be expected for a fast selloff, one-month *mom* did best. Position caps on equity positions (allowing only shorts) further improve the performance over this period by 5 to 9 percentage points for the three trend speeds considered.

Of the various quality strategies, profitability held up well during the recent selloff, as did growth. Safety did not do well, particularly when implemented as a beta-neutral strategy. This is similar to results seen during the Global Financial Crisis in 2007–2009. We argue this is due to tightening credit conditions. For example, if leverage is used to boost the returns of low-risk stocks, then a rise in borrowing costs can be damaging because it increases additional up-front costs and, as an indirect effect, it forces the unwinding of positions. Payout shows a small negative return over the recent selloff period.

It is perhaps surprising that the *mom* strategies did so well over the recent selloff, while the actual performance of trend followers over this period was slightly negative on average, albeit with considerable dispersion across managers, with some doing very well. This is illustrated in Figure 7.2, which shows that the cumulative return of the Société Générale (SG) CTA index over the COVID-19 equity selloff period was –4.8 percent. The trend-focused SG Trend index fared a bit better, and the trend-focused SG CTA Mutual Fund index, which is mostly simpler than the SG CTA index, was slightly positive. In particular, the first 10 days of the selloff were negative for these indices.

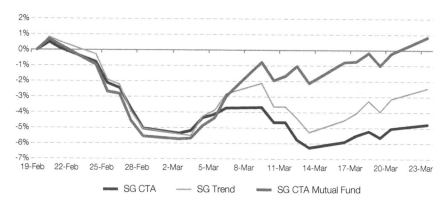

FIGURE 7.2 Performance SG CTA indices over the 2020 equity drawdown period. We show the cumulative performance over the COVID-19 equity selloff period from 19 February to 23 March 2020 for the SG CTA index, the SG Trend sub-index, and the SG CTA Mutual Fund index.

We have identified three possible explanations as to why our *mom* strategies perform so much better than the SG indices over the COVID-19 equity drawdown period. First, asset managers who purport to employ trend-following strategies often allocate to other strategies (e.g., carry) at the same time. Anecdotally, these non-trend strategies have not done well over the recent crisis period. This is consistent with the SG CTA index (which includes trend and non-trend strategies) performing the worst in Figure 7.2. Second, simpler trend strategies (like *mom*) seem to have worked better during this particular selloff. This is consistent with the performance of the SG CTA Mutual Fund index, which had the best results of the three. Third, trend followers typically employ slower models, and it is faster trend models that performed best during the COVID-19 equity drawdown.

This is consistent with the performance of our *mom* strategies, of which the one-month trend model was best (Table 7.1).

The second point deserves some elaboration. The *mom*(N) strategies introduced in Chapters 1 and 2 use as a signal the past return, divided by the volatility of returns, to create a value that approximates unit standard deviation. We limit values to be between −2 and 2 to prevent extreme views. For security k, at time t, the N-day momentum signal is given by:

$$\text{mom}_t^k(N) = \frac{\prod_{i=0}^{N-1}(1 + R_{t-i}^k) - 1}{\sigma_t^k(R^k)} \tag{7.1}$$

For the purpose of analysis, we consider 1-, 3-, and 12-month momentum strategies to capture short-, medium-, and long-term momentum trading. That is, N in Equation 7.1 is set to 22, 65, and 261 days, respectively.

In practice, trend followers often employ moving-average crossovers (*macs*) rather than the simpler *mom* strategies. During the most recent crisis, the simpler *mom* construction turned out to be a virtue. To illustrate this, we define a moving-average crossover of prices, where the two moving averages use exponentially decaying weights, one with a fast (short) and one with a slow (long) half-life. We divide by a volatility estimate for the difference of moving averages to again create a value that is approximately unit standard deviations, and limit values to be between −2 and 2:

$$\text{mac}_t^k(f, s) = \frac{\text{ma}_t^k(f) - \text{ma}_t^k(s)}{\sigma_t^k(\text{ma}^k(f) - \text{ma}^k(s))} \tag{7.2}$$

If we use fast and slow half-lives of 4 and 16 days, respectively, the *mac* behaves similar to the 1-month *mom* model; see Figure 7.3, where we compare the effective weight given to different lagged returns. Similarly, we can find *macs* that match the 3- and 12-month *mom* models reasonably well.

In Table 7.2, we see that correlations between paired *mac* and *mom* strategies are 0.9 or higher. However, one crucial difference is that *mac* models put relatively low weight on the most recent returns, making them slower to respond to a sudden selloff. The more gradual profile of *macs* helps to keep transaction costs under control. However, as can be seen in Table 7.3, during the recent, very fast equity selloff, *mac* models' more gradual trading led to substantially lower crisis performance compared to the simple *mom* strategy.

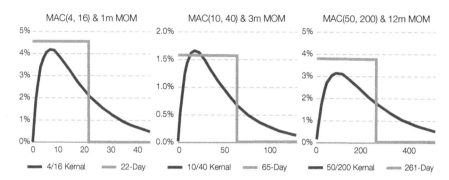

FIGURE 7.3 Moving-average crossover (*mac*) versus momentum (*mom*) **weight to lagged returns.** We show the weight effectively given to returns at different lags (in days) for *mac* and associated *mom* strategies.

For example, the *mac*(50, 200) is barely positive over the crisis period, while the associated 12-month *mom* had a +9.2 percent return.

TABLE 7.2 Moving-average crossover (*mac*) versus momentum (*mom*) correlations. We report correlations between the three moving-average crossovers (*mac*) and three momentum (*mom*) strategies considered.

	1m MOM	3m MOM	12m MOM	MAC(4, 16)	MAC(10, 40)	MAC(50, 200)
1m MOM		0.72	0.45	0.93	0.69	0.24
3m MOM	0.72		0.66	0.83	0.93	0.52
12m MOM	0.45	0.66		0.56	0.75	0.90
MAC(4, 16)	0.93	0.83	0.56		0.83	0.36
MAC(10, 40)	0.69	0.93	0.75	0.83		0.63
MAC(50, 200)	0.24	0.52	0.90	0.36	0.63	

In Table 7.3, we also report the asset class attribution of performance. Across all nine equity market selloffs, trends in fixed income are most profitable. In the most recent COVID-19 selloff, a main driver of the performance difference between *mac* and *mom* strategies is that *mom* strategies do better in equity indices.

TABLE 7.3 Performance of moving-average crossover (*mac*) versus momentum (*mom*). We report the total return of the S&P 500 and various trend (*mom*) and moving-average crossover (*mac*) strategies during the nine worst drawdowns for the S&P 500, the annualized (geometric) return during drawdown, normal, all periods, and the hit rate (percentage of drawdowns with positive return). The data are from January 1985 to March 2020.

Strategy	Black Monday	Gulf War	Asian crisis	Tech burst	Financial crisis	Euro crisis I	Euro crisis II	2018Q4	COVID-19	Draw-down (14%)	Normal (86%)	All (100%)	Hit rate %
					Total return						Annualized return		
S&P 500 (funded)	−32.9%	−19.2%	−19.2%	−47.4%	−55.2%	−15.6%	−18.6%	−19.4%	−33.8%	−48.2%	25.3%	10.6%	n.a.
S&P 500 (excess)	−33.5%	−20.7%	−19.7%	−51.0%	−56.3%	−15.7%	−18.6%	−19.8%	−33.9%	−49.6%	21.3%	7.1%	n.a.
1m MOM	5.6%	19.3%	9.0%	31.3%	28.6%	2.7%	4.9%	8.1%	40.8%	30.8%	5.7%	8.9%	100%
Commodities	0.2%	8.1%	0.5%	−2.9%	8.1%	−0.1%	−1.6%	1.8%	5.3%	3.8%	1.6%	1.9%	67%
Currencies	−0.3%	4.9%	0.9%	9.4%	7.1%	0.2%	−2.2%	−0.2%	5.6%	5.0%	1.1%	1.6%	67%
Equity indices	3.2%	5.8%	0.4%	7.1%	5.4%	−2.0%	1.1%	1.9%	19.3%	8.3%	0.6%	1.6%	89%
Fixed income	2.5%	−0.2%	7.1%	15.9%	6.1%	4.9%	8.0%	4.5%	6.7%	11.2%	2.5%	3.7%	89%
3m MOM	10.3%	10.5%	9.3%	50.7%	32.6%	0.5%	10.9%	0.8%	24.1%	30.1%	5.8%	8.9%	100%
Commodities	0.4%	5.8%	1.3%	1.6%	10.2%	−0.8%	−2.1%	0.0%	3.6%	3.9%	1.6%	1.9%	78%
Currencies	0.6%	7.4%	2.4%	10.3%	7.9%	−0.8%	−0.5%	−0.7%	6.6%	6.6%	1.2%	2.0%	67%
Equity indices	5.3%	0.0%	−1.9%	8.2%	3.3%	−3.2%	3.0%	2.3%	8.4%	5.0%	0.9%	1.5%	67%
Fixed income	3.7%	−2.6%	7.4%	24.8%	8.7%	5.6%	10.6%	−0.7%	4.0%	12.2%	2.0%	3.4%	78%
12m MOM	0.4%	12.2%	7.7%	52.3%	17.3%	−4.0%	−4.1%	−2.8%	9.2%	16.3%	11.0%	11.8%	67%
Commodities	2.2%	3.4%	1.8%	4.4%	4.6%	−2.5%	−2.6%	−1.5%	2.4%	2.4%	2.0%	2.1%	67%
Currencies	1.8%	7.4%	2.5%	10.2%	2.3%	−2.6%	−2.3%	1.3%	4.1%	4.9%	2.3%	2.7%	78%
Equity indices	−6.2%	−0.7%	−4.2%	8.3%	4.9%	−5.7%	−4.1%	−1.0%	−3.0%	−2.5%	3.0%	2.2%	22%
Fixed income	2.8%	1.9%	7.7%	22.5%	4.7%	7.1%	5.1%	−1.7%	5.7%	11.1%	3.3%	4.4%	89%

MAC(4, 16)	4.9%	16.1%	9.5%	47.4%	31.7%	2.9%	3.6%	5.1%	30.5%	30.6%	6.4%	9.5%	100%
Commodities	0.2%	7.3%	1.0%	−1.4%	11.1%	−0.9%	−1.3%	1.4%	4.3%	4.2%	1.7%	2.1%	67%
Currencies	0.2%	6.1%	1.6%	13.5%	6.7%	0.3%	−2.1%	−1.3%	4.4%	5.8%	1.5%	2.1%	78%
Equity indices	0.7%	4.2%	−0.8%	10.4%	5.0%	−1.7%	−0.6%	1.6%	12.6%	6.2%	0.5%	1.3%	67%
Fixed income	3.7%	−2.0%	7.6%	19.9%	6.3%	5.5%	8.1%	3.4%	6.9%	12.0%	2.7%	4.0%	89%
MAC(10, 40)	2.3%	11.1%	7.5%	52.0%	36.5%	1.0%	4.2%	2.9%	12.2%	25.4%	7.3%	9.7%	100%
Commodities	0.5%	4.9%	1.7%	1.3%	11.6%	−1.2%	−2.5%	0.0%	3.0%	3.8%	1.6%	1.9%	78%
Currencies	0.4%	7.3%	2.4%	11.1%	7.7%	−0.7%	−1.2%	0.2%	3.1%	6.0%	1.6%	2.2%	78%
Equity indices	0.4%	0.4%	−3.4%	10.6%	5.5%	−3.0%	−0.5%	1.7%	2.1%	2.1%	1.4%	1.5%	67%
Fixed income	3.6%	−1.6%	6.9%	22.7%	8.2%	6.2%	8.8%	1.0%	3.7%	11.9%	2.6%	3.9%	89%
MAC(50, 200)	−8.1%	4.9%	6.5%	32.1%	5.4%	2.3%	−3.3%	−4.7%	0.3%	6.2%	9.2%	8.8%	67%
Commodities	1.3%	2.7%	2.6%	2.4%	1.6%	−0.8%	−3.3%	−2.3%	1.1%	1.0%	1.1%	1.1%	67%
Currencies	1.8%	6.3%	3.4%	1.8%	−1.6%	−1.1%	−1.8%	1.9%	3.3%	2.8%	1.9%	2.0%	67%
Equity indices	−10.8%	−4.4%	−6.0%	8.5%	2.2%	−2.5%	−5.1%	−3.2%	−7.1%	−5.9%	3.4%	2.1%	22%
Fixed income	−0.2%	0.4%	6.8%	17.1%	3.2%	6.9%	7.3%	−1.1%	3.3%	8.7%	2.5%	3.4%	78%

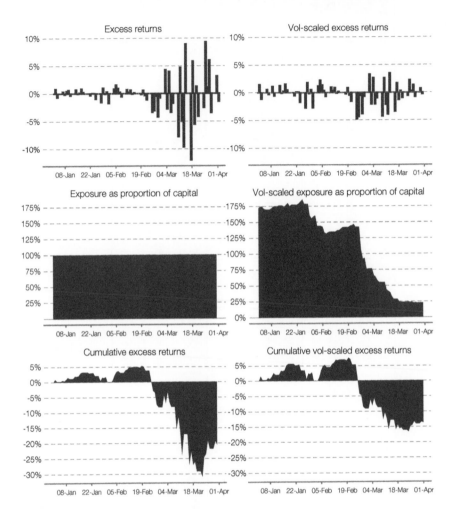

FIGURE 7.4 Volatility scaling of equity returns during the first quarter of 2020. The left panels show the statistics for investing a constant notional amount in U.S. equities, while the right panels show the case of volatility targeting. The top panels display daily returns (in excess of the T-bill rate) for the period. The middle panels show that notional exposure taken. The bottom panels show the cumulative returns.

VOLATILITY TARGETING

In Chapter 3 we showed that sizing holdings in an asset to target a constant ex-ante volatility, rather than targeting a constant notional exposure, leads to improved risk characteristics.[4] The explanation for this is that left-tail events tend to occur at times of elevated volatility, which is when a volatility-targeting portfolio has a relatively low notional exposure. In addition, for risk assets, such as equities and credit, we find that volatility targeting tends to improve the long-term Sharpe ratio of investment returns.

The first quarter of 2020 provides an interesting out-of-sample period to evaluate how volatility targeting performs. In Figure 7.4, we contrast the cases of constant notional (left panels) and volatility targeting (right panels) for U.S. equities. We use exponentially decaying weights for the volatility estimate with a half-life of 20 days.

The top panels show that the volatility-scaled returns (in excess of T-bills) are indeed more stable. This is achieved by holding more than a 100 percent exposure in January, when our volatility estimate is below the long-term value of 19.1 percent, and holding less than 100 percent exposure from the end of February, when volatility starts to pick up. In the four lower panels, a constant notional exposure leads to a much worse drawdown, with the cumulative return dipping below –30 percent, while for target-volatility investing, the trough is only around –17 percent.

STRATEGIC REBALANCING

In Chapter 4, we introduced a rebalancing rule for 60–40 stock-bond portfolios: Only rebalance the portfolio back to the target 60–40 stock-bond mix if the 1-, 3-, or 12-month trend in the stock-bond relative return is above its long-term historical average of 0.8 percent, 2.3 percent, and 9.1 percent (from Chapter 4), respectively. Moreover, if rebalancing, only move half of the distance back to a 60–40 mix.

In Table 7.4, we illustrate how our rule played out in the first quarter of 2020, assuming a 60–40 stock-bond mix at the start of the year. In Panel A, we show the stock, bond, 60–40, and stock-bond return. In all three months of the quarter, bonds outperformed. The only case where the stock-bond return differential is above its long-term average is for the three-month trend in January. In that case, Panel B shows a 50 percent rebalance back toward the target mix. In the first column, we also include the baseline case of always

TABLE 7.4 Strategic rebalancing in the first quarter of 2020. In Panel A, we report the monthly stock, bond, 60/40, and stock-bond returns for the US. In Panel B, we show the percent rebalancing toward a 60–40 equity-bond target mix at month-end for the baseline case of always rebalancing as well as when using strategic rebalancing rules based on the 1-, 3-, and 12-month trend in the stock-bond return. Panel C shows the resulting equity-bond mix after the rebalancing trade. Panel D reports the cumulative returns for the baseline case and under the strategic rebalancing rules. The data are monthly for the period.

	Panel A: monthly returns (US)					Panel B: Rebalance toward 60-40			
	Stock	Bond	60/40	Stock-Bond		Always	1m mom	3m mom	12m mom
1/31/2020	0.0%	4.0%	1.6%	−3.9%	1/31/2020	100%	0%	50%	0%
2/29/2020	−8.0%	3.7%	−3.3%	−11.7%	2/29/2020	100%	0%	0%	0%
3/31/2020	−13.4%	4.2%	−6.4%	−17.6%	3/31/2020	100%	0%	0%	0%

	Panel C: %stocks after EOM rebal					Panel D: cumulative returns			
	Always	1m mom	3m mom	12m mom		Always	1m mom	3m mom	12m mom
1/31/2020	60.0%	59.1%	59.5%	59.1%	1/31/2020	1.6%	1.6%	1.6%	1.6%
2/29/2020	60.0%	56.1%	56.6%	56.1%	2/29/2020	−1.8%	−1.6%	−1.7%	−1.6%
3/31/2020	60.0%	51.6%	52.0%	51.6%	3/31/2020	−8.0%	−7.2%	−7.4%	−7.2%

rebalancing 100 percent back to target. Panel C shows the allocation to stocks after the end-of-month rebalancing trade, where applicable. Finally, Panel D reports a cumulative return of −8.0 percent for the baseline case at the end of March versus −7.2 percent to −7.4 percent for the strategic rebalancing rules. That is, the strategic rebalancing rules reduce the drawdown by 0.6–0.8 percentage points (or, nearly 10 percent in relative terms). The impact of the rule is not as large as during the 2007–2009 Global Financial Crisis (about 5 percentage points then), when equities experienced a more gradual and larger underperformance. Nevertheless, the strategic rebalancing rule did reduce the COVID-19 drawdown, despite the suddenness of the crisis.

CONCLUDING REMARKS

The COVID-19 pandemic is the type of risk realization that provides an out-of-sample test of the ideas presented in the previous chapters.[5] We summarize three key ideas.

First, we examined various investment strategies and assessed how they performed during both drawdowns and recessions. For example, a program of buying put options performed very well during drawdowns but was infeasibly expensive during normal times. We found that gold was unreliable. Our research identified two strategies that were notable: allocation to trend following, and certain long-short equity strategies focused on quality, in particular, profitability. When updating our results for February and March 2020, we find that these two strategies performed particularly well during the pandemic selloff.

Second, we undertook a study of volatility targeting, which is both a risk management program (targeting constant risk exposure) as well as an investment strategy. Our research suggested this type of portfolio management was particularly beneficial for risk-oriented assets, such as equity and credit, over our sample. When we extended the sample through the first quarter of 2020, volatility targeting significantly outperformed, reducing drawdowns by one half. The spike in volatility led to sharp reductions in allocation to risk assets—at the right time.

Finally, we examined an important aspect of portfolio construction: rebalancing. We argued that rebalancing is an active strategy, since assets are sold after they rise in value and bought when they fall in value. Buying (rebalancing) when stocks are in a downtrend leads to larger drawdowns. We explored various heuristics to mitigate these larger drawdowns and introduced the concept of strategic rebalancing. Here, the rebalancing decision is conditioned on a trend-following signal. If the market is in a downtrend, then delay the rebalancing. At the end of February 2020, all of the trend signals we studied said to delay rebalancing. As such, the strategic rebalancing method outperformed a mechanical rebalancing rule.

In closing, we have argued that the separation of investment and risk management functions promotes suboptimal outcomes. For example, an investment manager may dismiss a diversifying strategy based on its standalone expected return or performance in normal market conditions, ignoring any beneficial impact it may have on the tail risk of the overall portfolio. Meanwhile, a risk manager may not be in a position to press for an allocation to the diversifying strategy if the investment manager sticks to predefined risk and exposure limits.

The design of many popular risk metrics also contributes to the poor alignment between the investment and risk management functions, with investment managers being more negatively affected. Metrics like skewness, kurtosis, and value-at-risk are expressed for a single period (day, week, or month), so they fail to pick up on price trends during crises that arise from a bad environment that is worsening. Such trends are often observed during prolonged periods of market distress. During these environments, the separation of investment and risk roles can be particularly problematic. The evidence presented in our book strongly supports an integrative approach to strategic risk management.

Notes

CHAPTER 1

1. This chapter is based on research conducted by Carl Hamill, Sandy Rattray, and Otto Van Hemert and published on SSRN: https://ssrn.com/abstract=2831926.
2. Kaminski (2011) defines crisis alpha as "profits which are gained by exploiting the persistent trends that occur across markets during times of crisis."
3. Some papers have accepted such simplifying assumptions for commodities (as well as other simplifying assumptions for the other asset classes) and studied trend-following strategies over multiple centuries. Examples include Hurst, Ooi, and Pedersen (2012), Lempérière et al. (2014), and Greyserman (2012), who start their analyses in 1903, 1800, and 1300, respectively.
4. As equity and bond data further back in time is only available at the monthly frequency, we need to conduct our entire analysis based on monthly data.
5. We estimate the standard deviation of returns using exponentially decaying weights. We take the maximum of an estimate based on a half-life of 6 months and 0.5 times an estimate based on a half-life of 24 months, where the latter acts as a floor in case the volatility is temporarily very low.
6. We also cap the signal value so that it is between –2 and 2, to prevent putting too much weight on outliers. We omit this step from the formula for ease of exposition.
7. Consider a simple example with 12-month momentum. Asset 1 has a past return of 0.10 and volatility of 0.20, so $mom_1 = 0.5$. Asset 2 has past return of 0.05 and volatility of 0.10, so the momentum signal is identical (i.e., $mom_2 = 0.5$). Cross-sectionally we need to divide again by the volatility for the dollar weights. So for asset 1, 0.5/0.2 = 2.5. For asset 2, 0.5/0.1 = 5. Hence, the dollar weight on asset 2 is double that of asset 1.
8. The gearing process starts with the individual securities, which are all scaled to 10 percent average ex-ante volatility using $mom * 10\%/\sigma$. Then, in each aggregation step (from individual securities to asset classes and then asset classes to the overall portfolio), we achieve a 10 percent average ex-ante portfolio volatility. This comes from multiplying by the weight given to a security or sector and then dividing by a factor $\sqrt{w'\Omega w}$, where w is a vector of relative weights (a vector of ones, except in the case of the commodities sector, as mentioned in the

main text) and Ω is the correlation matrix between constituent strategy returns based on exponentially decaying weights with a 24-month half-life.

9. For stocks, the predictive power does not seem confined to the first, say, six months. In fact, there is a lively academic debate on whether the first six lags are less predictive than the next six lags. See, for example, Novy-Marx (2012), Goyal and Wahal (2015).

10. To understand this, recall that the position of the lag 12 momentum strategy in, say, January 2000 will be based on the return over January 1999. On January 1, 2000, this means the position is based on returns up to 12 months ago. However, by the time it is January 15, 2000, the position is based on returns up to 12.5 months ago, and on January 31, 2000, it is based on returns up to 13 months ago. Returns just over 12 months ago are predictive with the opposite sign; see, for example, Baltas and Kosowski (2013), who show in their Figure 1 that past weekly returns are predictive with a positive sign up to lag 52 and predictive with a negative sign for lags 53 and 54. We find (in unreported results) that using daily data for the post-1985 period for which this is mostly available, the lag 12 momentum strategy does perform strongly, as then the position on January 15, 2000, would be based on returns over the January 15 to February 15, 1999, period (i.e., shifted forward by a half a month relative to the case of monthly returns).

11. The BTOP50 Index seeks to replicate the overall composition of the managed futures industry. For more information see: http://www.barclayhedge.com/research/indices/btop/.

12. Bowley's measure of skewness is defined as: $B(75, 25) = (Q_{75} + Q_{25} - 2Q_{50})/(Q_{75} - Q_{25})$, where Q_x is the xth percentile of the return distribution, making Q_{50} the median. We also confirmed robustness using $B(90, 10)$ and $B(95, 5)$ The Pearson skewness coefficient is determined as $Pearson = 3(\mu - Q_{50})/\sigma$, where μ and σ are the mean and standard deviation of returns, respectively.

13. A long straddle strategy involves holding both a long call option and a long put option with the same strike price and maturity on the same underlying asset.

14. Fung and Hsieh (2001) argue that trend-following strategies are theoretically more related to lookback straddles (an option that pays the holder the difference between the maximum and minimum of the underlying asset price over a given period), but find that empirically standard straddles explain trend-following returns as well as lookback straddles.

15. The analogy does not hold for a trend follower who takes a binary approach and either holds a fixed-size long or short position or a zero position, rather than gradually building up and down positions as the signal strength changes.

16. The delta of the straddle is given by $2N(d) - 1$, where $N(.)$ is the cumulative normal distribution function and $d = [\ln(S/K) + (r + \sigma^2/2)\tau]/(\sigma\sqrt{\tau})$, which for a small time to maturity, τ, is well approximated by the log return relative to the strike price, $\ln(S/K)$, scaled by $\sigma\sqrt{\tau}$, such that it is expressed as a number of standard deviation moves over the time to maturity period. For the illustration, we set the annual risk-free rate, $r = 1\%$, annual volatility, $\sigma = 15\%$, and time to maturity, $\tau = 1/12$years (1 month). We then vary moneyness, S/K, and plot the delta versus $\ln(S/K)/\sigma\sqrt{\tau}$.

17. A formal mathematical proof of how trend-following strategies naturally exhibit positively skewed strategy returns is given by Martin and Zou (2012).
18. A similar smile pattern is obtained when plotting the Sharpe ratio instead of annualized returns.
19. For currencies our data only starts in 1973; prior to that the risk is redistributed to the other sectors. We find that the percentage of observations for which currencies data is available is roughly equally spread among the different quintiles. As a robustness check we run our analysis from 1974 onwards; see Appendix 1A.

CHAPTER 2

1. This chapter is based on research conducted by Campbell R. Harvey, Edward Hoyle, Sandy Rattray, Matthew Sargaison, Dan Taylor, and Otto Van Hemert. See Harvey et al. (2019).
2. See Cook et al. (2017).
3. Also see, for example, Kaminski (2011).
4. Arnott et al. (2019) examine equity factor returns in equity up and down months, as well as recessions/expansions. An AQR whitepaper (2015) reports the average performance of various strategies over the worst quarters for equities markets.
5. For 1988-2018, daily total returns are available from Bloomberg. Prior to 1988, we use data on daily index percent changes (excluding dividends) and monthly total returns (including dividends), and we proxy the daily total return as the daily index percentage change plus the monthly dividend return spread equally over the days of the month.
6. The S&P 500 had recovered from the 2018Q4 drawdown by April 2019, after our sample period ends. The trough date remained December 24, 2018.
7. This means that we take into account that a +10 percent return followed by a −10 percent return actually means a loss of −1 percent (computed as 1.1 × 0.9 − 1). The annualized return is computed as (1 + geometric mean) days per year.
8. An investor's portfolio includes their human capital. A drawdown of X in a recession might be worse than a drawdown of 2X in a non-recession, for example, if the investor potentially loses her job during the recession or is faced with a lower compensation.
9. Asvanunt, Nielsen, and Villalon (2015) consider various ways to hedge the equity tails of a 60/40 portfolio, including option (collar) strategies.
10. Various approaches could be taken to mitigate the strategy's costs, but their benefits need to be carefully weighed against any loss of hedge efficacy, which is beyond the scope of this paper. First, one can generate income by selling out-of-the-money options, such as through put spreads or collars. Second, one can purchase protection where it is cheapest, by analyzing the cost across strikes, across tenors, or across markets. Third, one could employ a timing approach: buying more protection at times of stress and buying less when conditions are

loose. This might involve measuring market conditions, e.g., along the lines of the Chicago Fed's National Financial Conditions Index. Alternatively, one could forecast realized volatility directly using a statistical model (for example, Shepherd and Sheppard 2010), and then increase protection ahead of expected volatility spikes and the associated increased probability of market falls.

11. Before scaling, the volatility of the strategy is 2.7 percent.
12. Because historical data are limited, we did not use credit default swaps or CDX for our empirical analysis.
13. Based on our trading experience, we expect the transaction costs for implementing a short credit-risk strategy, implemented through synthetic indices such as CDX, to be less than 0.1 percent per year.
14. We focus on bonds issued by the U.S. federal government, which are believed to bear little to no credit risk. Bonds from other countries may have substantial credit risk and thus different return dynamics.
15. Throughout this chapter, a futures return is based on the near contract, rolled into the next contract shortly before the expiration date. The rolled futures returns data come from Man Group.
16. In Chapter 3, we argue that before the 1960s bond markets had very different return dynamics, so we start the quintile analysis in 1960.
17. While CTAs may often use moving average crossovers, Levine and Pedersen (2015) show that these are very similar to the time-series momentum strategies that we use in this chapter.
18. Based on execution analysis of live trades at Man Group over a 25-year history.
19. We also follow industry practice and restrict the signal value to between –2 and 2 to prevent putting too much weight on outliers. We omit this step from the formula for ease of exposition.
20. We also considered restrictions based on the beta of the equity or overall portfolio to the S&P 500 and found similar results.
21. In the Gordon growth model, price = dividend / (required return – growth). Using profitability = profit/B and payout ratio = dividend/profit, and then rearranging terms yields Equation 2.3.
22. Daily returns are available from: http://mba.tuck.dartmouth.edu/pages/faculty/ken.french/data_library.html and https://www.aqr.com/library/data-sets.
23. Lian, Tang, and Xu (2019) also find that profitability strategies perform better in months with negative equity returns.
24. Also, AFP use CRSP/XpressFeed Global data, while we use their Worldscope analogues. The accounting data are extracted from the Worldscope fundamental dataset, where we use annual, semi-annual, and quarterly data when available. We generate comparable numbers by constructing trailing 12-month averages for each frequency, per variable.
25. The deflation factor is proportional to the total return index of the S&P 500 (see Figure 2.1).
26. The relation between quality and different size metrics is discussed by Asness et al. (2018).
27. The low correlation between futures time-series momentum and quality stocks also obtains when considering just equity market drawdown or just normal periods.

CHAPTER 3

1. This chapter is based on research conducted by Campbell R. Harvey, Edward Hoyle, Russell Korgaonkar, Sandy Rattray, Matthew Sargaison and Otto Van Hemert, "The Impact of Volatility Targeting," *Journal of Portfolio Management*, Fall 2018, 45(1), 14–33; DOI: https://doi.org/10.3905/jpm.2018.45.1.014.

2. ARCH is autoregressive conditional heteroscedasticity. Robert Engle shared the 2003 Nobel Prize in Economics "for methods of analyzing economic time series with time-varying volatility (ARCH)" (https://www.nobelprize.org).

3. See, e.g., the August 6, 2017, *Wall Street Journal* article "What is risk parity?," https://www.wsj.com/articles/what-is-risk-parity-1502071260.

4. Under the common assumption of concave utility, investors dislike the left tail more than they like the right tail. Hence, for a given Sharpe ratio, investors are willing to give up some of the right tail to reduce the left tail.

5. See http://mba.tuck.dartmouth.edu/pages/faculty/ken.french/data_library.html. Until 1952, stocks on the NYSE traded on Saturday as well, and thus the data include the Saturday returns up to then.

6. Federal Reserve Economic Data (FRED), see https://fred.stlouisfed.org. To illustrate the return dynamics over a longer period of time, we will use monthly data in Figure 6 obtained from Global Financial Data (GFD) from July 1926 (to match the start date of the equity data).

7. Assuming that the 10-year yield is the par yield on a semiannual coupon-paying bond, we reprice the bond the following day using that day's 10-year yield, and assuming that all cash flows are now 1/261 years closer (with 261 the assumed number of weekdays per year). The return over the one-day period is new price minus one (par).

8. Moreira and Muir (2017) take the vantage point of a mean-variance investor and thus scale by variance for most of their analysis. However, in a robustness check, Moreira and Muir (2017) show that scaling by volatility empirically performs equally well. Volatility scaling, the focus in this chapter, leads to lower turnover than variance scaling does. Barroso and Santa-Clara (2015) and Daniel and Moskowitz (2016) study risk-managed momentum strategies.

9. We compute the standard deviation with a stated zero mean (i.e., based on squared returns), to prevent relying on mean returns estimated with large error over short time windows. In all cases, we require 270 trading days of data before we form volatility-scaled returns. This ensures that the slowest volatility estimate (using exponential-decaying weights with a 90-day half-life) has at least three half-lives' worth of data to warm up on.

10. Andersen et al. (2003) show that realized intraday volatility predicts daily return volatility well for a number of currencies.

11. This is the period with consistently liquid trading conditions over the full sample period and across both securities. Adding up the squared overnight return leads to slightly less persistence (not reported), which is consistent with Bollerslev, Hood, Huss, and Pedersen (2018), who find greater persistence of intraday volatility.

12. Saturdays are half-days before 1952. Volatility estimates will either count Saturday as a half-day (in case of equal-weight fixed window) or use double the Saturday return (in case of exponentially decaying weights).

13. We believe these estimates broadly reflect trading costs in these markets post the 2008 global financial crisis, but are not necessarily representative of trading cost further back in time. For credit, the estimate is reflective of trading the synthetic CDX investment grade index, which we noted before resembles a credit index exposure hedged with Treasuries. We note that while the trading costs for bonds and credit are lower than those of equities, for a given notional traded, we will show that one needs to trade larger notional quantities in these lower volatility fixed income assets in order to achieve a given volatility target, making equities ultimately the cheapest to trade of the assets considered on a "per unit of risk" basis.

14. We use Consumer Price Index (all urban consumers) data from U.S. Department of Labor, Bureau of Labor Statistics. See: https://fred.stlouisfed.org/graph/?id=CPIAUCSL,CPIAUCNS.

15. To test for the statistical significance of this improvement, we run a regression of volatility-scaled daily returns (20-day half-life) on unscaled returns. We find an intercept of 0.64bp with a t-stat of 3.05 (Newey-West corrected with 30 lags). The R-squared of the regression is 0.73.

16. Dopfel and Ramkumar (2013) and Moreira and Muir (2017) also find that volatility targeting improves the Sharpe ratio for equities since 1927.

17. For example, for the case of a 10-day half-life, the costs are about $2 \times 1bp \times 71\% \times 4.66 = 0.066\%$ per year for a 10 percent volatility strategy. The unrounded gross and net Sharpe ratio are then 0.4831 and 0.4766, but both are 0.48 after rounding.

18. See also Hocquard, Ng, and Papageorgiou (2013), who study how volatility targeting changes the tail risk properties of an equity portfolio since 1990.

19. These results are available upon request. In addition, this scaling is irrelevant for the results focus on drawdown/non-drawdown periods.

20. The vertical axis for the histograms is the normalized frequency (frequency / (number of observations × bar width)). In this way, the areas of the bars sum to unity, hence the "probability density" labels. Rescaling in this way eases comparison between the two histograms, particularly in cases where the bar widths of the two histograms differ.

21. For a discussion on the effect of the rebalancing frequency for a 60–40 balanced portfolio, see Granger et al. (2014).

22. Asvanunt, Nielsen, and Villalon (2015) consider various strategies to reduce the size of tail events for 60/40 equity/bond portfolios. These include options-based approaches, and shifting to a risk parity asset class allocation based on risk exposures.

23. Fleming, Kirby, and Ostdiek (2001, 2003) study the allocation across stocks, bonds, and gold using the conditional covariance matrix. Asness, Frazzini, and Pedersen (2012) compare the performance of balanced and risk parity portfolios using monthly data.

24. See also Christie (1982) for a discussion of the leverage effect. Bekaert and Wu (2000) argue that there is also a volatility feedback effect where the causality is

reversed compared to the leverage effect; volatility increases give rise to higher risk premia and so negative returns.

25. Dachraoui (2018) also argues there is a link between the presence of a leverage effect and the extent to which volatility targeting improves the performance for an asset.

26. Modeling of volatility, including autocorrelation analyses, is typically conducted with squared volatility (i.e., variance).

CHAPTER 4

1. This chapter is based on research conducted by Campbell R. Harvey, Edward Hoyle, Russell Korgaonkar, Sandy Rattray, Matthew Sargaison and Otto Van Hemert: "The Impact of Volatility Targeting," *The Journal of Portfolio Management*, Fall 2018, 45(1), 14–33; DOI: https://doi.org/10.3905/jpm.2018.45.1.014.

2. Among practitioners, the term *negative convexity* rather than *concavity* is often used. This stems from reading position exposures on risk sheets and so preferring a measure that can be either positive or negative, like beta or delta, rather than the more cumbersome switching between convex and concave when the direction changes.

3. While time-series momentum applied to macro markets (like a broad equity index or government bond) considered in this chapter tends to display positively convex returns, Daniel and Moskowitz (2016) argue that cross-sectional momentum applied to individual stocks is subject to crash risk.

4. We find that the performance of trend strategies is consistent over time, not driven by any particular sub-period.

5. See also Fernholz and Shay (1982), Booth and Fama (1992), Erb and Harvey (2006), and Brown (2015).

6. The focus of this paper is on 60/40 stocks/bonds in terms of capital allocation. More recently, volatility targeting has been gaining traction and we defer to Harvey et al. (2018) for a discussion on a 60/40 stocks/bonds portfolio in terms of risk allocation.

7. U.S. government debt has averaged around 60 percent of GDP since 1966: https://fred.stlouisfed.org/series/GFDEGDQ188S. The stock market capitalization-to-GDP ratio, also known as the Buffett Indicator, has averaged around 90 percent since 1975: https://fred.stlouisfed.org/series/DDDM01USA156NWDB. Note that both government debt and the stock market cap have trended upwards similarly as fraction of GDP since the 1970s.

8. Similarly, Perold and Sharpe (1988) note that constant-mix portfolios have less downside protection and less upside than a buy-and-hold strategy while performing better in relatively trendless but volatile environments.

9. Goetzmann et al. (2007) show that rebalancing strategies can make traditional performance metrics less reliable and suggest using manipulation-proof performance measures.

10. Fung and Hsieh (2001) argue that trend-following strategies are theoretically more related to lookback straddles, but find that empirically standard straddles explain trend-following returns as well as lookback straddles.

11. Israelov and Tummala (2017) consider an option selling overlay to augment portfolio rebalancing.
12. See http://mba.tuck.dartmouth.edu/pages/faculty/ken.french/data_library.html.
13. Federal Reserve Economic Data (FRED); see https://fred.stlouisfed.org.
14. As in Chapter 1, here we argue it is important to start as far back as 1960 so that the sample period includes a bond bear market environment (pre-1982).
15. Moskowitz, Ooi, and Pedersen (2012) and Levine and Pedersen (2016) use similar formulations.
16. There is no ex-post scaling to hit a particular level of volatility.
17. This is consistent with how practitioners implement such trend strategies.
18. Equal risk across asset classes (Panel C) is common in the managed futures space and will serve as our baseline case in subsequent analyses. Asvanunt, Nielsen, and Villalon (2015) also study the impact of adding a two-asset (equity and bond) trend strategy, like we show in Figure 4.4 (Panel C), to a 60/40 stock/bond portfolio.
19. Note that Black Monday refers to October 19, 1987, but that the market trough (using monthly data) is November 1987.
20. In Chapter 1, using data from 1960, we find that a simple trend strategy applied to 55 securities realizes a Sharpe ratio well above one.
21. Donohue and Yip (2003) and Masters (2003) link rebalancing rules to considerations like sensitivity to the tracking error with the constant-mix portfolio and transaction costs.
22. In this case, 6.2% means $6.2 gets traded for every $100 in a portfolio.
23. Driessen and Kuiper (2017), Ilmanen and Maloney (2015), Huss and Maloney (2017) argue that rebalancing less frequently is a way to exploit predictability in asset returns.
24. Here we use quarterly rebalancing per quarter-ends (Dec, Mar, Jun, Sep) and annual rebalancing per year-end (Dec). Using different months of the year leads to similar results.
25. We find that using a rule based on just the stock trend, rather than the stock-bond trend, leads to very similar results.
26. We set this at 0.8 percent, 2.3 percent, and 9.1 percent for 1-, 3-, and 12-month trend horizons, corresponding to the empirical evidence over the 1960–2017 period.
27. For example, if you start with a 70–30 asset mix, rebalancing halfway results in a 65–35 asset mix. The full move would result in 60–40.

CHAPTER 5

1. This chapter is based on research conducted by Campbell R. Harvey, Edward Hoyle, Russell Korgaonkar, Sandy Rattray, Matthew Sargaison and Otto Van Hemert: "The Impact of Volatility Targeting," *The Journal of Portfolio Management*, Fall 2018, 45(1), 14–33; DOI: https://doi.org/10.3905/jpm.2018.45.1.014.

2. See, for example, Magdon-Ismail et al. (2004), where they study the behavior of maximum drawdown for the case of a Brownian motion with drift and an analytic expression is derived for the expected value of maximum drawdown (with zero drift) and infinite series representation (for nonzero drift).

3. See also Harvey and Liu (2020) for an analysis of the tradeoff between Type I and Type II errors, as well as their differential costs.

4. This section adds to a vast literature on drawdowns that includes: (1) statistical characteristics, see, e.g., Douady, Shiryaev, and Yor (2000), Magdon-Ismail et al. (2004), Hadjiliadis and Vecer (2006), Casati and Tabachnik (2012), Bailey and Lopez de Prado (2015), and Busseti et al. (2016); (2) portfolio optimization, see, e.g., Grossman and Zhou (1993), Chekhlov, Uryasev and Zabarankin (2005), and Cvitanic et al. (2019); (3) hedging and risk management, see, e.g., Carr, Zhang, and Hadjiliadis (2011) and Leal and Mendes (2015); (4) trading strategies; see, e.g., Vecer (2006); (5) measurement, see, e.g., Korn, Möller, and Schwehm (2020); and (6) economic mechanisms, see, e.g., Sornette (2003).

5. Our analysis is based on monthly, rather than daily, return data for two reasons. First, we think investment and allocation decisions by large institutions are more likely to take place at a monthly frequency. Second, returns at the daily frequency are harder to model as they are influenced by a pronounced intra-month variation in the news flow (e.g., bigger moves on the day major economic news is released). Monthly returns are somewhat better behaved, as they reflect the combination of both high- and low-news days. The more complicated case of daily drawdown evaluation and replacement decisions is left for future research.

6. Bailey and Lopez de Prado (2015) argue that ignoring the effect of serial correlation in the return generating process leads to a gross underestimation of the downside potential of hedge fund strategies.

7. Both the variable we vary on the horizontal axis and the −2 sigma cutoff are based on the (ex-ante) standard deviation for the return process. Probabilities (vertical axis) are based on average realized values.

8. To motivate this statement, consider the monthly process defined above and set $\tilde{\mu} = 0$ for simplicity. If $R_t = +\tilde{\sigma}$, that means the annualized conditional Sharpe ratio $\frac{E_t[R_{t+1}]}{\sigma_t[R_{t+1}]} \sqrt{12} = \frac{\rho}{\sqrt{1-\rho^2}} \sqrt{12}$, which equals a value of 0.35 for a monthly autocorrelation of $\rho = 0.1$. And if $R_t = +2\tilde{\sigma}$, the annualized conditional Sharpe ratio is 0.70. These are high values compared to a typical annualized Sharpe ratio for general equities (say 8%/20% = 0.4) or a typical hedge fund (with Sharpe ratio of, say 0.5 to 1.0). Note that ex-post one can measure a higher realized autocorrelation for a given market; our statement is just that on an ex-ante basis, a monthly autocorrelation of 0.1 already provides a high degree of predictability.

9. This is an approach where one randomly selects (with replacement) blocks of consecutive observations from an actual distribution. As a robustness check, we reran our analysis with blocks longer than 24 months, and found similar results. See Efron and Tibshirani (1986) for an early discussion of bootstrap methods.

10. Under a normal distribution, a −5 sigma or worse monthly move happens less than once every 250,000 years.

11. Behavioral biases may arise because drawdowns can be attention grabbing when observed in a graph like Figure 5.5. Such an effect has its foundation in the salience theory; see Bordalo, Gennaioli, and Shleifer (2012). There is also a notion that after experiencing a painful loss, people become more sensitive to any additional losses—they just can't take any more pain (see e.g., Thaler and Johnson 1990). This could make a drawdown all the more salient: After experiencing initial painful losses, people are then subjected to more, which is likely to be extra painful.

12. To simplify the analysis, we abstain from adding a third Ugly type, sometimes considered in studies with heterogeneous agents.

13. Notice that in the case of monthly evaluation a maximum drawdown and a drawdown rule with the same cutoff value are equivalent. This holds because the maximum drawdown is determined using monthly data, and the evaluation of the rule occurs at the same monthly frequency, so a maximum drawdown and drawdown rule will both cross a cutoff value at the same moment for the first time, and so trigger at the same time.

14. It can be shown that a stop-loss policy adds value when the level of serial auto-correlation in an AR(1) process is greater than the Sharpe ratio of the process; see Kaminski and Lo (2014). Importantly, the Sharpe ratio should be measured at the same frequency as the autoregressive parameter. That is, annual Sharpe ratios are only used if the AR(1) parameter is estimated with annual data.

15. From K. French's website: https://mba.tuck.dartmouth.edu/pages/faculty/ken .french/data_library.html.

CHAPTER 6

1. This chapter is based on research conducted by Campbell R. Harvey, Edward Hoyle, Russell Korgaonkar, Sandy Rattray, Matthew Sargaison and Otto Van Hemert: "The Impact of Volatility Targeting," *The Journal of Portfolio Management*, Fall 2018, 45(1), 14–33; DOI: https://doi.org/10.3905/jpm.2018 .45.1.014.

2. The appraisal ratio is given by the ratio of the average risk-adjusted return and the standard deviation of the risk-adjusted return. It is the risk-adjusted ana-logue to the Sharpe ratio, which is based on the average and standard deviation of unadjusted returns.

3. For example, Fung and Hsieh (2002) mention that vendors started collecting hedge fund performance data in the early 1990s and that "post-1994 hedge fund data are less susceptible to measurement biases."

4. That said, as a robustness check, we confirmed that the alpha and exposure to factors for systematic and discretionary macro funds (which we will discuss later in this chapter) is comparable when using the HFR classifications for Macro instead.

5. Bloomberg tickers: SPX Index, LUATTRUU Index, and SBC2A10P Index for equity, bond, and credit, respectively.

6. Carhart (1997) introduces the use of a momentum factor in relation to mutual fund performance.

7. See http://mba.tuck.dartmouth.edu/pages/faculty/ken.french/data_library.html.

8. The G10 currencies are the U.S. dollar, Canadian dollar, Australian dollar, New Zealand dollar, euro, British pound, Swiss franc, Japanese yen, Swedish krona, and Norwegian krone.

9. Bloomberg ticker: DBHTG10U Index.

10. Alternatively, one can use listed S&P 500 options, expiring on the third Friday of the month. We confirmed that the volatility factor we use has similar return-and-risk characteristics and is highly correlated to this alternative volatility factor. We prefer to use options expiring at the end of the month, as it is a more natural match to the monthly data used for hedge fund returns.

11. The Fung and Hsieh (2001) PTFS risk factors require trading 26 pairs of straddles. The straddles are rolled to the new at-the-money contract whenever the underlying reaches a new high or low price, so as to replicate the behavior of a lookback straddle. Because several recent academic papers use the Fung and Hsieh volatility factors, we reran our regression analysis with them instead of the S&P 500 volatility factor and found that the risk-adjusted performance is similar for equity funds and slightly better for macro funds. To conserve space, these results are not included in this chapter.

12. The median is used here because it is robust to the occasional order-of-magnitude error we observe in the monthly AUM figures.

13. The significance levels are only suggestive. Given that hundreds of factors have been tested, we are fully aware that a coefficient that is only two standard errors from zero is unlikely to be "significant" at the 5% level. See Harvey, Liu, and Zhu (2016).

14. The average return approach essentially implies rebalancing fund weights to equal weights each month and, as such, is different from what a buy-and-hold position in each of the index constituents would give. See Granger et al. (2014) for a further discussion on this issue.

15. See https://www.hedgefundresearch.com/hfr-hedge-fund-strategy-classification-system for an overview of strategy and sub-strategy names and descriptions.

16. The cutoff values were chosen as the least-strict values for which only words that we consider germane to systematic strategies satisfy the criteria.

17. Abis (2016) studies man vs. machine performance in the context of mutual funds. Abis associates the word "quantitative" with her machine classification, like Chincarini (2014). Again, we argue that many discretionary funds use quantitative inputs which could lead to misclassification.

18. Kenneth French's website went live on December 18, 2001, and he shared data more informally before that date.

19. Newedge is now part of Société Générale.

CHAPTER 7

1. This chapter is based on research conducted in 2020. It was originally published as Campbell R. Harvey, Edward Hoyle, Sandy Rattray, and Otto Van Hemert (2020, July 18), "Strategic Risk Management: Out-of-Sample Evidence from the COVID-19 Equity Selloff." Available at SSRN: https://ssrn .com/abstract=3655196.
2. In Chapter 2, we study monthly returns of hedge funds and find that, in aggregate, macro funds are long volatility, a defensive property.
3. In Chapter 5 we focus on the drawdown statistic and find that heteroskedasticity (time variation in volatility) tends to lead to larger drawdowns.
4. Volatility targeting is also referred to as volatility scaling, since it involves sizing positions inversely proportional to the volatility of asset prices.
5. We note that for Chapter 2, the fourth-quarter 2018 selloff is also an out-of-sample data point, as we wrote the first version of the research in 2017 (and posted it online at SSRN.com).

About the Authors

CAMPBELL R. HARVEY

Professor Campbell R. Harvey, a leading financial economist, has been an Investment Strategy Advisor to Man Group since 2005 and has contributed to both research and product design.

He is a Professor of Finance at Duke University and Research Associate at the National Bureau of Economic Research in Cambridge, Massachusetts. He served as editor of the *Journal of Finance* from 2006 to 2012 and as the 2016 president of the American Finance Association.

Professor Harvey received the 2016 and 2015 Bernstein Fabozzi/Jacobs Levy Award for the Best Article from the *Journal of Portfolio Management* for his research on differentiating luck from skill. In January 2021, he was named "Quant of the Year" by the *Journal of Portfolio Management* for his outstanding contributions to the field of quantitative finance. He has also received eight Graham and Dodd Awards/Scrolls for excellence in financial writing from the CFA Institute. He has published over 150 scholarly articles on topics spanning investment finance, emerging markets, corporate finance, behavioral finance, financial econometrics, and computer science.

He holds a PhD in Finance from the University of Chicago.

***

SANDY RATTRAY

Sandy Rattray is Chief Investment Officer of Man Group and a member of the Man Group Executive Committee.

Before joining Man Group in 2007, Sandy spent 15 years at Goldman Sachs, where he was a managing director in charge of the Fundamental Strategy Group. He also ran Equity Derivatives Research at Goldman Sachs in London and New York.

Sandy is a co-inventor of the VIX index. He is a board director of MSCI Inc. and sits on the MSCI Advisory Council and the Jesus College Cambridge investment committee. Sandy is a governor of the Southbank Centre in London and is a founding patron of the London Cycling Campaign.

Sandy holds a Master's degree in Natural Sciences and Economics from the University of Cambridge.

***

OTTO VAN HEMERT

Otto Van Hemert is Director of Core Strategies and a member of Man AHL's management and investment committees.

He was previously Head of Macro Research at Man AHL. Prior to joining Man AHL in 2015, Otto ran a systematic global macro fund at IMC for more than three years. Before that, he headed Fixed Income Arbitrage, Credit, and Volatility strategies at AQR, and was on the Finance Faculty at the New York University Stern School of Business, where he published papers in leading academic finance journals.

Otto holds a Master's and PhD in Economics from the University of Amsterdam and a Master's in Mathematics from the University of Utrecht.

Index

Page references followed by *fig* indicate an illustrated figure; followed by *t* indicate a table